THE WINNING STREAK
Mark II

THE WINNING STREAK
Mark II

HOW THE WORLD'S MOST SUCCESSFUL
COMPANIES STAY ON TOP
THROUGH TODAY'S TURBULENT TIMES

*Walter Goldsmith
& David Clutterbuck*

ORION BUSINESS
BOOKS

First published in Great Britain in 1997 by
Orion Business
An imprint of The Orion Publishing Group Ltd
Orion House, 5 Upper St Martin's Lane, London WC2H 9EA

A CIP catalogue record for this book
is available from the British Library

ISBN 0 75280 778 1

Filmset by Selwood Systems, Midsomer Norton
Printed in Great Britain by
Butler & Tanner Ltd, Frome and London

CONTENTS

ACKNOWLEDGEMENTS

The authors are particularly grateful to the research team:

- Des Dearlove, who carried out so many interviews in our high-performing companies
- Philip Stiles, of the London Business School, who conducted interviews, researched the management literature and contributed Chapters Fourteen and Fifteen
- Barney Harford, of strategy consultants Kalchas
- Marilyn Small, who must have amended every page a dozen times over

and to the many executives around the world who gave their time to this project.

THE CAST LIST

Our thanks go in particular to the following chairmen and chief executives:

ASDA	Archie Norman, Chairman
Atlas Copco	Michael Treschow, President
The Berkeley Group	Tony Pidgley, Chief Executive
Boots	Lord Blyth, Chief Executive
Bowthorpe	Nicholas Brookes, Chief Executive
British Airways	Sir Colin Marshall, Chairman
	Robert Ayling, Chief Executive
N. Brown	Jim Martin, Chief Executive
Cadbury Schweppes	Dominic Cadbury, Chairman
Carrefour	Daniel Bernard, Chief Executive
Dr Pepper/Seven Up	John Brock, President and Chief Executive
Electrocomponents	Bob Lawson, Chief Executive
General Electric	Jack Welch, Chairman and Chief Executive
GKN	Sir David Lees, Chairman
Granada	Charles Allen, Chief Executive
IKEA of Sweden	Sven-Olof Kulldorff, Vice President
Microsoft	Bill Gates, Chief Executive
Rentokil Initial	Sir Clive Thompson, Chief Executive
Reuters	Peter Job, Chief Executive
SAP	Professor Henning Kagermann, Management Board Director
Siebe	Barrie Stephens, Chairman
	Allen Yurko, Chief Executive
Singapore Airlines	Cheong Choong Kong, Managing Director
Smiths Industries	Sir Roger Hurn, Chairman
SOL	Liisa Joronen, Chief Executive
Vodafone	Sir Gerald Whent, Chief Executive

Companies studied without Chief Executive or Chairman interview included ABB, Home Depot, JCB, Marks & Spencer, Southwest Airlines, Sony and Wal-Mart.

INTRODUCTION

In *The Winning Streak*, we identified eight characteristics of highly successful companies: leadership, autonomy, control, involvement, market orientation, zero-basing, innovation and integrity. Those characteristics – or rather the way in which the 23 companies studied built them into the day-to-day culture of the organisation – are still valid today. But the world has moved on and they are no longer enough to explain the phenomenon by which some companies consistently year-on-year outperform their competitors and deliver value to their shareholders.

It is as if, in 1983, we took a snapshot – a still picture. But companies, any more than people, are not frozen in time. To understand the dynamics of companies operating in the vastly more complex environment of the late 1990s, we need a series of snapshots, or better still, a video recording. What such a video would show is that increasing complexity in the external environment leads to an increasing complexity in the challenges facing top management, both internally and externally. The secret of success in the 1980s was a series of *ands* – do this and this and that, and your chances of being a world-beater are increased dramatically. No guarantees, of course, but it clearly improved the odds. Now to the *ands* have been added a host of *ors* – numerous issues that have to be managed, but for which there is no universally right answer.

Even in writing *The Winning Streak*, it was obvious that the ability to exert control and give autonomy were *prima facie* in conflict. High-performance companies tended to defuse that conflict by developing control systems that were welcomed by those they affected, who saw them as a practical aid to achieving the objectives they owned. What has become increasingly clear in this most recent study is that this *apparent* (and we emphasise the word apparent) conflict is inherent in all the key success factors for today's high-performance companies. These apparent conflicts give rise to critical questions that our high-performance companies ask themselves again and again, putting exceptional effort into making sure they have the balance right.

So what are these critical issues? Described in Chapter One and in more detail in Chapters Two to Eleven, they represent the balance of:

- control versus autonomy;
- long-term strategy versus short-term urgency;
- evolutionary versus revolutionary change;
- pride versus humility;

- focus versus breadth of vision;
- values versus rules;
- customer care versus customer count;
- challenging versus nurturing people;
- leaders versus managers; and
- gentle versus abrupt succession.

These ten balances are not the entire story. For a start, new balances arise while others fade. The ones that are echoed by the high-performance company CEOs and chairmen we interviewed represent a snapshot of the balances they perceived as most important in the late 1990s, and within another decade other balances may assume equal or greater importance. What is clear is that every time a company gets one or more of these balances wrong (and even the best companies do lose their balance occasionally) it becomes harder to sustain high performance. When they wobble, our high-performance companies usually have the insight, the tenacity and the commitment to their ambitious goals to pause, take breath and readjust themselves on the tightrope. When, however, high-performance companies lose that innate sense of balance, they are just as vulnerable as anyone else to falling off, although their momentum usually means it takes longer for that to happen (and therefore, as in the case of ASDA for example, there may be time for new leadership to drag it back to equilibrium).

An innate sense of balance is therefore an essential cornerstone for sustained high performance. But a building usually needs at least four cornerstones if it, too, is to be in balance.

The cornerstones of sustained performance

In addition to balance, long-term high-performing companies all place very high reliance on three other characteristics. These are

- a challenge culture;
- simple (but not simplistic) solutions to complex problems; and
- a highly developed sense of 'rightness'.

A CHALLENGE CULTURE

Early on in our interviews, we were led astray by frequent reference to companies being performance-driven or having a performance culture. In some ways this piece of management jargon has an attractive ring to it. It suggests relentless achievement, vigilance and devotion to winning. But it also suggests being hard-nosed, focused more on task than people, short- or at best medium-term in outlook. None of our high-performing companies would associate themselves with being short-term. As we interviewed more and more companies, we recognised that stretching targets and frequent measurement of performance were simply part of a broader attitude towards *challenge*. It was being challenged that encouraged and enabled people to achieve extraordinary performance, that enabled them to participate in the business dream and its fulfilment, adopting them as their own. Challenge can take many forms. It doesn't have to be imposed by managers, as our case study of Finnish Company SOL demonstrates; it is something internal, which high-performing companies release and harness as the primary source of motivation at all levels.

SIMPLE (BUT NOT SIMPLISTIC) SOLUTIONS

The most effective response to complexity is often simplicity. Alexander the Great knew this when he sliced through the Gordian knot. Thousands of factory managers and engineers discovered it and residcovered it in the 1980s when they tried to automate complex systems, only to find that they should first have simplified. Many companies attempting to implement business process re-engineering are belatedly learning the same lesson. *All* of our high-performance companies place simplicity at or near the top of their list of critical competencies, yet are able to operate effectively in increasingly complex environments. For want of a better word, we have called this combined competence *simplexity*.

A SENSE OF 'RIGHTNESS'

The concept of an innate sense of 'rightness' harks back to the original *The Winning Streak* study. At a late stage in the research, we added an eighth characteristic of highly successful companies, which we called integrity. At that time, we saw integrity primarily as something the organisation gained by reflection from its leaders, sometimes by generations of leaders. Because they cared passionately about the company's reputation, they set the tone of honesty and fair dealing that permeated the rest of the organisation. Our current research bears out that same conclusion still; however, it also suggests that a sense of rightness occurs when the majority of people in the organisation feel a clear alignment between their own basic values and those of the leadership.

Exactly what a sense of rightness is, is hard to explain. It is more than expressing a belief in truth, honesty and fair dealing. It involves an instinctive understanding of what the corporate community – the leadership, other employees and other stakeholders – would consider the appropriate response to be in any issue that has a moral dimension. That doesn't happen by itself. It happens because people self-select employers whose values they feel comfortable with, and because the organisation evolves a deep-seated consensus that may never be expressed in writing. It is intangible, difficult to describe, yet immeasurably powerful. It is, in effect, the soul (or conscience) of an organisation.

Digging for gold: the research method

Our original studies for *The Winning Streak* involved three stages. First, we employed a research team to trawl through the UK's top 1,000 quoted companies to weed out those that did not meet the basic financial criteria of at least ten years' continuous profit growth. This left us with about 80 companies, from which, secondly, we selected 25 on the additional criterion of reputation (among peers, informed observers and the public in general). One of these companies declined to take part on the grounds that it might 'tempt fate'; one other, on detailed inspection, simply didn't stand up (as it was facing problems that stemmed, interestingly, from a failure to plan succession effectively, and this led inevitably to inadequate leadership, a drift from the core values and a stagnation in innovation).

As the third stage, we visited all of the companies, interviewing the chairman and/or chief executive, and a variety of managers and employees at other levels to give a broad and deep perspective on the company. We were surprised at how accurately top management's perceptions of what was important about the company and its culture were echoed lower down. (Our experience within most large companies since then is that people become less and less in touch, the more layers they are above where the action is. In one experiment, in a major UK financial services company, we were able to plot the degree of alignment within stakeholders' views through each of the five most senior layers – the result was an almost straight line, with the most senior levels of management least in touch with the perceptions of the outside world.) At the time, we attributed that high level of alignment in high-performing companies to the style of leadership, and our current study reinforces that view.

Among all the experiences and anecdotes gleaned from those interviewed, we found a number of common themes, which became the eight characteristics of winning companies – control, autonomy, involvement, leadership, zero-basing (the ability to maintain contact with the funda-mentals of the business), market orientation, innovation, and integrity.

In the new study, we wanted to take an international look at high performance – not least because so many businesses are now international businesses. A new method of selection was essential, if only because it isn't practical to compare financial reporting across international borders in a meaningful way. So we looked instead for our starting point to surveys of company reputation. These included *Fortune* magazine's 'America's most admired companies'; *The Economist*'s 'Britain's most admired companies'; *Management Today*'s 'Britain's 250 most admired companies'; the *Far Eastern Economic Review*'s 'Review 200: Asia's leading companies'; the *Financial Times*' 'Europe's most admired companies'; and PA/Sundridge Park's 'Quality in Management' awards.

The companies of high reputation were then appraised on the basis of their financial performance – in particular, sustained growth and profit performance – with the result that a high proportion fell out of the frame immediately (particularly in continental Europe).

It also became clear that sustained success in financial terms was a lot harder in some business environments than others. The level of com-petition, the speed of change within the company's markets, the scope of transitions the company may have to make between fundamental technologies or between, say, a near-saturated home market and becoming a genuinely international (or global!) player: these all had a bearing on how we defined success.

After much debate we decided to conduct the research in two phases. Phase One consisted primarily of companies who met all our key selection criteria of:

- high reputation among peers;
- continuous growth in profits at annual rate above average for their industry for a minimum of ten years; and
- an emphasis on organic rather than acquisitive growth.

To these we added a handful of other companies, who were our 'con-trols'. These included companies, such as The Berkeley Group, with rela-tively short histories but which had remarkable performance against very powerful competition. They also included a few companies that had suffered relatively minor profit dips as they coped with radical change in their external environment – for example, the three airlines British Airways, Singapore Airlines and Southwest Airlines. For all three airlines, the effects of a vicious recession in air travel in the early 1990s were little more than an annoying blip on their profit record. We also decided to include one or two that had taken a dip in performance as they adjusted to a false step in their markets (for example, ASDA returning to its core values after a new CEO attempted to drive it in a different direction).

As in the first study, we omitted all financial services companies because of, again, difficulties of comparison. (It is quite feasible for a large financial services company to have decades of secured income and yet – or perhaps as a result – to be poorly managed.) And one other large group of companies left out of our study is most of the supercorporations. Giants like Shell or ITT are so large and dispersed that we wondered whether they have moved into a different paradigm of management, one where corporate decision-making is as much a political as a business institution. These 'business states' of course share many of the same problems as high-performing companies in general. However, they also have one major common factor between themselves: they are so large that the pace of growth has long ago had to slow down to more manageable proportions. Simple maths suggests, for example, that if any supercorporation were able to increase its size at ten per cent more than the average for large companies year-in-year-out, it would not take long for it to own everything in the world.

But it clearly is possible to stave off the corporate aging process, and many of our high-performing companies have successfully done so, many of them for two decades and more, with continued growth well above sector average year on year. Some of them have been continuously successful for 100 years and more. Microsoft is a good example. It has managed to increase revenues by 50 per cent or more a year, primarily by creating products that sell more products. From the start, it has aimed to achieve very large user bases, because that is the route to further sales. So, for example, selling its Q-DOS operating system cheaply to IBM (it received only $186,000) was a masterstroke, because it set the industry standard. Microsoft's system was then available to manufacturers of the many IBM clones, creating a much larger market. The same approach has worked well for Microsoft ever since. Says *Fortune*: 'Microsoft wins virtually every market share battle it enters, even when its products aren't necessarily the best.'[1]

In Phase Two of the research, we followed the same pattern – a majority of companies who met all the criteria, plus a proportion for whom a rational latitude was allowed by virtue of their competitive environment. By this time, we had sufficient clarity of the results of the study to describe them in outline. We knew we were on the right lines, when the CEOs of these companies responded with comments along the lines of 'That's right! That's us, exactly!'

In the original study, we also took a look at a control group of companies, which were manifestly less successful. Here we were fortunate enough to be able to draw upon a number of the original *Winning Streak* companies, which had lost their way. High performance has to be nurtured continuously if it is to be sustained and our appropriately numbered Chapter Fourteen examines the decline of some of these companies, together with several non-*Winning Streak* cases, against both the original criteria and those explained in this book. We also had the opportunity to observe one high-performing company as it lost its edge and began to pull it back again.

The majority of companies in *The Winning Streak Mark II* are from the UK, because of both the performance criteria we applied and the fact that companies in most other European community countries tend to be much less open to study than companies in the UK, Scandinavia and the United States. The research programme will continue in Asia–Pacific and North America, with a view to producing separate editions for those regions.

Of the UK companies that passed our original selection criteria, only one – ASDA – has been included in the main study this time around (Sainsbury forms a separate case study in Chapter Fourteen). Rentokil Initial was one of the few companies to decline to appear in *The Winning Streak* when asked; its Chief Executive Sir Clive Thompson now says it was one of the few major mistakes he has made!

The Winning Streak was portrayed – for better or worse – as a product of the 'back to basics' movement. If there ever really was such a movement, it was like the permissive society – an alluring idea, but where did you find a membership form? In essence, everything that emerged from the original study was common sense. A few commentators, expecting a new set of models and management jargon, were disappointed. What they had missed was that doing the basics well may be common sense, but it is without doubt uncommon practice. The reality is that managers are under greater and greater pressure to attend to more and more issues. Taking time out for reflection, for thinking through what is *really* important and focusing the majority of effort and time on those critical but few activities demands a level of introspection, humility and self-discipline most managers find it hard to muster. Yet doing a few things well must surely be preferable to doing a lot of things poorly.

We return to the 'back to basics' theme unashamedly. In the past decade, the usual waves of management fads have given business surfers a transitory thrill, before crashing onto the shore and dissipating their energy. Every touted panacea has turned out to have its bitter side-effects, or to deliver far less than it promised, from quality standards to business process re-engineering (BPR – often seemingly standing for Blights People Relationships!). Gurus recant and revise with monotonous regularity.

Yet the principle of doing fundamental things very well is as valid today as it was twelve years ago or a hundred years ago. All we have tried to achieve in this book is to identify what some of those fundamentals are, and how managers in very successful companies tackle them. If your response is, 'But we already do these things', then consider:

- Do you do them consistently, and consistently better than your competitors?
- Are these the absolute priorities for your time and energy?
- Are they genuinely a source of competitive advantage for your company?
- If not, why not?

Getting the balance right on the issues that matter isn't a matter for complex formulae or business models. It comes from experience, intuition, clarity of vision and example from the top. Any company *can* achieve it, no matter how big or small. Few *will* achieve it, because they are distracted by detail, short-term crises or sheer lack of commitment. There's always an element of luck, of course – indeed, Peter Job, Chief Executive of Reuters, refers to it as a key success factor – but how much luck did you make today?

About our high-performing companies

Excluding those in North America, our high-performing companies have a combined market value of well over £100 billion. They include 18 of the world's largest by market capitalisation, and 12 of the 120 top European companies. A more detailed description of each of the companies is contained in the Appendix: Case Study Company Profiles at the back of the book.

1 | TEN KEY BALANCES

The New Characteristics Of Sustained High Performance

'We have more questions than answers, but if we had the answers, we'd be asking the wrong questions.' *Bob Lawson, Chief Executive, Electrocomponents.*

High-performance companies are, almost by definition, unique within their own markets. They are companies that have followed their own path, developed their own culture and retained a refreshing individuality in comparison with the competition. In short, they stand out, not just for their results but also for their corporate personality.

So it is hardly surprising that they take very different views and approaches, not just compared with their competitors but with each other. That, of course, makes it a great deal more difficult to seek and find the common factors to their success. What commonality is there, for example, between a company like Microsoft, which sells the virtual product of computer software and, say, Siebe, which sells very tangible engineering products? The answer lies, we have found from our interviews and case study review, not in specific strategies or systems nor in a particular overriding philosophy or set of values. Rather, it lies in the dexterity with which they achieve a balance between the many pressures and demands upon them. They may not get every balance right all the time, but they get more right more consistently than either their rivals or companies in general. And they get them right more often because they do four things exceedingly well:

- They recognise that, when confronted by apparently conflicting demands, 'and' always gives a better result than 'either ... or' – so much so that, in many cases, they see *harmony of objectives* where lesser companies see only difficult choices.

- They are *challenge-driven*. If this conjures up an image of a culture where the only thing that matters is delivering the numbers, think again. These companies are in business for the long term; they want numbers now *and* in the future. And, by and large, they get both, because they recognise that people only deliver numbers long-term if they are both supported and challenged.

- They have a remarkable knack of tackling complex issues by creating simplicity – what we have called *simplexity*. This is not in the sense that politicians present simple solutions, tackling many-sided issues with clichés, but in the positive sense of breaking down complex issues to the point where they can be dealt with by a combination of simple solutions. So, for example, rather than attack a complex marketplace with complex marketing, they will instinctively organise into small units that can approach each market segment in its own context.

- They have a passionate belief in *doing the right thing* that enables people at all levels to steer a course between apparently conflicting demands. To some extent, this is dependent on the effectiveness of how they communicate and inculcate the corporate values; but, in reality, this sense of rightness – and the belief that the organisation expects people to exercise it – is an overlay to all the more specific values the organisation espouses. In *The Winning Streak*, we found that a high emphasis on integrity was an essential requirement for business excellence. It is probably true that such an emphasis remains a foundation for people's broader confidence in doing the right thing.

Creating balance
....

The concept of a healthy balance is innate in the philosophies of both East and West. The Chinese speak of yin and yang. The much maligned Epicureans of ancient Athens preached that happiness was a function of exercising discretion between too little and too much in every choice people are faced with. Moderation was an important part of the original thinking behind the Anglo-Saxon work ethic.

Built into most cultures is an appreciation that life is a process of managing between extremes. Yet, in business, companies expend great effort in seeking black and white solutions.

One of the problems with any kind of business issues research is that people often only spend time thinking about issues if they perceive them as a problem, or if they have consciously addressed them. Because our high-performance companies manage many of these balances instinctively, they are not necessarily aware that they are doing anything special. So many of the initial clues to where the critical balances might lie came in our research from less successful companies.

The ten characteristic balances of high performance that emerged from our interviews are all issues that have caused great difficulty to less successful companies. Each was recognised by the vast majority of our high-performance companies as being a 'real' issue; most companies recognised them all. However, because they generally manage these issues well; and often instinctively rather than with great deliberation, the chairmen and CEOs rarely referred to a specific strategy for dealing with them. Maintaining the right balance on these complex issues had simply become part of 'the way we do things here'. They do, however, discuss and review these issues frequently. Says Electrocomponents CEO, Bob Lawson: 'They key is bringing these balances to the surface, so you can discuss them and dedicate time to solving them. You may not be able to get the balance you want straight away, so you have to be able to plan step by step how you'll get there.'

Does this mean that other companies cannot duplicate their success? In one sense, yes, for each high-performing company has found and continually evolves the right set of balances for its own circumstances. However, these instinctive behaviours started at some point as deliberate behaviours; so the company aspiring to high performance should, in theory at least, be able to gradually develop its own instinctive right balances and then manage the inevitable adjustments that these will need. In doing so, it stands to free up the energies of the organisation and the people in it to concentrate on both organisational and personal achievement – with all the bottom line implications of so doing.

Let us look briefly then, at our ten key balances:

- control versus autonomy;
- long-term strategy versus short-term urgency;
- evolutionary versus revolutionary change;
- pride versus humility;
- focus versus breadth of vision;
- values versus rules;
- customer care versus customer count;
- challenging people versus nurturing people;
- leaders versus managers; and
- gentle versus abrupt succession.

These ten balances are set out below in outline, for greater development in the chapters following.

CONTROL VERSUS AUTONOMY

The first, as we have already indicated, concerns the balance between control and autonomy. High-performance companies are constantly questioning *how they give people the maximum freedom to get on with the job and act as if they were owners of their slice of the business, yet exert just enough control to ensure the organisation gains the maximum benefit from its size and from a common sense of direction.*

There are strong parallels here between such an organisation and society at large. Society grants its citizens wide freedoms, which in most of the world include the freedom to travel, to congregate, to learn and to have different opinions. In return, it imposes a number of rules that set out boundaries around those freedoms – for example, the speed at which we can drive, the degree to which we can express opinions that might incite hatred or violence. Even Paradise had its rules. The more enduring and successful societies are those that manage the balance between freedom and responsibility with the greatest sensitivity. This doesn't mean that there is a right answer or a single right model – the currently high-performing economies of Singapore, Sweden and Switzerland, for example, all have slightly different balances that reflect their culture, economic history and geographical size, among other factors. Several of our high-performing companies refer to a sense of citizenship within the organisation as a source of both control and creative activity on the part of their managers away from headquarters. We refer to this phenomenon, for reasons that will become obvious, as **mission control**.

Among the common factors we observed in our high performance companies were:

- clarity of role and responsibility between headquarters and operating units;
- an absence of headquarters' bureaucracy;
- consensus between the centre and the operating units about what should be controlled where;
- an emphasis on no surprises;
- structures that maintain the benefits of smallness and simplicity;
- an emphasis on speed of information and decision-making; and
- a balance between strategic control and financial control.

LONG-TERM STRATEGY VERSUS SHORT-TERM URGENCY

The second critical question relates to *how companies persuade their managers to think long-term while maintaining urgency and action in the present.* Maintaining a healthy balance between spending quality time on strategic issues and getting the job done today is a familiar problem for managers everywhere – especially if they have a sense of always firefighting. Yet the experience of our high-performance companies is that tackling tomorrow's problems today leads to less firefighting and more strategic thinking;

getting every manager involved in continually thinking about the future provides a cohesion of effort that reduces the amount of firefighting. As with autonomy and control, getting the balance right creates a virtuous circle that supports continued high performance. This issue can be described as **strategic urgency**.

Our high-performing companies held to a number of common principles, which could be described as:

- strategy belongs where the action is;
- clarity is more important than cleverness; and
- instinct is how we put the urgency into strategy.

EVOLUTIONARY VERSUS REVOLUTIONARY CHANGE

Closely linked to item (2) above is the issue of how companies approach change: *how can we ensure an effective balance between evolutionary and revolutionary change?* All of our high-performance companies have a strong preference for evolutionary rather than revolutionary change – although the pace of evolution may be faster than in their competitors. This is, to some extent, a natural outcome of continued success. Several of the chairmen and chief executives poured scorn on the notion of 'if it ain't broke, fix it'. They preferred instead for people to focus on the things that are not working well and on those things that need to be changed to meet the demand for constant and substantial improvements in performance. When and only when that demand cannot be met by continued evolutionary change do they look to revolutionary change and embrace it with enthusiasm and (of course) a sense of urgency.

Some of our companies started out with revolutionary change – for example, both GKN and Smiths Industries switched markets almost entirely. Having achieved a high momentum of change, however, they have not relaxed. Instead, they have readjusted the *focus* of change from structural issues to technology and system issues, recognising as they do so that change in those areas may in turn lead to a demand for further structural change. This capacity to perceive evolutionary and revolutionary change as faces of the same coin, and to recognise when each is appropriate, permeates our high-performance companies from top to bottom. We refer to this process as **accelerated evolution**.

Among the common factors we found amongst our high-performance companies were:

- doing different things or doing things differently;
- putting innovation centre-stage as the source of maintaining differentiation;

- giving bright people the space to drive change around them;
- using customers as change partners;
- recognising that well understood constraints can encourage rather than diminish creative innovation;
- experimenting widely but putting effort behind the chosen few ideas;
- demonstrating remarkable persistence;
- spreading innovation rapidly among operating units;
- making change happen fast; and
- staying nimble.

PRIDE VERSUS HUMILITY

Success often – perhaps always – carries with it the seeds of ultimate failure. A source of competitive advantage today may all too easily become a millstone tomorrow. All of our high-performance companies were acutely aware of this, recognising that the longer high performance continues, the greater the risk of developing a complacent arrogance. Yet, at the same time, they perceive a strong sense of pride in the organisation to be an important (sometimes vital) element in attracting, keeping and motivating their people. For them, the question, *how can we sustain justified pride in our achievements without slipping into dangerous complacency?* is a very real preoccupation. We call this phenomenon **underweening pride**.

Among common approaches adopted by our high-performing companies are:

- choosing to compete and compare with the best;
- working with demanding customers;
- encouraging challenge within the core values;
- not letting the seat get too warm; and
- nothing is ever good enough.

FOCUS VERSUS BREADTH OF VISION

Although conglomerates are now largely out of fashion, several of our high-performing businesses have more than one area of business. And even those in an apparently unitary business are in fact spread across a number of different businesses. For example, Singapore Airlines is more than just an airline: it is also an operator of airports, and a major maintainer of aircraft. 'Sticking to the knitting' is all very well, but growth comes from knowing when and how to move the boundaries of what that business is. The issue is, in essence, about whether the business looks at itself through a convex or a concave lens.

A convex perspective leads to a high degree of focus, doing a few things exceedingly well and ignoring opportunities to slip into other markets. Herman Simon, in a recent book,[1] provides example after example of companies that have survived and in many cases prospered by sitting firmly within one niche and seeking a high proportion of the world market within that niche. A concave perspective, on the other hand, views the core business as a jumping-off point for all sorts of potential ventures. While the convex perspective acts to narrow down the options for growth, the concave perspective opens them out. The greater the concave curve, the broader the horizon of opportunity.

Our high-performance companies wear the equivalent of bifocal lenses, able to stick close to their core business(es) and core competencies, yet able to put these into context within the broader environment, sensing when and how it is appropriate to use a convex or concave perspective. Not surprisingly, we refer to this skill as **bifocal perspective**. For the busy manager, bifocal perspective offers an answer to the critical question: *how do I focus on the core business and new opportunities at the same time?*

Our high-performing businesses manage the delicate balance between convex and concave activity by:

- being very clear about the boundaries of the business they are in;
- ensuring that core competencies are the organisational glue;
- being intolerant of dog businesses; and
- investing in success not failure.

VALUES VERSUS RULES

A similar process of judgment occurs around business values and the role they play in making things happen. All our high-performance companies have strong values that underpin decision making at all levels. These are usually clearly articulated, but may also simply be broadly understood, shared beliefs. Like most other companies, those in the high-performance category also have systems and rules that tell people what to do. In the gaps between the rules lie what we can call operating principles: extrapolations from the values that provide effective guidelines where there are no rules or systems, or where the rules or systems come into conflict with the values.

The key here is the clarity with which high-performing companies instinctively distinguish between these three layers of decision-making aids. The values are to all extents and purposes immutable, fixed for the long term; on the few occasions when the values change, it is in response to or as a precursor to a radical change in the nature and personality of the business. (That is, *evolutionary* change is never allowed to undermine the core values.) The rules and systems, on the other hand, are constantly up for grabs. If they interfere with the achievement of the business vision or goals, or do not provide sufficient support, they must be changed – and rapidly. Operating principles, again, lie somewhere in the middle. They *can* be changed, but usually only after considerable debate or the need to carry out a radical realignment of the business in its markets.

To manage a business in this way requires a high degree of alignment between the values of the organisation and the values held by the people in it. Companies that fail to achieve that sense of alignment have to have lots of rules to force people to behave in a consistent manner. Companies that do have it can place much greater emphasis on achievement through values and operating principles – as do all our high-performing companies. In these companies, such rules as there are make sense to ordinary employees because they are related to broader values; and if they don't, the contrast is usually enough to stir debate that will likely as not get the rules changed. The key question here, then, is *how do I get people to do the right thing with the minimum of rules?* We describe this process as **living the values**.

Our high-performing companies use their values to generate consistency of approach and decision-making across the organisation by:

- having the right role models where they make a difference;
- managing the unconscious messages;
- continually looking for opportunities to communicate and demonstrate the values; and
- managing the operating principles, keeping the rules at bay.

They also share a number of values, not least that business should be exciting and fun.

CUSTOMER CARE VERSUS CUSTOMER COUNT

It's a classic paradox. The bigger a business gets, the more customers it needs to fuel the system. But the more customers it gets, the more difficult it becomes to look after them. So you end up chasing more and more customers to stand still. If any market illustrates this phenomenon, it is mobile phone networking. To gain the required return on investment, Vodafone has to secure a large market share. Yet the mobile phone market is characterised by very low levels of customer loyalty. Maintaining the balance between attention to market share (an issue in this case largely of price and short-term value) and building customer loyalty (an issue of longer-term value) is far from easy.

Of course, most managers in most companies would agree intellectually that the surest way to high market share lies in a high quality of customer service, but the reality is much more complex than that. For a start, service quality is generally a fairly slow means of building market share, so what do you do if you are in a hurry? Moreover, many companies (especially in financial services) have invested tens of millions of pounds in service-quality improvements, improving systems and changing employee attitudes, without seizing any significant competitive advantage over equally high-spending competitors.

For the questioning manager, the critical question here is: *how do I balance the need for customer volume against the need to make every customer feel uniquely served?* Our high-performing companies do this in a number of ways, but the common factors include:

- a recognition that the best customer is usually an existing customer;
- a talent for focusing on the customers they really want to keep;
- building relationships with 'character'; and
- putting competitive advantage before cost.

Overall, we can describe this mixture of common approaches as **customer focus** – not in the very general sense that the phrase is usually used (where it usually implies little more than finally noticing that the customer matters) but in the sense of focusing very sharply on who the customer is, why they do business with the company and how the relationship can be developed to the maximum benefit of both the customer and the company.

CHALLENGING PEOPLE VERSUS NURTURING PEOPLE

How can I get extraordinary performance out of ordinary people? was a question posed in the original *The Winning Streak* study. It remains a valid and important question. Our high-performing companies don't see a conflict between being hard and soft on their people; they believe in being both at once. Hard, in the sense of setting challenging, sometimes incredibly tough targets; soft, in the sense of understanding that people need support, encouragement and motivation if they are to succeed in meeting those challenges.

The evidence that stretching targets do result in higher levels of performance and commitment is strong, and not just from this study. According to classical goal-setting theory, goal difficulty, which includes a degree of stretch, is associated with greater individual effort and persistence.[2]

Among the common factors to managing this balance of soft and hard (we call it **tough but fun**) are:

- recruiting the best people possible for each job;
- nurturing creativity and proactive behaviour;
- providing the training and development to achieve great things;
- encouraging a genuine sense of ownership at all levels of the business;
- recognising and rewarding achievement; and
- using communication as the driving engine of commitment.

LEADERS VERSUS MANAGERS

Our high-performance companies were in no doubt that they expect their managers generally to spend more time on leading than managing, although they regarded both as important. Leadership style varied considerably, but common factors included:

- reliance on values rather than systems to influence other people's behaviour;
- taking seriously a manager's role as chief coach;
- an expectation that leaders set the example for others to follow;
- identifying with the 'big idea'; and
- an emphasis on inclusion as opposed to exclusion (that is, on leaders being part of 'us' rather than 'them').

In describing this issue as **values-based leadership**, we are building on a great deal of recent thinking elsewhere about the nature of leadership and management. Our own conclusion, in brief, is that the *function* of management is greatly enhanced by the effective use of the *role* of leadership; and that being effective as both manager and leader demands a high degree of sensitivity to stakeholders and their concerns.

GENTLE VERSUS ABRUPT SUCCESSION

High-performing companies tend to manage the transition between one chief executive and the next with remarkable smoothness; **seamless succession** is something they all take a degree of pride in. How they achieve it varies considerably – from a five-year apprenticeship for Allen Yurko at Siebe to a contest between equals elsewhere. However, with few exceptions, all of the successions to the top job have been internal appointments. There has been continuity of the core values, the broad strategy of the organisation and, indeed, the company's approach to all of the nine other balances.

That is not to say that a new CEO is a clone of his or her predecessor. Far from it. But each makes his mark by building on the successes of the past. What a contrast with the situation that occurs in so many companies! The new CEO feels it incumbent to introduce some dramatic change that emphasises his or her presence. But our high-performance companies are not looking for a new broom, but for one that will continue the process of evolutionary change. They do so by:

- building a high degree of strategic consensus among the top team;
- ensuring that potential CEOs spend long enough in the company to really understand how it works; and
- using the retiring CEO as a chairman mentor.

In summary . . .

The rest of this book is devoted to exploring in more detail – and in the interviewees' own words – how the high-performing companies achieve each of these balances. The lessons from their experience are pragmatic and, to a remarkable extent, duplicable in other companies, given a sufficient will from top management.

Among those lessons is that high-performing companies never assume that the balance on each of these issues is right. It's a bit like sailing a dinghy: there is a constant need to watch the signs of wind and water, the direction and shape of the waves, what is happening to the sails of competing vessels and to adjust the rigging accordingly. Such constant fine-tuning is the essence of high performance. Daniel Bernard, Chief Executive of Carrefour, expresses it well: 'We have to live with very big tensions (I agree with the ideas in your book). Very important is that we have to offer customers a large assortment of goods but we also have to rotate stock and keep prices down while increasing our margins and levels of service. Another tension is that we have to be fully global and fully decentralised while maintaining standards and quality.

'In the next five years, it will be difficult. We have to keep finding new tools to harmonise these impossible tensions.'

2 | MISSION CONTROL
Control versus autonomy

'If you don't need a policy from the centre, you shouldn't have it.' *Lord Blyth, Chief Executive, Boots.*

'We have to make the right balance between individual responsibility and control from the centre.' *Daniel Bernard, Chief Executive, Carrefour.*

A recent study by the UK's Institute of Management looked, among other things, at the extent of resources and the influence held by managers in companies with a high emphasis on 'empowering' staff at all levels.[1] It found, rather like the Biblical tale of the five loaves and two fishes, that the more managers shared power, the more authority and resources they gained. It is a principle that most, if not all, our high-performance companies would endorse. The way to exert the most effective control is to limit it to the few simple, readily understandable processes that have the greatest impact on group performance, and to maximise the freedom that managers at all levels have to achieve clear goals in their own way. And the more rigidly those core controls are enforced, the greater are the other freedoms people need in order to compensate and to release their creativity, initiative and proactivity.

Control and autonomy are therefore two sides of the same coin. Significantly, managing this particular duality is the only core characteristic of success that was both common to our research 12 years ago and remains so today. So it is fitting that we deal with it first.

For Allen Yurko, Chief Executive of Siebe, balancing control and autonomy remains 'the cornerstone of our management philosophy'. He explained in an interview: 'We're loose because we say to our operating companies, they've got the ball. We're a holding company which chooses to be close to the action, but no one can make all the decisions at the centre. Our approach is multi-local management.'[2] Balancing that looseness are stringent financial measurements and targets set with the centre.

What do we mean by control and autonomy? Formal control seems to be exercised in three main ways: through setting or agreeing targets for performance (mainly but not exclusively financial); through measurement and reporting systems; and through requiring certain decisions to be made centrally or corporately. Autonomy is, in essence, an absence of formal control: once clear goals are set, the individual manager has greater or lesser freedom to determine how they will be met. There *are* still controls in place, but they are much less obvious or intrusive. They are the controls exerted by the personal and organisational values, which form part of the 'sense of rightness' we have already referred to in the Introduction and the first part of Chapter One.

The analogy we draw here is with a manned mission into near space, perhaps to the Moon. The astronauts are surrounded by restrictions that would not be tolerable under normal circumstances: the need to carry out frequent and detailed safety checks, to wear cumbersome protective clothing and to take orders from ground control about almost everything they do, including when to eat and sleep. So why do they do it? It's not just for the pay – there are a lot of easier ways of making a living; and it's not because they are forced to. No, they do it fundamentally for the freedom and adventure that the restraints give them, for the sense of personal achievement and of taking part in something greater than themselves.

If that analogy doesn't work for you, try a comparison with scuba diving or Formula One racing. Whichever analogy you choose, the individuals who accept the restraints:

- understand and respect the reasons for the constraints;
- value the freedom the restraints grant them; and
- accept the restraints as being there to help them do what they wish.

The nature of control

Like most companies, our high performers exert control over their operating businesses through three main methods:

- setting targets;
- measurement and information; and
- highly selective central decision making.

Nothing remarkable there. What stands out, however, is how much effort they put into ensuring that they manage each of these processes with the maximum of consensus and goodwill from the businesses they control.

Roger Mavity, managing director of Granada Rentals (a subsidiary of Granada), says: 'At Granada, the process of setting a target for each of the four operating divisions starts with the divisional head agreeing his own target with his own team, which is then proposed to the Group Board. All the divisional targets are added together, and the Group Board then takes a view on whether more is needed. All the divisional heads are told together how much more is needed collectively, and each one then works out how much more he can contribute. The whole process takes time, but the emphasis is on the divisional head feeling ownership of his target, because he has played the pivotal part in setting the figure himself.'

CONTROL THROUGH SETTING TARGETS

High-performing companies vary considerably in how they set targets, from those who believe strongly in imposing challenge from above in order to motivate people to higher and higher performance, to those who allow people to set their own targets and generate their own challenge. Whether the companies are at one extreme of this spectrum or somewhere in the middle is not the issue; what counts is the fit between the method of target setting and the behaviours, which both sides of the arrangement expect the targets to elicit. In essence, targets are a means of focusing attention and effort on the things that matter to the company: who sets the targets is less important than who *owns* them and the degree of influence people feel they have in making them happen. (*Please refer to the addendum* at the end of Chapter Three for more details.)

CONTROL THROUGH MEASUREMENT AND INFORMATION

The information that comes into the headquarters of our case study companies is almost always simple, brief, relevant and locally accountable. Nothing else will do. The group CEOs have their own ideas about what constitutes the critical data they require, but they are uniformly intolerant of lengthy reports. (Please refer to part of the addendum at the end of Chapter Three, *Standard reporting keeps it simple*, for more details.)

CONTROL THROUGH HIGHLY SELECTIVE CENTRAL DECISION MAKING

The range of what our selected companies feel they have to control from the centre is understandably diverse. We shall explore some of them later in this chapter. The common factors, insofar as there are any, lie in the group's sense of identity and how the centre sees itself as adding value. The more the value of the group lies in the corporate brand (for example, Marks & Spencer or Rentokil Initial), the more they are likely to want to decide at the centre. Conversely, where the brand strength lies in the operating businesses, the fewer are the decisions that have to be referred to the centre.

All of our high-performing companies try to limit what they decide on behalf of the businesses to the minimum possible. A critical factor in their thinking is not to hold up action with structures that require deliberation at the centre.

ESTABLISHING BUY-IN TO CONTROLS

The 'fit' of controls demands not only that they are functional and appropriate but that they are seen to be so. It's the perception of the managers, who have to work within the control systems, that determines their attitude towards them (and by association, towards the centre). And it is their attitudes that determine whether they use the controls as important elements of their drive to meet challenging targets – as a motivator, therefore – or whether they spend time trying to work round them.

Says Graham Thomson, Chairman of Berkeley Homes (North London) Ltd (part of The Berkeley Group): 'The role of the centre is to offer guidance. They're our bankers. We set our cash requirements and targets with the centre. That's important, otherwise we could say they aren't our targets and they're unrealistic. But if [Berkeley Homes] North London gave a profit forecast of say £5 million and Kent had a different forecast using the same amount of cash, then the centre would ask why and offer guidance. Competition between the different traders in the group is very important. It's something we thrive on.'

Says Dominic Cadbury, Chairman of Cadbury Schweppes: 'You have got to distinguish between those things which you want to control and those things where you are happy to have your management make decisions for themselves. The overall benefit to the organisation of having the business properly controlled has to be seen to be greater than any reduction in autonomy that takes place.

'People accept control where they believe it's in the interests of the business to do so. If the controls go beyond what people think is sensible, you are quickly going to run into morale problems, where people see themselves as being controlled excessively by head office. Head office is seen as there to stop you using your initiative, penalising the people who take risks. If the organisation is going to do that, you are going to finish up with a management team and a culture that is cautious, involves a high degree of consultation and committee work, often bringing in consultants. That's always a sign that people are not prepared to take decisions. It tells you the business is over controlled.

'The process of getting people signed up is quite a lengthy one. We want to make sure that we get people onside for a long-term commitment, so that once the control is in place, it's in there for good. If you are going to do that, you've got to get it right. You need to be quite clear what are the places that you need to control and what are the things where you want to encourage local discretion, responsibility and accountability, because you are going to hold somebody in that operation accountable and he or she is on the line to deliver the budgeted result. If that person doesn't feel they have sufficient autonomy to achieve that result, then you have really got a problem, because they are not going to feel that they are genuinely accountable.'

An example is how Cadbury Schweppes tightened up its control over its brands. It wasn't always so, says Dominic Cadbury: 'Brands are fundamental to the company. I can remember doing a study back in about 1976. I went round the world visiting various markets and our brands were presented in quite different ways. We wrote 'Cadbury' five different ways. There was little consistency and what there was really depended on the fact that the same people had been working in England together. They had gone out into the various markets and had done what they had learnt in the UK. Now, in a market which is moving closer and closer together, it would be ridiculous to let people run those brands completely as they wish. To achieve the maximum value for our brands, you've got to achieve a degree of consistency, which can only be achieved through a level of control. We have done that over a period of time, getting people's agreement that this was the optimum positioning of a brand and through discussion. Then having agreed that optimum position, we say, "Right, we will stick to that. This product is going to be sold in this way, presented in this way and you cannot make massive changes to the brand on your own." We have taken away the autonomy that existed before, but with their involvement and agreement.'

Buy-in is largely a matter of perspective, according to Patrick Mannix, Director of Personnel and Quality Programmes at Reuters. 'Many people perceive performance measurement as a restrictive cage. I liken it, however, to an aviary. A cage is restrictive, an aviary allows freedom to fly; but within some bounds. How do you create a framework to ensure that entrepreneurs are taking the business where you want to go, but which is big enough to allow them the freedom to succeed?' he asks.

Says Colin Hutchinson, Managing Director of Berkeley Homes (Hampshire) Limited: 'The key difference between Berkeley and other companies is the autonomy of the trading companies. With your own board of directors you are running your own business. The centre watches carefully but we make the day-to-day decisions because we know our patch. I know Hampshire inside and out, but put me in North London

and it might be a different story. The centre puts in chairmen, but providing you run your business according to the rules and criteria – primarily
to achieve an acceptable return on capital – then they let you make your
own decisions.'

At first sight, there is little pattern to what these companies choose to
control closely. What is common is the deep thought and discussion that
has gone into defining and constantly reviewing these controls. All are
very clear about *why* they need to control these specific issues, and about
the link between these tight controls and their strategic competencies.
Some examples:

- At Rentokil Initial, says Chief Executive Sir Clive Thompson: 'The UK
  corporate HQ is a banker. We control marketing, strategy, the weighting
  of services, and we have total control over acquisitions. Acquisitions
  have to be driven by strategy not by opportunity alone. Then the day-
  to-day activities are controlled from within the individual country. We
  use branches – typically 30, 40 or 50 people in each. So in each branch
  there will be 30–40 service people, 5–10 sales people; all report to the
  branch manager. Each branch is a profit centre.

  'The branch managers are responsible for achieving targets. They
  report to an area manager, who reports to a regional manager. They all
  report to the country MD. Everyone above the branch manager is simply
  there because we recognise that branch managers aren't perfect.

  'We also maintain central control over other areas. Marketing, for
  example, in all our services is in exactly the same style in every country –
  like McDonald's. We say: "This is what we provide, this is what we are
  good at." By restricting the areas we get into we probably cut off 10–15
  per cent of potential markets. Take pest control, for example: the pests
  vary – we handle poisonous spiders in Australia for example – but our
  approach to service is similar. We get the same excellence in Indonesia
  as in Holland.'

- 'At Electrocomponents', says CEO Bob Lawson, 'We do control:

  → Measurements of customer service. They are on my desk every
    Tuesday morning. That says "It's important and Bob knows about it."
  → Availability of range.
  → Capability of supply – we aim to ship every order on the same day;
    within some major cities, within two hours.
  → Daily/weekly sales. I knew this morning at 10.00 a.m. that two of our
    businesses had had record sales the day before. So I went out and
    shouted it across the floor – you have to share success while you are
    still buoyed up by it.

We run two levels of overall control: the business plan, with up to three years' outlook; and the annual budget, which is rolling and covers initiatives people will deliver.'

• IKEA has set itself very firmly at the control end of the control–autonomy spectrum in most aspects of store management. Jan Kjellman, head of the Swedish division, explained to the *Financial Times*: 'There is always a conflict between the local store and IKEA of Sweden. They want to follow local market trends, but that is not in line with the IKEA identity. We have to safeguard our identity.' The company's five per cent share of the German market could have been much greater, for example,' said CEO Moberg, 'if we had adapted to more traditional German styles and tastes ... but we would have had a different profile. We believe in the long run we will win the customers over to our Swedish way of thinking on furniture and home furnishing.'[3]

Yet in spite of its rigid control over product and store design, IKEA has become progressively more liberal towards its operations in terms of financial control. Partly because of its initial failure to crack the North American market, in 1992 the company stopped asking its operating divisions for annual budgets. CEO Anders Moberg told *The Economist*: 'We realised our business planning system was getting too heavy; we can use the time saved for doing other things better.'[4]

IKEA also believes it has to control product development. That, says Sven-Olof Kulldorff, Vice President of its Swedish operations, is critical to maintaining low prices and high quality. IKEA not only creates the designs, but it specifies to suppliers how the product will be made, so as to maximise quality and efficiency – even down to how the raw materials are cut.

• Reuters, too, leans towards control. Explains main board Director David Ure: 'I don't know if it makes us control freaks, but there's more and more integration. Why? Because as barriers to entry lower, we are open to more competition. A lot of our competitive advantage is the integrated nature of our business in terms of pricing, product etc. These are the macro-barriers to entry. To unpick that integration would be dangerous.'

• Marcus Beresford, Managing Director of Industrial Services of GKN points to 'a structure that carries with it accountability. The review process for budgets, for company strategies – they all happen with regularity. The chief executives of the businesses have to come and explain what they are doing to the Chief Executive, myself and a couple of others and they are accountable monthly. They can't invest large sums without there being an involvement from the centre.'

- Marks & Spencer, like most successful retailers, imposes a common formula from the centre. From the head office building in Baker Street, not far from the home of the fictional Sherlock Holmes, the company has functional departments controlling all buying, merchandising, logistics, finance, land and building management, pricing and quality standards. It also sets basic standards for a wide range of other activities, such as recruitment.

  This might not seem to leave much for the store manager to do. But his or her job is about dealing with people – staff and customers – and with being the company's eyes and ears in the marketplace. Local markets have local needs. A completely rigid system of control from the centre would have distinct disadvantages. So the branch manager monitors what his or her customers want and negotiates with head office about which products to assign to the store. Detailed knowledge of the demographics of each store's customers helps make these discussions constructive and avoid over-reaction to freak events.

  The store manager is supported by a staff manager, who also reports to human resource functions at divisional level and at headquarters. Recruitment, training, welfare and almost all other people activities are decentralised to the stores.

- Boots, like Marks & Spencer, needs to maintain a degree of homogeneity about its stores – familiarity breeds sales. Says Personnel Director David Kissman: 'We have more controls than we would like – we have to maintain standards. If you have 1,200 stores and you want people to have the same shopping experience when they go into these stores, then you have to have certain rules. But we may be a bit top heavy. If you want people to be really innovative, then you have to allow them to take risks.'

- Says ASDA Chairman Archie Norman: 'I don't believe in our sort of business in letting people get away with the idea that what you need is a high level of autonomy. What you want is a high level of discretion on a narrow front. There are a few things that we ask the stores to exercise discretion over. We give them autonomy, we expect them to perform. There are many, many things that are very highly centralised here, as they are in any retail organisation. We make no bones about it, it is not a democratic organisation. It is an involvement company, but it is not a democratic company. The two are very different.'

- At The Berkeley Group, the centre sets return on capital (unusual for a housebuilder) and gross margins. Almost everything else is left to the operating companies – including what they want to call themselves.

Says Chief Executive Tony Pidgley: 'In our business, the traders must not be seen to be part of a big corporation. When we changed our name, for example, to St David in Wales, some people thought we'd gone mad, but we have to be seen as local to the area we are operating in.'

The nature of autonomy

High-performing companies promote autonomy by being very clear about what they want to control from the centre, and as a consequence about what they *don't*.

Says British Airways' Chairman, Sir Colin Marshall: 'In our business, some control systems, such as safety, security and financial, need to be kept very tight at all times. In other areas, central control has been loosened considerably, with managers encouraged to take the initiative of running their own "businesses". The different areas of the route network, for instance, have to compete with each other for use of expensive capacity on existing routes.'

Bob Stack, Personnel Director at Cadbury Schweppes, often disappoints people carrying out surveys of group HR practice. He has to tell them he can't give them data – because he hasn't got it himself. Not only would the operating companies object if he did try to gather the data; they would ask questions about why he was wasting his and their time.

Autonomy is rarely, if ever, absolute. Most of the time, however, autonomy is a 'licence to operate' – the freedom to make one's own decisions within an agreed framework of accountability. It is expressed well by Carrefour CEO Daniel Bernard: 'Everybody takes decisions at all levels. I have no impact on the daily running of stores around the world – how could I? In our organisation, it is clearly decentralised. But we discuss our ideas, and make sure we transfer know-how.'

And Granada's Roger Mavity declares: 'Once a month, I'm accountable for what I'm doing; and, just like Christmas, that meeting is never cancelled ... in between, I have a lot of freedom.'

At Microsoft, says Mike Murray, Vice President Human Resources and Administration: 'The balance we have struck is that while we recognise the critical need to have agreement on corporate direction, especially on product strategies and technologies, implementation belongs at the local level. We have to trust local management to figure out how to solve the problems. But it's not entirely hands-off – we insist on a continuous feedback loop.'

Genuine autonomy has a number of characteristics:

- it is earned through trust, which is earned through performance;
- it involves a sense of personal ownership of the responsibilities; and
- people always feel they have space – the scope to reach out and do more, without touching the walls of their job.

AUTONOMY IS EARNED THROUGH PERFORMANCE

None of our case study companies has central controls for their own sake. Top management recognises that the more time it spends poring over figures, the less it has for longer-term tasks such as envisioning the future, and for the hands-on activities that characterise effective leadership. So they work hard to recruit and develop people they can trust. The more trust, the less need to monitor and control. In effect, autonomy in most of these companies is something you earn.

Says Stephanie Monk, Human Resources Director of Granada: 'If a business commits to meeting its objectives or growing its market share or acquiring a bigger part of its sector, it has a lot of autonomy as to how it does that, how it structures itself, how it uses its resources, how ambitious it is in going for something. Where people are proving to be successful they are given a lot of freedom to operate. The relationship gets a bit closer when people are not performing and then the magnifying glass is applied and the level of frequency and intensity of discussion, from brainstorming to review, increases. You can earn the right to your autonomy and you sustain your autonomy through the quality of your performance.

'Granada is absolutely dedicated to achieving an outstanding level of financial improvement year on year. Everyone knows that, it's the religion. You make your numbers, because that earns you the right to create your strategic future.' Or, as Charles Allen, CEO puts it: 'Our organisations are tightly controlled in some respects and people are given tremendous autonomy when things are going well. But as soon as they are not, everything is pulled in very tightly. I always say: "The ticket to autonomy is complying with effective forms of control."'

Granada's *modus operandi* ensures that managers report upwards on trading performance, with great discipline and great regularity; yet they have very wide freedom of operation. As long as the information reporting shows that the results are coming in satisfactorily, that freedom of operation continues. But as soon as the information flow indicates trouble coming, then the manager has to justify his operational decisions much more fully. The underlying concept is to ensure that managers have the freedom to succeed on their own, but do not have the freedom to fail on their own.

Says Jim Martin at N. Brown: 'Discussions with managers at budget time can be quite vigorous, but once they are agreed it's up to them. This gives them considerable flexibility, but they must deliver. If they don't, they get a lot of help from the centre.'

By measuring performance through the few but powerful measures the group does insist on – and in particular, through meeting financial targets – Cadbury Schweppes feels able to let people make their own mistakes in other areas. 'You could have a disastrous marketing campaign, for example,' says Personnel Director Bob Stack, 'and no-one from outside the operating company would ask to review it.' Only if the figures start going wrong is there intervention from the centre.

A SENSE OF PERSONAL OWNERSHIP OF THE ISSUES

Every time the centre takes a decision out of the hands of a manager, that affects that manager's area of responsibility, it is in effect saying that it is not his or her issue to worry about. Or it is saying it does not trust the manager to make the right decision. Or both. Says Bob Lawson, at Electrocomponents: 'We put a lot of time into deciding what is important. A lot of things you can control aren't worth controlling. We apply the "So what?" test. So, for example, if I say, "I'm going to control your expenses" you could say, "Either you trust me or you don't; if you do trust me, you don't need to control them."'

Liisa Joronen, CEO of SOL, is also a fierce believer in trusting people to manage themselves. 'Our people measure themselves because they are so honest. When you really trust people, they are more honest. They don't set low targets; they always set them very high, although they know if they don't reach them they are not paid bonuses. If it's one-hundred-per-cent *your* target, you always overoptimise yourself. It amazes me.

'My most important task is to arrange celebrations and thank those who produced excellent work. My most important and very difficult duty is not to tell people if they have not met their targets and not to tell them what they have done wrong or what they should do. People are clever enough to realise themselves what is good and what not; it's their work not mine. If I interfere in their work it soon becomes mine and they start finding excuses. It has taken a long time to learn that lesson. It is so much easier to tell others what they should do than to let them discover it themselves.'

Other companies try to develop personal ownership of the issues in different ways. For example Wal-Mart encourages department managers and their assistants to operate as 'stores within stores'. They receive weekly figures on sales, profit and loss, mark-up and inventory, both for their department and compared with others across the company.[5]

THE SCOPE TO REACH OUT

When managers who are frustrated and angry about their jobs describe their feelings, they rarely, if ever, complain about having too much opportunity. Rather, they complain about being 'boxed in', 'prevented from doing what I see to be necessary', 'weighed down with paper and meetings'. They talk about having to adopt a short-term focus most of or all the time.

They also talk about being stressed. Significantly, one of the main causes of stress is feeling personal lack of control over events around you. For example, the person who is stressed out by overwork is often affected less by the work itself than by the powerlessness to control the amount or timing of it. The more autonomy a person has, the more potential they have to exert control over events. Of course, there are other factors involved – among others, their skill and ability, their level of confidence and how clearly they understand the issues. Nonetheless, when people feel they are in control, they are much more likely to take intuitively right decisions, to take sensible risks, to experiment and to motivate those around them. In short, autonomy is the bedrock of entrepreneurship within large and small organisations.

The sense of having wide boundaries to operate within comes across time and again from our interviews with line managers. Take John Brock, President/CEO of Cadbury Schweppes' subsidiary Dr Pepper/Seven Up: 'We really are a devolved company. In the US alone, we're a $1.3 billion-turnover business. We have an annual operating plan and a long-range plan (three years). We come to the UK in November for the annual plan review and April for the long-term plan. Once they are approved, we go make them happen. As long as there are no financial surprises, and our financial guys keep talking to the financial guys over there, we have the freedom to get on with it. As the senior guy in the US operation, I've also made it my responsibility to come to the UK on a regular basis, not to ask permission for what I'm doing but to let people know what's going on and keep them informed.'

Similarly, at Siebe, Sergei Fangi, Managing Director of the Italian-headquartered subsidiary Ranco Controls Europe, finds that ambitious targets and close monitoring from the centre still allow a great deal of freedom. Target setting is a collaborative process and once targets are set, he has significant scope in deciding how to achieve them.

A final point about the nature of autonomy is that it takes time to achieve. Building people's confidence in their own ability to take decisions, overcoming the natural suspicion that the company will think better of it and pull back on the reins, equipping people with the skills and support systems to operate more autonomously – these things all take time. So, when Granada acquired hotel chain Forte through a hostile acquisition (Forte was an original company in *The Winning Streak* but had gradually succumbed to organisational arthritis – among the symptoms was an oversized headquarters), many Forte managers were fearful of the new owners. Recalls Granada's Human Resources Director Stephanie Monk: 'While one level of people were thrilled to have autonomy, those at another level initially kept looking to us to provide the answers. "When is Granada going to tell us what our culture is going to be, when is Granada going to tell us what we're going to do?" I said, "It's not like that. This is what we are and we can commend some of these things to you, but you determine what your future is going to be and you will need to establish your own new culture and values."

'You just can't change the structure and say the byword now is autonomy and expect people to go away and try. You actually have to help people through that transition because it's quite hard, when you have had to constantly go through a process of checks and balances, to suddenly find you have the freedom to propose and implement things and to realise you stand or fall by them. So it's stimulating, but a bit more threatening, to be in an environment where there is a high degree of local autonomy.'

AUTONOMY, DELEGATION AND EMPOWERMENT

It is probably useful at this point to emphasise the difference between autonomy, delegation and empowerment:

- Autonomy is essentially a licence to operate within preset boundaries.
- Delegation is giving someone responsibility for achieving a specific task or tasks.
- Empowerment is creating the environment where people feel willing and able to take responsibility for themselves.

Delegation and empowerment are therefore alternative routes to achieving autonomous operation. Our high-performing companies use both, extensively. Delegation happens because flat structures and stretching targets demand it. There simply isn't time for managers to do their direct reports' jobs.

Empowerment, however, demands much greater proactive effort on the part of the company and its top management. It requires continuous attention to:

- the processes of decision-making;
- developing the capabilities of people in the organisation to accept greater responsibility; and
- the style of leadership and management.

These latter two themes are developed elsewhere in this book (*see* Chapters Ten and Eleven), but it is appropriate to say a few words here about the processes of decision making. There will, in all companies, be a trade-off to make between the need to take an organisational perspective on issues, and the need to base decisions on the knowledge and understanding of the person on the spot. Many companies take away critical decisions from the front line, because they fear that front-line employees don't have sufficient organisational perspective to make the right decision. Our high-performing companies, in the main, prefer to turn this issue on its head. They ask instead: 'What can we do to equip front-line people to take more decisions more effectively?' The answer usually amounts either to educating them, so they understand the issues better, or to providing them with the relevant information to make decisions, or both.

Few companies in our study go so far in this direction as SOL. CEO Liisa Joronen explains how a work team would approach a new contract: 'They will sit down with today's supervisor and think through the goals of the work together. What are we doing here and why? They set the goals together – for example, customer satisfaction, handling the costs, profitability. The first few times, the supervisor or team leader has to explain these things, to increase their knowledge of the business, but after that the cleaners and supervisor together have the responsibility to set the goals and to plan together how to achieve them.' Each month, the supervisor receives a full breakdown of financial performance, customer by customer, and other key measures such as customer satisfaction. The team use this information to manage the customer relationship and to plan how to reach their profit targets.

In summary . . .

This chapter has begun to answer, in very broad terms, the question of how high-performance companies manage to balance giving people the maximum freedom to get on with the job and act as if owners of their slice of the business, against exerting the controls needed to ensure the organisation benefits from its size and a common sense of direction. The key, in most cases, appears to be a clear understanding of what has to be controlled and why, together with a determination to let people use their initiative in every other matter. Chapter Three examines this process in more detail.

3 | MISSION IN ACTION
Balancing control and autonomy

'Providing you deliver at the end of the day, you like to be left alone.' *Gerry Robinson, Chairman, Granada.*

'Don't prevent your people from using their own brain's and don't prevent your people from doing good work and good quality.' *Liisa Joronen, Chief Executive, Sol.*

'We always require a result, but almost never specify a method of getting there. An empowering organisation still has to specify what has to be done. For example, Welch says there has to be a 360-degree appraisal process, but there is a wide variety of approaches across the company in how they do it.' *Steven Kerr, Vice President for Corporate Leadership Development, General Electric.*

Given the great variation in type and style of business among our case studies, it would not be surprising if we had found very different solutions to how they achieved a workable balance between control and autonomy. In practice, however, we found a remarkable degree of commonality in approach. In particular, they all placed great importance on:

- ensuring clarity of role and responsibility between headquarters and operating units;
- preventing headquarters bureaucracy;
- consensus about what should be controlled where;
- no surprises;
- the value of small size and simplicity;
- emphasising speed of information and decision-making; and
- balancing strategic and financial control.

Clarity begins at home

There are two critical questions that our case study companies ask themselves frequently. The first is, 'Where does the control for each business issue have to be vested in order to fulfil the business objectives most effectively?' And the second is, 'Do people in the business understand where the control lies and accept that this is appropriate?' Both questions need to be asked frequently because the answers may change. For example, IKEA's ventures into the United States obliged the company to reassess radically the central control it exerted over product range and supply.

The answers to the two questions will almost always be positive where there is a high degree of clarity around three things:

- the role of the centre;
- how to achieve co-ordination and consensus on new ideas and policies; and
- what each individual is accountable for.

The source of this clarity is without doubt the centre and, in particular, top management. If they can articulate easily and credibly who is responsible for what and why, it is relatively simple for the message to percolate down. In this sense, clarity truly does begin at the corporate home! 'The key is absolute openness,' says Bob Lawson, CEO of Electrocomponents. 'People don't care too much about what the mix is between autonomy and control, provided they know what it is. They can't cope with lack of clarity.'

Clarity is a virtue greatly espoused in business, but all too rarely practised. It is a natural instinct to fudge issues at all levels where being precise might cause conflict, or invite embarrassing questions or comparisons. Achieving clarity requires significant time spent and reflective space devoted to:

- understanding an issue and its context;
- determining the relative importance of different factors;
- considering carefully how to communicate that understanding to others; and
- checking that others have acquired the same understanding.

So often, in business, managers say they can't find the time to do this properly. Yet what could be a more valuable use of the manager's time than to ensure people understand what is needed of them and why? The higher up the organisation, the more important clarity becomes. At junior management levels, the task is relatively simple and the manager is generally on hand to answer queries and redirect effort. If he or she isn't there, more experienced colleagues with similar jobs can step in with advice and guidance. At the top, by contrast, most of the work is remote and intuitive in nature. If a senior manager puts a different interpretation on a goal, for example, it may be much harder and take much longer to detect. Indeed, it is not uncommon, we have found, for directors on the same board to have very different understandings of policies they have all agreed to.

So our high performing companies balance an instinctive action orientation against the discipline to establish great clarity about objectives and priorities. For example: 'At Boots,' says Personnel Director David Kissman, 'We have worked very hard on the link between where the business is going and what we expect of people. The real skill is to break this down and demonstrate at each level how this fits into the big picture. We split what we do into output and a development review. The output was linked into the development review and is based on competencies, which in turn are translated into behaviours.'

THE ROLE OF THE CENTRE

What does the centre do? At Granada: 'The how of running the businesses was and is determined within the businesses. The role of centre has been predominantly to challenge, to allocate resources, to stimulate, to propose, to test and provoke people within the businesses to do things beyond what they probably thought themselves able to do, left to their own devices,' says Stephanie Monk. 'Holding the strategic ring comes from the centre. It determines which will be the businesses in which we invest and seek to grow in the future.'

An important part of the centre's role is to promote good practice, by suggesting ways in which business units might achieve their targets. It is a delicate balance. Too little forcefulness and the businesses may ignore the underlying message. Too much and they may feel obliged to go along with projects or trends they do not believe in. Explains Michael Treschow, Managing Director of Sweden's Atlas Copco: 'We probably do a little or a lot with quality circles or re-engineering or whatever the buzz-words are, but we are very careful that we don't run centrally promoted activities. We'd rather have a menu of concepts and processes and give it to the operating companies, saying "You have a tough target. Here's a toolbox. You are there to pick the tools that you like, that fit your timing, personality or strategy." It's no fun as a manager to be told "Now you are going to have quality circles" or "This is the year of customer focus". I'm very allergic to that sort of concept. Rather, we'd say, "This is the year of even tougher targets than last year and in order to make those targets, you will have to do something. Some of these proven ideas might help, but you have to own them."'

For SAP, a critical role for the centre is 'development, both managerial and technical', says main board Director Professor Henning Kagermann. This reflects the bias in background of most of the senior people in the company – and is one of its core strengths. The centre also monitors customer satisfaction, to ensure that the businesses keep a balance between the short and long term.

SOL supports best practice from the centre by developing guidelines and tools its supervisors can use to manage their operations more effectively. Says Jukka Suuniitty, a SOL employee at the centre: 'I came here first as a supervisor in the field, while I was studying. After I graduated, I made an appointment with Liisa Joronen and told her I had ideas about developing supervisors' work. I had a one-year project to develop lists to manage customers and employees – for example, one computer table lists all the details they ought to know about a customer's premises. Another is a planning tool where you plan your whole year's customers; it also helps you see how the customer's inspection goes, monthly and by every customer. Another tool helps them manage salary memos.'

If Sunniitty or any of his colleagues wants to promote a new way of working, they have to sell the idea individually to all the supervisors and their teams. For example, he explains: 'When I go to talk to cleaners about teamwork, I tell them what teamwork means and why we encourage teams. They then make a decision whether they take the challenge or not. My task is to sell the idea. They make the decision, whether they are ready to do what's needed. Voting is a bad idea. There has to be some kind of consensus.'

Hans Ola Meyer, Finance Director of Atlas Copco, continues the theme: 'We accept the basic underlying reasons and philosophy of the decentralised structure of the group – because we're into machining industry and not finance. We understand that. The model then, as I see it, is to try to achieve as much as possible of the co-ordination benefits that you can without challenging the basic underlying decentralisation philosophy. OK, so the way we attack it is to set up a system internally – we actually call it an internal bank structure, we use that name even – and to set up a system in terms of structure and how you communicate and who executes trades etc. as efficiently as possible so that the operational divisions will use that service without even contemplating otherwise.'

The same applies to major change initiatives. It is not the centre's role at Atlas Copco to impose them on the businesses. Atlas Copco takes the notion of the centre as a bank much farther than most companies. As a benevolent bank, it demands a dividend from its operating companies. Says Meyer: 'We try to create a true commercial environment, so they pay market-based interest rates from the internal bank and they get market-based rates on their internal deposits. We evaluate their credit-worthiness as an external bank would. On top of that, we also charge them a high requirement for the equity they use, which is our money, loaned to them to use. There's not much admin with this internal dividend system. It works very smoothly. But it supports the whole idea of decentralisation. Otherwise, no one would really care about risk capital versus borrowed funds and you haven't created a true balance sheet responsibility.'

Adds Lennart Johansson, Atlas Copco's Business Controller: 'We have never given out an instruction since I've been here saying "Now everybody has to cut costs, now everybody has to stop hiring people, or now everyone has to postpone this or that to adjust." Even when some divisions went into recession we didn't restrict the businesses that had new products and were going for growth. It's the guys that have the big problems who must cut the costs. In the same way, we'd never launch a big culture change from the centre; it's up to the businesses to decide.'

Another role for the centre is to act the same part as an effective non-executive might at main board level – questioning, challenging and asking naive questions. Says GKN's Managing Director of Industrial Services, Marcus Beresford: 'Even the most stupid questions can be important. They can be absolutely at the core.'

SOL's head office operates in much the same way. Indeed, that is almost the only reason for its existence. Says Liisa Joronen: 'We don't give any support from headquarters to any area, and they can grow as fast as they want. But all the figures must be good.'

Atlas Copco has effectively taken the decision not to try to impose a common culture. So has Bowthorpe where, says CEO Nicholas Brookes, it 'would smother the creativity and entrepreneurship. What I do encourage is a culture based on five tenets of customer love, achievement, development of people, integrity and creativity – these elements are general to all our businesses.' Other companies, notably Rentokil Initial and Siebe, appear to have taken the opposite view, preferring to establish a common culture around the world. Says Rentokil Initial's Sir Clive Thompson: 'We have encountered problems imposing our culture in other countries/cultures. I use the word "imposing" rightly as we transcend the national culture. We have had a lot of problems as we have developed a presence in developed countries – which are the best markets for us. Yes, we have taken our company culture to North America, Europe and Asia–Pacific. We've done it. We've established a global culture. That's the difficult bit.' However, on closer examination, what they have really developed is less a culture than a management approach. The behaviours they expect, and in some cases have imposed, are those that are essential to delivering their particular balance of control and autonomy.

More typical is the approach followed by SAP. Says Henning Kagermann: 'The culture in the countries was only to a certain extent shared. There are some common guidelines. There is local management in place in the countries, though there may be some German managers in place in the start-up days of the subsidiary. The influence of the local culture is strongly in evidence. There is a different culture, for example, in SAP in Japan. There is more hierarchy in the US than in Germany, where the corporate style is more one of informality and a family atmosphere.'

The role of the centre, then, varies considerably across our high-performance companies. Each has made a series of decisions about the degree to which it wishes to play the following roles:

- holder of the purse strings;
- source of *internally* driven challenge and high standards (supplementing, not duplicating challenge from the companies' own markets);
- source of culture and shared values; and
- a resource for advice and best practice.

To a large extent, it doesn't matter which of these roles they play, nor how intrusively they do so. What does matter is how clearly those roles are understood both by the people in the centre and the people in the operations. As long as they are in agreement about what the proper role is, and as long as there is continuous discussion to ensure that the balance is generally correct, it is relatively easy. Even where controls are tightly applied, understanding the limits and reasons of the centre's need to control each area empowers managers to find a great deal of scope to work within the controls.

THE CO-ORDINATION PROBLEM

The more decentralised a company is, the more difficult it becomes to gain consensus about new ideas and policies, to share good practice, and to stimulate teamwork between operating units. High-performing companies tend to seek informal ways of adding value by bringing people together. For example, General Electric (GE) has tackled this issue in several ways. Firstly, Chairman and CEO Jack Welch brings together the top 30 or so most senior executives into a Corporate Executive Council, which meets regularly to explore issues that have impact across the group. Says Noel Tichy, a professor at the University of Michigan, who has worked closely with Welch: 'This executive council has little overt authority and no clear role in decision making, yet has come to function effectively as GE's political centre ... by design, [it] is a workshop in GE's core values.'[1]

At Smiths Industries, too, says Human Resources Director David Spencer: 'We have lots of meetings to exchange information around the group and make deals between units.' Bowthorpe is just facing up to these issues. Says CEO Nicholas Brookes: 'When I came here, our 97 companies had never all come together at the same time. I brought all the managing directors into one place for two-and-a-half days. We covered a lot of topics, such as our strengths and weaknesses and our future direction. A professor from Stanford University led a day's session on global strategy. It all generated discussion between companies realising they could get benefits from other members of the group and ideas for going forward.'

In a heavily decentralised organisation, there will always be a certain amount of reinventing the wheel. The key to keeping this in check appears to be raising the threshold of expectations to a level where no one can afford to adopt a 'not-invented-here' attitude. The divisions of high-performance companies *have* to be alert to new technology, new sales approaches, new methods of organisation and people management, because they cannot otherwise achieve challenging goals. Sharing of good ideas occurs because people value the trades they can make. In essence, an internal market develops, independent of the centre, to spread good practice – it is almost a black economy within the formal economy of the company. Coalitions also develop, less to influence the thinking of the centre than the thinking of the organisation. (This is an important difference, because the latter approach is by its very nature much less political.)

CLARITY THROUGH ACCOUNTABILITY

Gerry Robinson at Granada insists that managers have clear objectives, that progress should be monitored once a month, and that they should then be left alone to get on with it. He told *Management Today*: 'When I was a junior, I always hated having to explain the detail of what I was doing to someone else. Providing you deliver at the end of the day, you like to be left alone. Most people I know manage things like that.'[2]

Gerry Whent at Vodafone agrees. He sees his role as being to 'develop local chief executives and give them their heads'. Sam Walton, founder of Wal-Mart, maintained similarly that a manager's primary task is 'simply to get the right people in the right places to do a job, and then encourage them to use their own inventiveness to accomplish the job at hand'.[3]

The Berkeley Group also takes great care not to intrude on local managers' areas of accountability. Says Geoff Hutchinson, Chairman of Crosby Homes: 'We occasionally have a conference with talks about a particular aspect such as inner-city developments and workshops, which is very useful. But part of our culture is that we don't believe in central control. Each business is very local. That is reflected in the way that the main board directors act. They wouldn't dream of calling you into the head office. As far as they are concerned, your head office is your business wherever you are. If they want to talk to you about your business, they expect to get in a car and come to you.

'I was talking to them for about six months before I joined. What really struck about Berkeley wasn't just the product but the culture and passion for the business. I can remember walking into Tony [Pidgley]'s office the first time and being surprised at the way they conducted themselves. It was so unlike the normal corporate style. They just came straight to the point and said this is a very autonomous company: if we pay you a salary, we expect you to run your own show – we don't expect to have to tell you what to do.'

The high-performance companies in our study are also very clear about the reason for having the controls they do have. These can usually be expressed as either:

→ to promote cohesion across the group *in the few areas where this is a critical competitive advantage*; or
→ to share good practice between autonomous units.

A useful concept for establishing clarity through accountability is what Boots calls 'dual citizenship'. Explains Chief Executive Lord Blyth: 'We continue to reduce the amount of central policy-making. Our broad rule is that, if you don't need to have a policy from the centre, then you shouldn't have it. We do without central policies by driving the business through dual citizenship and a culture of no surprises. ... The first dual citizenship question is: "Is this good for my business?" If the answer is yes, then the second question is: "Is it good for the corporation?" If the answer to that is yes, you proceed; if not, you don't.' He admits this has been a difficult philosophy to spread. It relies partly on educating people so they have the background knowledge to be able to make these judgments themselves, and partly on ensuring that people understand that they are accountable for making such judgments.

Just as it is important to have clear and universal understanding about the role of the centre, people in the operations also need to have a very clear understanding of what their individual roles are. We have found the following checklist to be very helpful in this respect.

• Are you clear about the critical measures of your performance? At most, managers can cope with four or five key measures. Of these, at least one should be financial; one on outputs (eg sales or productivity); one on developing people (ideally, including themselves); one on customer satisfaction (which can include internal customers). Trying to focus on too many objectives usually means that none will be achieved well and many won't be achieved at all. Effective managers concentrate on the big measures and link other measures to those as closely as they can.

- Do you have a regular and effective method of checking your priorities against shifting corporate needs? It can be very easy to lose sight of corporate thinking when you are in the field. Although CEOs of our high-performance companies spend a lot of time visiting the operations to keep managers up-to-date, the system works best when managers themselves take the initiative to keep in touch, not just with the centre, but with each other.

- Are you able to explain precisely what your key priorities are to your direct reports and internal suppliers? If they are going to support the manager in delivering the required performance, they have to share that clarity of understanding, because that is what gives them the context in which to manage their own priorities.

- Can you relate each of your priority objectives to one or more core corporate values, and to one or more core business objectives? If the manager cannot see a direct link between his or her activities and the broader business picture, he or she is almost certainly heading in the wrong direction!

An absence of headquarters bureaucracy

Do complex organisations need complex headquarters' operations? Not in the view of most of our high-performing companies. Like the companies in *The Winning Streak*, they have the smallest headquarters they can. Siebe, for example, has only five people to run a $5 billion company. Allen Yurko sees this less as a structural issue than a people issue. 'Why do I say that? Because the kind of person who will work in a culture that's decentralised with a very small headquarters has to have a high internal locus of control.[4] They have to know they have the ball and they have to want it.' With people like that, he concludes, a large headquarters staff would not only be unnecessary and wasteful, but obstructive and dysfunctional.

The chairmen and CEOs of most of our high-performance companies feel passionately about this. For them, empires are built at the frontiers, never at court. Charles Allen's view of the company Forte had become is aptly symbolised by its headquarters. 'Forte had a fifth company – headquarters.' It was, of course, one of the first things to go after Granada took the hotel company over.

For Clive Thompson at Rentokil Initial, keeping headquarters small is part of a much larger issue, that of maintaining simplicity of structure by constraining staff posts at all levels to the minimum possible. In principle, if a job doesn't add value to the business, or to customers, then it shouldn't exist. 'We hate functional people,' he declares. 'They are parasites.'

Rentokil Initial's acquisition of BET brought with it an implicit assumption that there would be radical changes in the structure of the new subsidiary. Among Thompson's immediate priorities was to 'break BET, which already was 52 businesses, into 100'. At IKEA, says Vice President Sven-Olof Kulldorff: 'We never use the word headquarters. It is an ugly word within IKEA.' Percy Barnevik, CEO at ABB, cut the headquarters staff from 2,000 to 170 in a rapid exercise that fired 30 per cent of the staff, and allocated the rest between the operating companies and the profit centres.

At Bowthorpe, too, says CEO Nicholas Brookes. 'We keep a keen headquarters with no large functional structure. We have no corporate HR or marketing at the centre. The thing that attracted me to this company was the degree of independence given to the businesses. If you can give the responsibility to the entrepreneurial experts, who really run the businesses, and then support them, it really breeds success. As for acquisitions, many companies find the entrepreneur takes his money and goes off to do something else. For us, one measure of success is that, in many cases, the entrepreneurial management is still with us and still thriving. That's to do with the way we run the company – in an environment which encourages creativity and innovation and values the technical community and entrepreneurs. I believe you can do all that, even in a large company.'

None of our high-performing companies likes spending money at the centre, except for major acquisitions. The headquarters of most of them are functional rather than palatial, and this attitude often permeates right through the non-customer-facing parts of the business.

To emphasise the fact that Wal-Mart's head office must be as a low-cost an overhead as possible, it is very unassuming. *Business Week* described it as a warehouse, with a lobby style reminiscent of 'Early Bus Station'.

Daniel Bernard, Chief Executive of Carrefour, comments: 'We have a very small centre. We have 110,000 people worldwide, but only 35 people in central HQ. The centre is for organising countries, finance, control, and organising for synergies, and to shape overall strategy. Management by charter is not for us. The executive board meets three days a month. It is permanently informal, a very close style of operation.'

Says Tony Pidgely, Chief Executive of The Berkeley Group: 'When we were talking about moving here [Berkeley House in Cobham, Surrey, UK] I was scared to death about the big corporate image of a head office like this. In fact, I was so nervous about it that I changed my mind three times – it even made the press that I couldn't make my mind up about a land deal. But when we moved here we lost three of our old receptionists who really fitted into our culture and had the Berkeley passion. We still haven't managed to replace them.'

ASDA does have a substantial corporate headquarters in Leeds but, says Chairman Archie Norman: 'We always say we aren't interested in pushing bits of paper around in some head office building. The only interesting thing in retailing is selling; selling to customers happens in the stores. We try to create a company where people behave as if there's only one store, in other words they live above the shop and they live in the shop. I often reflect on the fact that if we did that, had ASDA House above a store somewhere, people would behave and work more effectively.'

In SOL's egalitarian society, there are no organisation charts – no one is more important than anyone else. At the head office, there are no status symbols, nor any job titles, simply a broad, primary responsibility for a particular area of activity, such as salary administration, book-keeping and computing. They also have one or more secondary responsibilities, areas they must be familiar with so they can step in while the person with primary accountability is away. Behind this concern to keep headquarters small are a number of very practical considerations. Among them:

- The more people there are at the centre, the more the centre is likely to interfere (after all, these people all have to justify their existence).
- The larger the centre, the more likely people in the field are to perceive it as the place to be. If the action and glory is all in the field, the high performers will prefer to be there instead!
- If the centre has enough staff to create policy on its own, then its motivation to consult and involve the operations in policy development is reduced. Keeping the centre staff small obliges them to distribute responsibility for policy development to a wider group, which promotes much wider ownership.
- The bigger the centre, the less trust between people there and in the operations. This is in large part a clarity issue – the more people see it as their task to educate the field, the greater likelihood of conflicting and confusing messages.

Consensus about what should be controlled where

When Cadbury Schweppes made a global decision to swing the pendulum a little more towards central co-ordination, it was not the headquarters that drove the discussion. It was the operating company CEOs around the world, who perceived greater added value for their businesses from increased consistency in the global brand and increased collaboration between operations.

We found very few examples of high-performance companies imposing new controls on their subsidiaries, and then only after extensive consultation and buy-in. For example, Smiths Industries' Sir Roger Hurn admits that he only introduced internal audit into the company with a great deal of reluctance, and only as a result of external pressure to conform with recommended standards of corporate governance. He explains: We have always believed that the right way to control a business is to delegate power to the chap running it – the managing director – and to put alongside him a chief accountant and to give that chief accountant a dotted line responsibility through the accounting chain to the (group) managing director. If for any reason, the chief accountant feels lent on by the local managing director to bend the rules or not to report things, he knows he has a line of appeal. I believe passionately in that system.' Cadbury Schweppes, which has a similar approach, moves chief accountants on every few years 'to stop them going native'.

To a certain extent, the group CEO and his colleagues are seen in many of our companies not as the source of further controls, but as a bulwark against an external world that seeks to create unnecessary complexity within the company. Certainly, managers at Smiths Industries are aware of and supporting of Hurn's efforts to resist bureaucracy, wherever it originates.

At Singapore Airlines, significant autonomy is given to operating subsidiaries such as SATS Airport Services, a service provider at Changi Airport. SIA provides between 40 and 45 per cent of SATS' business, but leaves all day-to-day operational and strategic matters to the subsidiary. 'SIA would like us to wear their uniforms when we work for them, but we refuse, because it would send the wrong message to the other clients. SIA accepts that we operate to the benefit of all our clients,' says SATS Chief Executive Tan Hui Boon. SATS' freedom to make such a stand is in large part a result of its adherence to the key control system – the company's six core values and, in this particular case, the core value of customer awareness. Control by values creates a framework that makes 'dual citizenship' issues between the parent and the subsidiary transparent and relatively easy to resolve.

At GKN, the corporate human resources function is very careful not to overplay its role, says the function head, John Rugman: 'If you centralise, it makes all the issues much more complicated. So we have resisted any attempts to centralise the management of employee relations. We have made it clear that accountability is with line management. Our role is to challenge them: "How good are you in terms of flexibility and productivity? What challenges do you face which require you to change how you use manpower?" We are constantly probing and pushing, making sure that they approach current problems and address future needs. Decentralisation does not mean neglect. You have got to be smart enough at the centre to make sure they are not going to sleep. That's how we add value from the centre.'

Maintaining a consensus about what should be controlled where is a matter of constant vigilance. The centre needs to be sure it is not encroaching unnecessarily; and the operating units need to understand their responsibility for sharing the management of the consensus-building process. The businesses need, for example, to recognise that they are not baronies, and to value the benefits of co-ordination, while fiercely defending the right to meet the requirements of their local markets. Once again, it comes down to mutual benefit – does the location of control on a specific issue benefit both the business and the group? It can be very easy for creeping centralisation to occur without this kind of debate, so constant vigilance is essential both at the centre and in the businesses. Says John Rugman of GKN: 'We have always had a decentralised structure and preserved it, though at times there were temptations to tidy things up to take a more central direction. One of the things we have succeeded in doing is resisting those temptations. ... The more you centralise, the more complicated it makes all the issues.'

No surprises

What emerges from all of our interviews in the high-performing companies, whether with people at headquarters or in the field, is a remarkable degree of trust in the quality of the information that flows each way and in the goodwill of the people providing it. Says Lord Blyth: 'You can't dismantle the control apparatus of 100 years unless you have cumulatively built up quite a deep sense of trust that you can leave the businesses not to surprise you with failures or mistakes.' The phrase 'no surprises culture' echoes throughout our companies. For example, says David Kappler, Finance Director of Cadbury Schweppes. 'The greatest crime you can commit is not being open about a problem in your region.' Also at Cadbury Schweppes, John Brock, President and CEO of Dr Pepper/Seven Up declares: 'We are a very devolved company. As long as there are no surprises, you have the freedom to get on with it.'

Clive Thompson, CEO of Rentokil Initial, agrees: 'We have a philosophy: this is not your business, it is our business. Share your problems with us now, not six months later when you've been covering them up. Our branch structure – 600 branches all reporting back – makes it very difficult to cover up poor performance and problems.' Adds Martin Ellis, General Manager of UK Healthcare (a Rentokil subsidiary): 'I've been involved in acquisitions. The existing managers don't always understand profit in the same way we do. You tend to get a lot of excuses from them too – the weather was bad or it was holiday time. When you grow up with the Rentokil Initial culture you learn there's no hiding place. The company will accept reasons but not excuses.'

What happens when things go wrong? Says Michael Treschow of Atlas Copco: 'Sure, then we come down hard. If you don't want any "help" from the centre, then make sure you follow your plan, otherwise you will get a lot of help. For me, it's not the importance of having the good figures – that's something for time. For me, it's important that people have control over their business. Control means it becomes as you said it was going to be. I'm not saying prediction in detail, but you should be able to tell roughly what the numbers are going to be next month.'

Atlas Copco manages 'no surprises' by very close monitoring of performance against targets. If an operating unit sets a target, but does not meet its budgets in the first couple of months, that attracts a lot of attention. Says Lennart Johansson, Business Controller: 'For us it is OK to miss the target, but it's not OK to miss very early in the process. It's not OK to have a very long starting track before you start to do anything about it; it's not OK to be inflexible in how you adjust. If the business overruns its marketing expenses, for example, it is not acceptably simply to cut back on marketing later in the year. The manager has to look for more flexible solutions to bring the budget back on track.'

At SOL, says Liisa Joronen: 'We cannot have surprises, because we have clear targets and a rapid information system. Our company culture emphasises that everyone should keep his or her eyes and ears open all the time.'

'Surprises tend to come when people are scared' says Granada's Charles Allen. ' "No surprises" is probably the most important cultural value at Granada. It's easy to say but hard to do. In reporting, I always ask for highs and lows. That makes it easier for people to tell you about problems before they become serious. If the high for a certain month is taking grandma for dinner, then I know that it is not a good month.'

The 'no surprises' rule also works from top management to the board. Says Sir Gerald Whent at Vodafone: 'If there is something that isn't quite right, then we tell them. We are close to being good everywhere but we have our horrors. We don't hide them either; we do tell the board. We say that's a problem and this is what we are doing about it and what are your ideas? We promote this thought all the way down the line. The only thing you will get clobbered for here is hiding your problems.'

No surprises is in essence an attitude of mind. It requires courage and a sense of both timing and proportion. It doesn't mean covering one's back by deluging other people with memos about possible problems and being able to say 'Well, I did warn you'. It means constantly assessing and re-assessing in a realistic way what is happening in every activity and on every issue of importance to the business. It means recognising when something apparently insignificant – for example, a small increase in customer complaints about a particular product or a series of minor falls in margins for a service – has the potential to grow into something more significant. It means building in the leeway to react to missed targets in time to take sufficient remedial action – so it requires a great deal of thinking ahead. It requires a determined mixture of discipline and creative flexibility (in themselves yet another difficult balance for companies to achieve). And it requires a supporting climate, where people know they will not be punished for failing to achieve the impossible, but will be energetically encouraged to go back and try again.

This last point is a particularly strong belief of GE's Jack Welch. Says Steve Kerr, the company's Vice-President for Corporate Leadership Development: 'Respect for mistakes and errors is implicit in GE. It's a balancing act we are good at. It's not OK to miss your numbers. But if you make the punishment too heavy, people will set goals that are too low. Jack Welch often says: "Most people, if they had the same information that you had, would have made the same decision." The issue then becomes, "If someone makes a mistake, why didn't the system make sure that that person had the information and how can we change it so they do have the information in future?"'

Keep it small, keep it simple

How big does an operation have to be before the team at the top begin to lose touch with what their employees and customers are thinking? How big before the core of their role shifts from managing downwards to managing upwards? How big before people in one part of the business lose contact with what people in other parts of the business do, and what other departments' current key issues are?

Of course, the answer varies from company to company, but it will always be 'not very large at all'. Our high-performance companies gen-erally work hard at keeping their units small, self-contained and with identities of their own. This was a trend we found in our original study; since then, it has become much more pronounced among high-performance companies.

The modern classic of this devolved approach is, of course, the Swedish–Swiss engineering giant ABB. CEO Percy Barnevik doesn't say whether he came to the same conclusions independently or through observing other companies such as Siebe or (from the original *The Winning Streak* companies) Racal. In a now-famous spree of corporate dismemberment, Percy Barnevik broke apart an unwieldy divisional structure into 1,000 smaller companies that were close to the customer. These were then subdivided into 5,000 profit centres, each containing on average about 40 people. The leaders of these profit centres know what they have to achieve, they are familiar with their markets and their products, and they are responsible for their own profit-and-loss accounts. Each month, Barnevik sees the P&L from every one of the profit centres through an online computer system. However, the control over each business is exercised through a very short chain of command – through the company manager, who reports both to a business manager and a country manager, who in turn report to two members of the executive committee (one of three regional managers and one of three business sector managers). It sounds complex, but it provides young managers with a high degree of freedom to develop their own ideas, build their own confidence and feel a real sense of ownership for part of the business. They can also show what they are made of, in the knowledge that excellent performance will be noticed all the way up the line to the CEO's office. Says Barnevik: 'If you can overcome the disadvantages of big-company bureaucracy and still get the advantages of size, you have a fantastic edge that is very difficult to copy.'

Microsoft's remarkable ability to develop just the right product at the right time is attributed by various commentators to maintaining business units at a manageable size – on average about 30 people, small enough to get together in one room to talk about a project. Bill Gates told *Fortune*: 'It's very important to me and to the guys that work for us that Microsoft feels like a small company, even though it isn't one any more. I remember how much fun it is to be small, and the business units help preserve that feeling.'[5]

The Berkeley Group has a similar philosophy. Explains Colin Hutchinson: 'We know that every trading company in the group has its limitations, so we keep breaking them down into units of a certain turnover. That way you keep them small and controllable. That's where our strength will be now and in the future. You can bring passion to the job when you have 70 or so staff. But once you get to 250 you lose that personal touch. If you start doing too much you lose the detail which is vital to keeping a superior product. As a board of a small company, we'll talk about every single bathroom suite and toilet-roll holder that goes into every property we build this year.'

Berkeley also insists on local names for the businesses. Identification with the group is not a priority, nor even an issue. What does matter is the association by customers, employees and contractors with a local firm that has local understanding and local interests at heart. Similarly, the name N. Brown is probably unfamiliar to its thousands of customers – they recognise only the catalogue brand directed at them.

Granada's rentals division recently reorganised a centralised national structure into 20 much smaller units, each of which competed with the others. The intention was to drive quality up by creating a competitive, entrepreneurial culture within each of the 20 business units. It not only succeeded in that, but the newly created business units became much more accountable and responsible. That in turn meant that the management control they needed from head office was greatly simplified, and a huge amount of cost was saved in head office.

Where practical, many of the high-performance companies share this preference for emphasising the identity of the individual operating units, rather than of the group as a whole. Says Sir Roger Hurn of Smiths Industries: 'We practically don't use the name Smiths on anything we produce. At Hythe, our plastics company in Kent, people think of themselves as working for Portex and quite rightly so. They may not even know they are part of Smith's Industries and I don't mind. ... We want a clear identification of people with the business in which they work, an awareness that we promote that business not the corporation. If you look at any of the trade magazines for the businesses we are in, you will see lots of specific advertising for our 60 ancillary companies, but none for Smiths itself.'

At Bowthorpe, too, says CEO Nicholas Brookes: 'The companies operate as attachments to Bowthorpe. No way do I want to stamp these companies with the Bowthorpe name. We are deliberately very low profile.'

At Siebe, Allen Yurko aims to 'keep our companies and divisions as small as practical. Back in the 1970s and 1980s, there was a huge move in American business to divisionalise everything. We never did that in Siebe. Yes, we streamlined the business culture and structure, but people still had their own little business team and focused on their own business. Now at Siebe we have thousands of little teams focused on individual products. We've never had to do anything but share the same culture and keep the business teams in place. 'Occasionally, someone comes to me and says: "I've found a way of taking out four controllers and ending up with one." The reality is that that's a divisionalist philosophy and we won't allow it.

I don't have a hard and fast rule about how small a division should be. If it gets to the sub-critical point, we'll make it part of another division. It's whatever you feel is right. If they get big enough, we'll divide them into more focused groups again.'

At Reuters, the sheer global reach of the company keeps numbers down in any one location and each location is encouraged to behave as a separate business. Says Chief Executive Peter Job: 'We have very large numbers of small-to-middlesize units, so all around the world we've got countries, even like Germany, which wouldn't have more than 450 people in – Japan probably about 380. That is not a huge size and its one where people can have considerable enthusiasm about what they are doing without feeling part of a massive bureaucracy. Even in our large units, such as the United States, there are probably not more than 2,000 people.'

At Vodafone, says Julian Horn-Smith, Managing Director of International Operations: 'We tend to stay small. We are very decentralised. We like to empower managing directors of the businesses – they are little emperors in their own fiefdoms. We tie managers in with share incentive schemes. We are very actively looking at a business when it gets to a certain size, because in a service-provision business you can quickly get diseconomies of scale.'

Similarly at SAP, where growth is largely in the international markets, says Henning Kagermann: 'If the subsidiaries grow too big, we split them up.' Having large numbers of small units also reduces business risk, claims Rentokil Initial's Chief Executive Sir Clive Thompson. He explains: 'You can either make lots of small mistakes or one large mistake. Six hundred different branches mean its hard to make large mistakes. The large mistakes are likely to be in uncertainties coming through from acquisitions – for example, companies not what you thought, or putting the wrong person in to run it.' To reduce the risk from its acquisition of BET, one of Rentokil Initial's first steps has been to break up the business into smaller units.

An emphasis on speed of information and decision making

To an outsider, Singapore Airlines looks like one big company. But in reality it is, says Managing Director Cheong Choong Kong, 'an amorphous mass of 101 companies operating independently.' This independence is important in ensuring that customer needs get the priority attention they deserve. So, for example, says Tan Hui Boon, Chief Executive of SATS Airport Services, the SIA subsidiary which is a service provider at Changi Airport: 'Our autonomy means we can make decisions – especially spending decisions – much more quickly. For instance, if one of the tugs that moves aircraft around broke down, that would be a priority for SIA, but if a high loader used for loading cargo broke down, it wouldn't, because that's not central to the group's core business. As an independent operator, we can react much more quickly, because it is central to ours.'

Rapid decision making permeates all our high-performance companies. For example:

- Speed is one of GE's core values, a fundamental characteristic not just of manufacturing processes but of decision making, communication and response to market changes.

- At ABB, speed of decision making is helped by rapid communication systems, including satellite links, and an emphasis on talking ideas through with knowledgeable colleagues, whether they be in Zurich or deepest Siberia. When the merger that formed ABB was announced, it took just six weeks for Percy Barnevik to set up the combined operation. He personally interviewed 400 staff to choose the team he needed.

- At Microsoft, says Mike Murray, Vice President Human Resources and Administration: 'In a highly iterative business, where things change so rapidly, we often need to change course midstream, so we must have an efficient feedback loop. Our e-mail system, with its lack of hierarchy, ensures that everyone who needs to know about a problem is informed within 48 hours.'

- Says Graham Thomson, Chairman of Berkeley Homes (North London) Limited: 'The chain of command to get decisions made is very simple here. If some of my chaps came in to me today with a piece of land where we needed to move fast I could react very quickly. If need be, I could pick up a mobile phone on the way out the door, call Tony [Pidgley] on the way – not for his permission but out of courtesy and know that he'd back my judgment – and I could exchange contracts this afternoon. With some other companies that decision would have to go to the main board, which slows everything down.'

Similar reasoning lies behind the business structures and systems of most other high-performing companies. They recognise that speed – of both decision making and carrying out decisions – is fundamental to their competitive advantage. To reinforce speedy decision making and action, they keep structures simple and flat and avoid paperwork wherever possible (both of which ideas are explored further below).

- Chris Pearce, Finance Director of Rentokil Initial sums this approach up when he says: 'The better people prefer our simple structures. There's not a lot of waffling around in our culture. There's not a foot-and-a-half-high pile of paper at the end of the process; there's a pile about a quarter of an inch, which as these things go is very little.'

- At ASDA, says Archie Norman: 'Competing in food retail is about pace – about being able to innovate, develop, change faster than the competition. You'll never achieve that pace if your system is anarchic, in other words if everyone has autonomy and every management action is discretionary, because by definition you'll move with the pace of your slowest or your weakest manager. So we regard ourselves as quite 'command and control,' as very fast moving. We have very few layers of management, we are very direct in what we want to do, but we make that work through a culture which encourages people to be involved and which always treats colleagues with respect. Treating people with respect is critical to service because if you do that, if someone says: "Hey, this is a crazy idea", then you listen: we overdose on opportunities for creating improvement, for listening.'

- The key to rapid decision making at the centre, says Siebe Finance Director Roger Mann is: 'Culture with a capital C. It comes back to planning within the businesses. They have to know what they are going to do. If it's not planned correctly, they won't ask in time to get the approval.'

KEEPING STRUCTURES SIMPLE AND FLAT

There are only four layers separating the most junior employees in IKEA's workforce of 33,400 from the chief executive, so decisions tend to be taken very quickly. *The Economist* refers to 'a management structure that is as ruthlessly flat as the firm's knock-down furniture kits'.[6]

'In making commercial decisions and reacting to information coming from the market place, we are much faster than most because you're not going through layers of management. And because there's a lot of local autonomy, a lot of things don't even need to come here for approval at all,' says Robert Stack at Cadbury Schweppes' headquarters.

Kevin Hayes, Managing Director of Cadbury's Asian–Pacific operations agrees: 'We're very fast-moving and nimble on our feet. We have a very fast approval process. If I need something I get a very quick answer. It doesn't matter if its a 'no', as is the case sometimes – its much better than death by a 1000 cuts.'

At Vodafone, says International Managing Director Julian Horn-Smith: 'We want simple decision-making. The structures in the company are very flat, there is the chief executive and an executive committee plus the plc board. Decisions can be made very quickly. We tend to empower people to make decisions. This is an entrepreneurial culture, driven by shareholder value. Every week, the chief executive reviews commercial policy. He looks at the headlines from the business – we make decisions there and then. On investments, we review these every four months (and we have monthly accounts meetings too).'

So complex structures are also to be avoided. Says GKN's David Lees: 'It is unrealistic to pretend that managing a global business, at whatever level, is not complex, so the key issue is how to reduce complexity and increase simplicity. Clarity of organisation is perhaps the most important contributor to the reduction of complexity, thereby establishing clear-cut lines of authority and responsibility.

'I have always felt that the priorities for GKN have been, firstly, the avoidance of a matrix organisation with the attendant potential problems of defining who is responsible for what. Secondly, the reduction of management layers where possible to avoid distortion of the message; thirdly, on occasions when it may be expedient to miss out a link in the management chain, to ensure that the intermediate link is kept informed.'

It could be argued that flat hierarchies are simply the current fad. Lots of other, less successful companies have reduced the number of layers over the past decade and more, sometimes driven by the need to cut costs (ie to 'downsize'), sometimes as part of some overall logistic, such as Business Process Re-engineering. What makes the difference in our high-performance companies is that they are committed to the notion of flat hierarchies as an essential part of their management philosophy. They believe, in general, that you cannot decentralise effectively if there are intermediaries to get in the way. They perceive short lines of communication as vital to creating and sustaining clarity. The more layers there are, the easier it is to avoid responsibility and the greater the potential for surprises to sneak in. And they believe passionately that people need large spans of opportunity to grow, to take initiative and to react flexibly to changing needs. In short, without a very flat structure, it becomes difficult, if not impossible, to establish a balance between control and autonomy that works for both the centre and the operations.

AVOIDING PAPERWORK

On way of keeping the bureaucracy at bay is constantly to monitor the paperwork that is generated at the instigation of headquarters. Is it needed? Could it be done more simply? At Siebe, for example, says Finance Director Roger Mann: 'We have maintenance of paperwork as well as maintenance schedules for machinery. We are continuously reviewing our paperwork systems. For example, within each business unit we have a standard code of overheads, which goes down into the divisions. We expect all business units to complete these schedules every month. Previously we had them sent through to Windsor [Berks, UK]. We now get a summarised version and what we also ask for is + or − so we get the exceptions. It doesn't bog people down with paper at president or subdivision level.'

One of the abiding stories about Marks & Spencer is how it launched a company-wide programme to root out excessive paper. The aim wasn't just to recapture some space (its London office was bulging with filing cabinets full of documents no one ever needed again) but to emphasise the importance of direct rather than indirect communication. High-performance firms often have what might be called 'memophobia' – they hate writing and receiving memos unless absolutely necessary. Says Geoff Hutchinson, Chairman of Crosby Homes, part of The Berkeley Group: We send a few memos but not many. By the time you've dictated it and had it typed, it's a lot quicker to just pick up the phone and say "sort it". All companies have their weekly management meetings to review the business, but we don't have a secretary sit in to take notes. The conversation goes straight into a Dictaphone, and as the tapes fill they are fed to secretaries who type them up. It means that as you walk out of the meeting you pick up a copy of the minutes and within one or two days all the items have been actioned. That is taken for granted, unless there's a good reason why not. Berkeley's culture says management is not about talking, but about doing. Once that culture is in place is just keeps going.'

Telephone or face-to-face meetings are almost always the preferred form of communication. Says Kevin Hayes, Chairman and CEO of Cadbury Schweppes Australasia and MD for Asian–Pacific: 'If people have a problem in this company they will get on the phone – it's a quick and painless way to resolve issues.

'In my role as head of this region I meet up regularly – once every four months – with London to iron out issues. There is also a very strong informal network which [is] as effective as the formal [one]. For example, I can call the MD of Ireland or South Africa without going through the centre with all the filtering that could involve. The same applies on a smaller scale within the Australasian business; people can pick up the phone and talk to one another.'

At Wal-Mart, each of the 12 regional vice presidents lives near the headquarters at Bentonville, USA, flying out to their region on a Monday and visiting stores till Thursday. On Friday, they come together at the centre to share what they have learned in the field. On Saturday, they meet together with the chairman or vice chairman and 250 other key staff to review the previous week and plan for the week ahead. The discussion is sent by satellite to the stores. By store close that day, store managers have discussed the issues with their department managers, who put the decisions into action.[7]

At Siebe, the things headquarters wants to control get dealt with without delay. Says Allen Yurko: 'If a manager is on budget and has a long-term strategic plan that we've endorsed, and they're hitting their five new product launches a year, what happens when he sends in a request for $3 million for a new plant in Mexico? We sign it the same day. It goes back, no board review. Done. Typically in this company, if you're a general manager on schedule, you can get a major capital programme approved within 48 hours, assuming of course you've done your homework. We flip through it. We look at the paybacks. We look at the risk analysis and so on, but the point is in 48 hours you've got approval. It's a very fast process. Why? Because we know this guy. We see him ten times a year and he's delivering all those other programmes. Why shouldn't he deliver another good $3 million expansion for us? He certainly knows that if he screws it up he's going to screw up his bonus, his budget performance, everything, so he's not going to submit something stupid.'

Balance between strategic control and financial control

Says Bob Lawson, CEO of Electrocomponents: 'Strategic control is absolute. There is only one strategy. Financial control is variable. We use the "so what?" test on both.'

High-performing companies keep their operating businesses in line with a mixture of strategic and financial control. Strategic control in this context is about defining a group vision of the kind of businesses the company should be in and the broad image and reputation that should be echoed throughout the group. The more brand-conscious businesses – such as IKEA and Cadbury Schweppes – tend to exert the strongest strategic control, but most high-performing companies give it equal or near-equal priority to financial control.

The issue is neatly summed up by Todd Jick, managing partner of the Centre for Executive Development in Boston, Massachusetts, working with Cadbury Schweppes: 'The balance Cadbury is trying to strike is to allow leaders to have enough local freedom or autonomy to get the job done, but to do so within a larger strategic framework. It's the classic tension between delegation and control. Cadbury Schweppes are clear that they don't want a control culture, but neither do they want anarchy. It must be devolved responsibility within a strategic framework.'

The need for both financial and strategic control is emphasised by Martin Ellis, General Manager of UK Healthcare at Rentokil Initial, for whom the financial objective is the starting point and the strategic control is the route for getting there: 'The key thing for me is focus – 20 per cent profit growth for ever. That message has never changed in all the time since I started with the company as a technician. People here talk about it all the time. The next bit after the 20 per cent profit is important – for ever. You can achieve good results for a while by cutting costs, but you can't sustain it for ever. That forces managers to motivate their people, not simply to take a knife to the business when they're having problems. Simplicity and focus and rigid and regular review of trading are the key factors.'

At Siebe, Allen Yurko, like his predecessor, spends most of his time meeting subsidiary company top teams, listening to what they say about their businesses and giving a gentle steer as needed. A minimum of ten times a year, he or one of his top team colleagues meet with each business team. The purpose of these two meetings is not primarily to chew over the numbers. With clear, frequent data flowing backwards and forwards, that doesn't need a lot of time in most cases. People know what their targets are and how they are doing against them; the only discussion needed is around how they plan to achieve them.

Although there are formal meetings to control the business, they are characterised by a high degree of informality. Says Yurko: 'We are part of the informal network and informal structures. We sit there and we talk about the products and we are part of their team. On occasions, of course, they'll recognise where we sit, but they know they can bounce ideas off us informally. It's how a lot of our new products arise.'

At the same time he says: 'We watch cash vigilantly in all our companies. A problem with the cash is always a precursor to a bigger problem. Lots of companies, when they go global, allow bad asset management to creep in. We never make that mistake.'

GKN's David Lees also feels strongly about the need to separate strategic and financial control. He explains: 'If the two become merged, the danger is that financial control issues are glossed over in the interest of the pursuit of strategy, and the strategic issues become increasingly the focus of short-term considerations. I believe, therefore, that the business processes adopted by companies should reflect this distinction and that operational and financial reviews with line management, which may be shorter but occur at more frequent intervals, should be kept apart from the strategic reviews which are likely to take longer but occur less frequently.'

As these examples demonstrate, high-performance companies recognise the need for top management to remind people constantly of the need to apply both financial and strategic controls. GKN's emphasis on separating the two reflects the fact that they are different in both nature and timing – at least, in the way they are applied in high-performance companies. Financial controls tend to be set at the broadest level from the centre and require detailed short-term feedback, from which trends can be extrapolated. They are primarily about *outputs*. Strategic controls are set with the businesses, look at the medium to long term (however that is defined in the business) and are primarily about *processes*. The key concern for top management insofar as a business's strategy is concerned is to ensure that it fits within the broad corporate strategy and that the executives' thinking is sufficiently rigorous, wide-ranging, visionary and pragmatic.

In summary . . .

This is the only issue in the book to require two chapters – a reflection of how important it is to maintain the right balance between keeping people in check and harnessing their energy and enthusiasm. Get it wrong and people look for their excitement and fulfilment outside the job; get it right and you capture not only their minds but their very essence as well.

High-performance companies develop a high degree of clarity about what they need to control and why, and equally about what they want the operational businesses, and the managers within them, to be accountable for. Along with clarity, they develop consensus – about the importance, relevance and usefulness of controls – and therefore buy-in. Above all, they work hard to keep controls as simple and few as possible. Then they pursue them with the utmost vigour.

These themes – and especially those of clarity, consensus and excitement – will echo throughout the following chapters. In Chapter Four, we pick up the theme of the strategic context, which in large part defines the nature of the controls and freedoms a company operates.

ADDENDUM: TARGETS AND STANDARDS

Who sets the targets?

Roger Mavity, Managing Director of Granada Rentals, puts it succinctly: 'Unwavering attention to the few critical objectives creates a single-mindedness that is itself a key success factor. ... I know there are only a few things I have to do – achieve the numbers promised, and rethink the strategy to increase profits in the future. Having targets, you stick to them. Trying to justify missing a budget on the basis that we had missed it by only a small amount would be like trying to justify to your wife that you slept with other women, but it wasn't important as it didn't happen that often.'

At the 'targets from above' end of the target-setting spectrum are Rentokil Initial, which has the objective of increasing profits and earnings per share by at least 20 per cent per annum, and clothing catalogue company N. Brown, which requires a minimum of 15 per cent. Says Martin Ellis, General Manager of UK Healthcare at Rentokil Initial: 'No one is interested in my qualifications before I joined the company; what matters is what I've done here. But if you have a failure or a difficult patch, the company is interested in not just what's going wrong but what you're going to do about it and how you plan to get back on track. As long as you've understood the reasons and show that you've learned from the problem then that's OK. You have to justify performance in terms of the numbers and the trading account. The trading performance is the ultimate measure. At the end of the day, in the Rentokil Initial culture the only truth is the trading account – profit and loss. That's it. End of story. It produces a competitive atmosphere between managers, which most of us enjoy.'

At N. Brown, for example, says Iain MacFarlane, Director of Administration: 'Over the past ten years, we have devolved greater responsibility to a wider management group. We've had to relax some controls, but we've kept tight financial controls. As a company, we're very keen on budget control. We expect people to deliver on those targets. There is some flexibility around how you do that but there have to be good reasons for changes. We're very performance-oriented. Employees right across the spectrum know what is expected of them. They know the parameters of their jobs, both qualitatively and quantitatively. If you're a mail opener, for example, you know you have to run at a certain quality and pace and that you will be monitored, not every day maybe but regularly. Similarly, a telephonist knows that we're monitoring calls, breaks etc. That's true throughout the business. The discipline to perform is there. I think it's hard to find any successful business that isn't like that.'

At the other extreme of the target-setting spectrum are Berkeley, Reuters, Electrocomponents and SOL. Says The Berkeley Group Chief Executive Tony Pidgley: 'We're not really driven from a plc perspective. It goes back to how you look at the business. We are not a corporate machine. Central HQ is not allowed. All right, so we're meeting here today, but as far as I'm concerned the word 'HQ' is not allowed. We have a different business philosophy to other companies. We believe managers must be autonomous. They must be accountable for performance and setting targets. We don't play the main board game of setting targets. We don't tell them to grow the business by 30 per cent. We say, you run the business. What we do set at the centre is the return on capital (that's something too few housebuilders do) and the gross margin. We set those very clearly.'

At Reuters, says CEO Peter Job: 'We actively manage the business. We don't manage on financial targets. That is not intended as any disrespect to anyone else. It's just the way we do it. We tend not to set very high hurdles in order to get better performance out of people. It can work; but it can also have the opposite effect. No one will ever tell the king that he doesn't have any clothes on.'

As Electrocomponents internationalised, says CEO Bob Lawson, it recognised that: 'We can't run [the Electrocomponents subsidiary in] France but we can give them clarity and enable them to buy in to our goals. They come up with substantially better objectives than we could set for them.'

In Finnish cleaning company SOL, all the supervisors have been given training in computerised budget management. SOL's supervisors set their own performance targets, their budgets – and the salaries of their team of cleaners. They decide where, how and when to do the work. To balance this high level of discretion, they are expected to measure a wide range of factors affecting the margins of the job, from customer satisfaction, to time spent on each job, to the cost of cleaning materials used. This information is needed, not by the head office, but for them to manage very tight margins.

The supervisors base their performance targets on the targets that employees set for themselves in consultation with the supervisors. These targets – and how people are performing against them – are posted in the office for all to see. Targets are set annually, and reviewed twice during the year.

Says Chief Executive Liisa Joronen: 'We don't set an overall target for profit, turnover, anything. I have no idea what my budget for next year will be. My people always set their own targets. That's one of the key reasons why we have been so successful. If they set targets that are a bit unrealistic, they still reach them easily because they are theirs. If I set a high target, they might say they can't do it because the competition is too high.

'Targets are set annually for each month and reported continuously, at least once a month. Our information system is very fast. All monthly information is ready on the second or third day after the end of the month. It is spread immediately to the supervisors and around SOL. When the figures are excellent we celebrate them in many ways. Quick and correct information is a key success factor for us, because the supervisors can immediately start the correcting or improving actions. I need only a few basic figures to see that everything is all right – customer satisfaction, employee satisfaction, profit, and turnover. Sometimes I look at the detailed figures for curiosity or if the basic figures are not good.'

Standard reporting keeps it simple

Cadbury Schweppes' Group Finance Director David Kappler describes how the confectionery and soft drinks manufacturer handles the gathering of financial information: 'Cadbury Schweppes is a pretty autonomous organisation. On finance, we demand reports, accounts, forecasts etc. in a predetermined format at the centre and to our time-scale. So we have the numbers coming from around the world which we can consolidate to see the big picture. You need a process to add up those numbers that is beyond simply getting a sale and profits figure. We tell the operating companies how we want the measures and numbers defined. But within the businesses, they are free to report how they choose to their own boards (although we also demand a copy of those reports on a monthly basis).

'That's the way the thing has been set up traditionally, although I would say the pendulum in financial control terms is moving now more to control at the centre and away from autonomy. To some extent that reflects my own style – I've been in this job about two years now – but it also reflects a broader trend with financial controls.'

The reliability of the figures they receive is a matter for constant vigilance by the CEOs of our case-study companies. All spend considerable time coaching senior managers in how to avoid surprises in the figures. To a large extent this process is about developing the CEO's confidence in each manager and the manager's confidence in his or her own predictions. Clive Thompson again: 'Once a month I receive a forecast from every area/branch for the year (it's very important to have a full breakdown, as consolidated forecasts can often cover up poor performance in one place).

These are reviewed each month. Because I know the individual managers – which ones are optimists and which are pessimists – I know from those forecasts what the profit will be for the year.' With a new acquisition, such as BET, however, he needs a lot more information: 'I have no idea what their forecasts mean,' he says.

Atlas Copco is moving the balance slightly in the opposite direction. Says Hans Ola Meyer, Finance Director: 'From the beginning of the eighties and even seventies, a real treasury and central finance function was created. Since then I would argue that if anything we have gone slightly back again and pushed more of the day-to-day treasury matters out again, so we only focus on getting the flows and the exposures within the group as much as possible. That allows us to control and offset the risk without instructing them how to act. It is very much a balancing act.'

Adds Lennart Johansson, Business Controller: 'We try to operate with very few instructions. Messages from the centre saying "This is what you have to do and this is how it will be done" would become very obsolete very quickly. It's an impossible task to ask this of 16 divisions, which are actually quite different. So we try to limit that. The only area where we do have instructions is in financial reporting, which simply means that we want everyone to report in the same format and have the same definitions. So if we want to compare notes between different businesses we are sure we are talking about the same things. We try to be very, very precise about the definition of gross profit margin for example, or what is supply cost, what are admin costs. Even when we make acquisitions we want new companies to adopt that standard format in a reasonably short time.' Financial reporting to the centre needs to focus on trends and short-term forecasts, rather than historical data, continues Johansson. The fact that the divisions and business unit managers are able to predict profits a month ahead with reasonable accuracy gives the centre confidence they are in control of their operations. And if they are in control, then the centre doesn't need to be.

4 STRATEGIC URGENCY

Long-term strategy versus short-term urgency

'It's much easier to focus on the long term if the short term is going well.' *Sir Roger Hurn, Chairman, Smiths Industries*

'You can have an urgency about a long-term strategy. And we do.' *Dominic Cadbury, Chairman, Cadbury Schweppes*

'The strategy is very clear. We've set it out as a company without any great secrets. But the purpose of communicating strategy is to give people a sense of direction and focus. There's no point having strategies if people are not organised around them to deliver; therefore you have to find points where you're going to focus the fire power and the capacity to change fast if necessary.' *Archie Norman, Chairman, ASDA*

'We must be willing to invest in the long term, yet at the same time our fortunes are made in three month increments.' *Mike Murray, Vice President Human Resources and Administration, Microsoft.*

It's a truism that most people in business regard time to strategise as both a necessity and a luxury at the same time. The urgent needs of today always seem to overshadow the need to think about the long term. Yet balancing short-term action against long-term thinking becomes more and more of a critical skill. Not only is it essential from an organisational point of view to retain the ability to respond with forethought to events in a rapidly changing external environment, but the advent of flatter hierarchies means that managers are increasingly likely to have to live with the consequences of their short-term decisions – if only because it takes longer to move onwards and up.

Although all of our high-performance companies have a very strong emphasis on delivering promised results today, they maintain an equal emphasis on delivering results tomorrow. The regular discussions between group top management and the operating companies focus on two topics:

- Is there anything that will prevent you from delivering to target (and, if so, do you know precisely how you are going to overcome it)?

• What are you doing today that will deliver results next year, and the year after, and the year after that?

To have this kind of discussion and be sure it will result in the right level of action, they need to have the right people in place. Says Siebe's Allen Yurko: 'We have a no-nonsense approach – we want a cash profit. We spend a lot of time searching for people who understand the profit motive.'

Managers who can think in several time-frames (present-, near- and medium-term future) simultaneously don't grow on trees. All of the chief executives we interviewed spent a lot of their time finding, recruiting and nurturing such people. They set the example from the top. For example, says Lord Blyth of Boots: 'We don't review the performance numbers of the business at the board meetings. The board get a note of the figures in advance of the meeting and they ask questions about the numbers before the meeting. We don't spend more than ten minutes talking about numbers in a historical sense. Nearly all the conversation is about critical challenges and growth opportunities.'

They also seek to create the kind of operating environments where people have the personal space both to tackle what needs to be done now and to think deep and hard about the future. Setting tough goals, paradoxically, seems to be more of a reinforcement than a barrier to this kind of environment; because the goals aren't achievable through incremental growth or doing the same things, they force people into taking the time to think more radically and more strategically.

Some insights into the difference between urgency and strategy come from management writer Michael Porter, who explains: 'Trade-offs are essential to strategy. They create the need for choice and purposefully limit what a company offers. Operational effectiveness and strategy are both essential to superior performance, which is, after all, the primary goal of any enterprise. But they work in very different ways. ... Overall competitive advantage or disadvantage results from all a company's activities, not just a few. Operational effectiveness means performing similar activities better than rivals perform them. ... In contrast, strategic positioning means performing different activities from rivals' or performing similar activities in different ways.'[1]

The importance of the long-term view
....

As far back as 1956, Soichiro Honda was explaining the importance of sacrificing 'short-term profits in an effort to contribute to and achieve harmony with our society. As an example, I would point out that Honda's motorcycles, cars and parts are manufactured and assembled around the world.' This wasn't just a matter of do-gooding; Honda was looking commercially to the future and recognising that 'if we want to be well received in the countries where we do business, it is imperative that we contribute to those countries' economic and industrial development and create employment opportunities.' It took most of his contemporaries another 25 years to get the same message.[2]

At IKEA, allowing managers to get on with running their own business in the short term frees up the top team to concentrate on the longer-term strategic issues, says Vice President Sven-Olof Kulldorff. He explains: 'We have one big advantage. We are not listed on the stock market. That means that management doesn't have to make constant reports and projections, and can think very long-term.'

Several of our case-study companies have been accused of being short-term in their thinking, because of their emphasis on achieving year-on-year hefty improvements in their returns to shareholders. If the description were true, they have been short-term for a very long time. The reality is that all are driven by very large goals that demand a steady ratcheting up of the business. The bigger the goal, the greater the sense of urgency needed to bring it about and the bigger the steps needed to get there.

Siebe's investment in bright young undergraduates around the world is typical of the long-term pay-off that high-performing companies look to. Says Chairman Barrie Stephens: 'We have 549 youngsters in universities getting degrees at our expense. We spend seven to eight per cent of sales (sometimes higher) on sunrise engineering R&D, on new technology and on new and replacement assets every year. We do it to make sure the orchestra plays to packed houses five and ten years down the pike. If you are getting your money's worth from graduates who stay, from high technology investment and asset acquisition, then you are three-quarters of the way there. Couple all of these with natural leaders and you have a good chance of success. It works!'

Chasing big goals

Big goals give shape and structure to the high-performing companies' activities. Described by two writers in the *Harvard Business Review* as big, hairy, audacious goals (BHAGs),[3] they provide the challenge and motivation for people to perceive today's achievements as no more than stepping stones on the way to something greater, but still achievable within their lifetimes or at least the lifetime of their children. General Electric's Jack Welch puts it succinctly when he says that 'companies need overarching themes to create change.'

What makes these ideas so alluring and so galvanising to employees is that they are big enough to make people gulp, but within the bounds of human hope, and they are also simple and clear. The following provide a useful reminder of the kinds of big idea that high-performing company CEOs spend so much of their time selling:

- 'The first objective is to be number-one supplier to the financial community in all market segments in all countries. Our cup is already half-full – we are unquestionably the leading vendor worldwide – but we concentrate on the half which is empty. The second objective is to continue to be the leading media supplier internationally.' – Peter Job, CEO of Reuters, writing in the firm's 1995 annual report.

- For Rentokil Initial, says Chris Pearce, Group Finance Director: 'Clive Thompson as Chief Executive is very important. I'm a great believer that all institutions – whether its a school, a theatre or a company – depend on having a good leader. You need a good team, too, but the role of the chief executive or leader is the most important, not least in setting a very clear objective – in our case to grow the business by 20 per cent a year for ever, although the "for ever" part is perhaps not possible. But having one very clear objective is the key.'

- JCB is clear about its grand design: it wants to be number one in the marketplace and has already achieved this with its range of Loadall telescopic handlers and its backhoe loaders, the ubiquitous yellow digger. The founder is quoted as saying: 'Our greatest moment hasn't been reached yet. I really do believe we've only just started in business and there's a long way to go.'[4]

- Sony, as a similar example, aims to become 'the leading maker of consumer electronics in the digital age', says its President Nobuyuki Idei. To help employees envision the necessary move from the company's analogue past to a digital figure, he talks of 'digital dream kids'.[5]

- 'Bowthorpe wants to be number one,' says CEO Nicholas Brookes. 'Our "BHAG" is to be "the global leader in selected markets by providing creative solutions which improve the performance of customers' complex electrical and electronic systems" – the two hairy bits are deciding to shoot for the number-one spot and concentrating on creative solutions as the way to get there.'

- Microsoft's vision, says Bill Gates is 'a computer on every desk and in every home, all running Microsoft software'.[6]

- GKN's pallet business expresses its big goal in terms of market share. Managing Director of Industrial Services, Marcus Beresford, explains that the company intends to turn its current global ten per cent market share into a dominant 40 per cent. In Europe it is already more than half-way there, but the big challenges will be in the fast-expanding markets of Asia–Pacific, where there is 'nothing that you would recognise as a Western FMCG logistics infrastructure'.

- 'SOL's big goal is to be the best in all the areas we measure, not only in Finland but worldwide,' says Liisa Joronen.

- Noel Tichy describes GE's original 'big ideas' as speed, simplicity and self-confidence. To these have been added 'boundarylessness' – breaking down the internal barriers of hierarchy, geography and function, to promote teamwork.[7]

- Atlas Copco's Chief Executive Michael Treschow says: 'Our vision is to be the global leader in our businesses – compressors, power tools, and rock drilling equipment and services. We will be the global leader when we are the first choice of our customers everywhere by giving best value.'

The relationship between big goals and strategic-planning processes can get very complex. The farther you are away from achieving the goal, the more options you have available to you. At the risk of being simplistic, it is sometimes helpful to define vision as being 'the picture of where we are going' and strategy as 'the broad route to getting there'. A useful comparison is thinking about next year's winter holiday. The vision would encompass all the remembered sensations of the ski resort (the feelings, the sights, the sounds), or perhaps the expected sensations if you had never been skiing before. The strategies would include more prosaic issues such as how to get there (by plane or by train, for example); which airline to choose; which flight; what to pack; and so on. However, strategies can also be visionary in the sense that they may stir strong sensual feedback, ranging from the pleasant (for example, partying all night on the ski-train) to the unpleasant (for example, fear of flying). They also tend to be relatively long-term. Says Rentokil Initial's Sir Clive Thompson: 'Strategy we think about every ten years or so. A good strategy lasts; only a lousy strategy needs revising all the time.'

What makes the strategic vision so powerful is the intensity with which it is portrayed. Effective leaders (*see* Chapter Eleven) find the language to capture people's imagination about what it would mean to achieve the goals. They also find ways to make each key step of the goal meaningful to the people who have to make it happen, no matter what level they are in the organisation. For example, Granada got its motorway service station employees to envision the ideal scene at their counters at various times of day. It was a very practical way to make the vision relevant and compelling to these staff.

Unlike the business values, the vision can and does change in high-performing companies as it becomes a near-reality and thus loses its power to challenge and inspire. Says Siebe's Yurko: 'We used to aim to be in the top three of each of our core businesses. Now we want to be the best company in each of those markets.'

Although some businesses have to plan in detail 20 years ahead (for example, it can take that long to write down an oil refinery or a chemical factory), by and large our high-performing companies tend to differentiate between long-term vision and strategy. The strategies they adopt to achieve their big goals are on the whole relatively short-term, rarely looking above three years ahead. Knowing the direction they are heading, they concentrate on the current and next page of the road map rather than the destination.

Even General Electric, whose strategic planning expertise has been the much-praised subject of numerous business school cases, recognises the limitations of strategic planning in the classical sense. Indeed, Steven Kerr, Vice President for Corporate Leadership Development says: 'GE gave the world models of centralised planning. But while everyone else was writing up the case studies, GE had moved on. The future comes so fast you can't afford to spend lots of time planning in detail.' Says Jack Welch: 'Trying to define what will happen three to five years out in specific, quantifiable terms, is a futile exercise. The world is moving too fast for that. What should a company do instead? First of all, define its vision and its destiny in clear, broad terms. Second, maximise its own productivity. Finally, be organisationally and culturally flexible enough to meet massive change. The way to control your destiny in a global environment of change and uncertainty is simple: Be the highest value supplier in your marketplace.'[8]

Liisa Joronen at SOL goes even further, rejecting strategic planning altogether. She explains: 'Top management decides what businesses SOL is in. In these businesses SOL has no other strategy than to be the best.

Our business moves so fast and is done only by people so we cannot have strategic planning. We have had Total Quality Management since 1979. That includes everything, and can be called our strategic planning.'

Southwest Airlines doesn't have a ten-year strategy, or anything like it. It knows what business it is in and sticks to its niche. Beyond that, however, strategy consists of frequent reviews where the top team (and others) step outside the box and look at the business as a whole. Says CEO Herb Kelleher: 'We sit down and say, "We have to re-examine this whole airline, and how it's operating, how we are serving the public, and what changes are taking place outside." '[9]

Reuters is even wary of having a vision. Says Chief Executive Peter Job: 'We are slightly uncomfortable in this company with visions. So often they prove to be nightmares. Vision seems to be a word that new CEOs in US companies use when they are trying to make their mark.'

Creating urgency

'It's very easy for a business to lose its sense of urgency,' says Dominic Cadbury. 'They may feel that their long-term strategy has set it all out and, therefore, provided you stick to the long-term strategy, that this is going to produce success. Your industry may be incredibly stable and predictable but, if everything is not being tackled with urgency all of the time, you are not going to be successful.'

Says Archie Norman, chairman of ASDA: 'I think if you want to create that continual process of urgency, you've got to attack it from every direction; you've got to have a leadership that's got that urgency; you've to be prepared, when people become complacent, to change them and if necessary move them out; you need to have the customer volume turned up loud so that the complaints and dissatisfactions and desires of the customers and colleagues are always reverberating through the business. That creates a sense of urgency. You need to create a sense of performance culture right through the business. You need to have people from outside who are firing in new ideas. As soon as we stand still you'll see the business sink. We have to have our foot down on the accelerator and through the floor all the time.'

Nicholas Brookes, CEO of Bowthorpe, maintains: 'Strategy is all about urgency. If you don't plan now and fast, you are never going to get to where you want to get to. The tendency can be to say, "We don't need to plan, because there's plenty of time." But there isn't plenty of time; you've got to do it today.'

Vodafone's Sir Gerald Whent sets an example from the top in reacting swiftly to market change. 'I look at the competition every Monday morning. We have a meeting of 14 people and from that I will know exactly what is going on in every part of the network in all the countries, and particularly in this country. I will know every trick and tariff. That is a regular thing, because of the fast-moving market. When you have a team of bright directors meeting like this, they in their turn become aware, because they know it's their job to do it.'

Continuous evaluation and re-evaluation of their environment enables high-performance companies to make radical shifts in direction, sometimes long before the competition. Chief Executive of The Berkeley Group, Tony Pidgley, for example, astounded competitors by going liquid, selling off as much as possible of the company's houses and land in 1988, when land prices were still going through the roof. 'It wasn't a hard choice to make', he says. 'We weren't making money through our expertise but through inflation. It was unreal. We bought a small company in Dorking which built some flats in the area, and they jumped in value from £60,000 to £90,000 in months. We bought a piece of land for £2 million, held it for seven days and then sold it for £7 million.

'That November, we debated what to do. We felt that the market couldn't go on the way it was. We had to protect the assets of the business. In the following February, we announced it to the City and instructed our MDs to go liquid. That's probably the only time we've ever brought them all together at one time. We never summon them all together, but on this occasion we told them to sell anything and everything. We knew that if we were wrong and had gone too early, we might miss out on some profits, but if we went too late, we could lose the business.' Not long after, the bottom fell out of the market.

'How did we do it? Simple. We call it "Indian signs". Indian signs are the smoke signals that indicate a change is coming. When you see the signs, you use good old-fashioned common sense, something we're good at. Property is a feast or famine business. History shows us what happens if you don't make the right adjustments at the right time.'

Smiths Industries was able to make a relatively rapid strategic about-turn when it became clear to Sir Roger Hurn that the commercial aerospace industry was heading for a slump. He explains: 'We were very early in taking costs out of our business, when others were not yet recognising what we were seeing. We did it over a three-year period, because we were close to our customers and because we had *feel*.' By feel, Sir Roger means an intuitive recognition of what is happening in an industry. Feel is very difficult to define, but it is undoubtedly a strategic competence – the ability to assess trends from unorthodox perspectives.

In this case, a critical factor was how Sir Roger and his colleagues analysed the underlying dynamics of customer behaviour. 'Airlines' own performance was going down and yet their orders for new aeroplanes were continuing at a high level,' he explains. 'It seemed to me that they weren't going to be able to afford them, come the day. And that's what happened.' Because Smiths Industries had already battened down the hatches, it was better able to ride the storm than rivals, who had simply watched sales trends, and it was able to take more rapid and effective advantage of the subsequent upturn in sales when that eventually occurred.

'Strategy belongs where the action is' comes with one big caveat, however. As the Smiths Industries example above illustrates, sometimes it is important to have people at the corporate centre looking at a much wider horizon than those in the individual businesses. It is unlikely that many of the individual companies within Smiths would have had the sensitivity of antennae to recognise the big game that was about to be played out. As so often is the case, it is an issue Peter Drucker has already considered. Reports Steven Kerr, Vice President for Corporate Leadership Development at GE: 'When Peter Drucker was interviewed recently about his biggest learning point as a consultant, he said it was at GE – he learned he should never put the same guy in charge of today, who is in charge of tomorrow. We have to make sure there are people looking at the long view and we have to protect them.'

The role of these people – whether strategic planners or the top team – is to ensure that strategic thinking takes place and to mould the context. In some cases, it can be to think the unthinkable – what will we do if our whole market changes dramatically? Microsoft's Bill Gates is a master of such thinking (Mike Murray, Microsoft's Vice President of Human Relations and Administration describes him as 'one of the best game players ever to run a business . . . always thinking three or four moves ahead of the competition'). What they must never do – and what characterised so many strategic planning functions in the 1980s and led to the demise of many of them – is to remove *ownership* of the strategy from the senior managers in the operations. These longer-range thinkers are the scouts who climb tall trees in the forest and relay what they see down to the captains below. Very often, however, the people who can make best sense of the vista, and therefore the people who have to climb tall trees themselves, are the top people in the business. Says Murray: 'In any large organisation, there need to be four or five key players, who have the interest and understanding of the game to understand what could change and how.' When these people are at the top, they have the capacity to share what they see and inspire those who need to make the change of direction happen.

Balancing the long term and the short term

Later in this book, we use the analogy of the primitive (emotional) and evolved (rational) brain to explore the apparent conflict between values and rules. However, most people are more familiar with the notion of right and left brain. When neurologists investigated the interaction between vision and thought, they found that the right eye (connected to the left side of the brain) concentrated more on the large picture, while the left eye (connected to the right side of the brain) focused more on the details. What fascinated them was not the mechanics of the individual halves, but how the whole brain synthesised detail and the big picture into an effective appreciation of what the eyes observed in the world around them.

In large part, the balance between strategic focus and action orientation is a similar synthesis. The strategic focus, with its longer and wider horizon, gives the big picture. The short-term action orientation tackles the immediate steps along the way and overcomes current barriers and crises. Synthesising the two is essential to maintain the pace of the organisation in the desired direction. Too much focus on one, to the detriment of the other, inevitably leads either to a slowing down of progress or a preoccupation with inessentials.

Says Granada's Human Resources Director Stephanie Monk: 'You can't afford a choice between long-term strategy and short-term urgency. Meeting the challenge in the short term means being flexible. Charles [Allen] has a very clever notion about contingency planning for the unknown. You start the year knowing something will go wrong and you plan against that eventuality. You are on the front foot not on the back foot. By doing that you actually create the space and time to be thinking about the longer term. Our view is that is most appropriately done by the businesses in the first instance. Across a spectrum of companies we would certainly veer towards short-term delivery and urgency, but that has actually been the route through which we've been able to work strategically as well.'

Granada's pragmatic approach is typical of how the high-performing companies tackle this issue. Looking to both the short and long term isn't an option for their managers – it is a basic requirement. They create the environment for these expectations to be fulfilled in several ways:

- recognising that strategy belongs where the action is, and acting accordingly;
- emphasising that clarity of strategy is more important than how clever it is; and

• using instinct to put the urgency into strategy.

STRATEGY BELONGS WHERE THE ACTION IS

Strategic planning has undergone something of a revolution in recent years. The old dictum 'structure follows strategy', though valid in context, was used in the 1970s and 1980s to justify large, central strategic-planning departments. Strategy became the responsibility of strategists and managers were expected to stick to managing. Two factors combined to make organisations reject this approach. Firstly, it didn't work. Phalanxes of MBAs trained in the same strategic theories tended to come up with the same answers whatever organisation they worked in, so there was little opportunity for companies to differentiate themselves through the originality of their strategic approach. Managers who didn't have responsibility for generating strategy had no ownership of strategy. When it went wrong, the strategists blamed the managers for inadequacy of implementation and the managers complained that the strategy was flawed. Secondly, the return to fashion of leadership – an unexpected but common by-product of downsizing amongst management ranks – encouraged entrepreneurial people to demand that the centre should return accountability for strategy to those who had to make it work.

Our high-performance companies, by and large, never fell into the centralised strategy trap in the first place. Rather, they have held closely to the rule that *strategy belongs where the action is*. This rule is based on several well-founded assumptions:

• the people running a business unit are usually best placed to understand how their markets are developing;
• strategic planning is a continuous, evolutionary process; and
• ownership and implementation of strategy are indivisible.

Cadbury Schweppes, for example, has no central strategy department; strategy is the responsibility of the two business streams, Beverages and Confectionery. The only strategic decisions made at the centre relate to acquisitions and a balancing of the two businesses. SOL, too, reserves strategic control solely for deciding where to invest in new ventures, either as home-grown new business areas or as acquisitions. It takes few risks – it paid cash for its recent acquisition of a waste management company. 'The strategy is now to grow and be the best by all measurements,' says CEO Liisa Joronen.

Where they do have central strategy departments, our high-performing companies put them to one or more of three very specific uses:

- gathering data on competition, technology development and market development across a much wider market segment, to inform the thinking of the strategic teams belonging to the business units;
- acting as a conduit for new concepts and technology in strategic analysis; or
- helping to co-ordinate the strategy of individual business units.

We use the word 'helping' in the last bullet point deliberately. The CEO and group top team in all our high-performance companies see their role very much as strategic co-ordination. By discussing strategic issues frequently with the top teams of the business units, they ensure that strategic thinking is a continuous process, rather than a once-a-year event.

GKN's approach is typical. Says Sir David Lees: 'Every month I sit down with the managing directors [of the divisions] and we go through every business. Then every month, we do one or two strategy reviews of particular businesses, where the managing director of that business will go through his strategies. We try to divide the short-term financial performance from where the business is going. We try not to have set time horizons on strategy because it's quite different between the businesses. Outside of this formal review, there are informal strategy reviews going on [in the business units] all the time.' One of the benefits of this approach, he maintains, is to ensure that division heads aren't allowed to let sentimentality cloud their judgment about underperforming businesses.

The CEO and board in most of our high-performance companies create the broad strategic framework – the key things that matter – and allow unit top management to *sell them* on the strategies they have devised within that framework. For example, Siebe's Allen Yurko has regular meetings with operating companies, where he says: 'The individual managing directors basically get to customise their strategy presentation to us however they see fit. The only thing we ask for is don't bore us with detail. The top five or six things you're going to do, that's what we want to monitor. We don't want to see the objectives of all 47 managers in the business; what we want to see is strategy, a person's name, and a date. That's the bottom line, how are you going to do organic growth within your division? How are you going to get those products out there? How are you going to improve your quality? How are you going to beat the competition? How are you going to penetrate new markets?'

All of the companies emphasise the importance of having the businesses own their strategies. Where they do use strategic consultancy it is to complement rather than replace management responsibility. 'We aren't the sort of people who just bring in consultants because we need to get new ideas. What I cannot stand is when you bring in consultants to help you with the strategy. If you can't figure out your own strategy, then there is something wrong. You should probably wheel in the consultants and take out the management,' says Michael Treschow of Atlas Copco. Southwest Airlines' Herb Kelleher makes a similar point: 'When an outside consultant comes to Southwest and says, "We want to ... show your people how to do their jobs better", I tell them, "If you can do that, I'm firing all of them and hiring you!" Because, if an outsider can do that, we've got the wrong people in our jobs. They need to solve their own problems.'[10]

Rob Rowley, Finance Director at Reuters, makes a similar point about consultants. 'We listen to them', he says, 'but we don't tend to allow consultants to do anything substantial in the organisation. We will use people to help us do things better, but we will not allow people to take control of the organisation and tell us what we should do.'

CLARITY IS MORE IMPORTANT THAN CLEVERNESS

When a large European aerospace manufacturer decided to share its business plan with every one of its 22,000 employees, it was a bold step. Before then, only an inner cadre of 20 or so people had access to the whole plan. Communicating it more widely meant that it had to be turned into plain language and presented using straightforward, easily understood graphics. Some months later, a couple of members of the inner core admitted that this was the first time *they* had understood the plan fully and that one of the benefits of the exercise was that they were much clearer about what they had to do. The clarity of their understanding led them to more incisive decision making and this was echoed layer by layer down the organisation.

The generic principle that these managers had learned was that *strategies work best when they are readily understandable*. It is a good example of 'simplexity' at work. To motivate people to deliver the strategy, the strategy must be crystal clear, unambiguous and easy to explain to others. In short, if it is beyond the ability of the ordinary frontline employee to articulate the strategy to a third party, then the strategy itself is almost certainly too complex to be implemented effectively.

At Atlas Copco the business strategy, along with the vision and values that go with it, are spelt out in a picture book. 'It tells you all about Atlas Copco' says President Michael Treschow, 'our products, history, structure. You should always be able to explain to your grandmother what Atlas Copco is about in three minutes. If you can't do that, then there is something you have missed.'

'I'm a great believer in over-simplifying the objectives of the business so that everyone knows what they are,' says Granada's Charles Allen. 'In most cases, that has been "keep it, grow it".'

For David Lees at GKN, strategic clarity 'is one of our core competencies. ... Knowing where you are going and why you are going there is very important.' Even long before GKN began its switch away from its traditional businesses, this was a value branded into the culture. GKN was among the first companies in the world to insist that every operating company and every manufacturing site gave all employees a detailed annual report and an opportunity to discuss plans for the next year.

Likewise Sir Roger Hurn at Smiths Industries: 'My experience says that people really do welcome change when they understand the reasons for it. Managers should tell people in clear language, not prevaricating or pretending it's secret.'

'Planning,' says IKEA founder Ingvar Kamprad, 'is often synonymous with red tape. Of course, planning is necessary to establish guidelines for your work and make the company function in the long run, but do not forget that exaggerated planning can be fatal! Exaggerated planning restrains your freedom of action and reduces your time for the actual performance. A complicated planning process paralyses. Let simplicity and common sense characterise your planning.'[11]

One of the benefits is better and faster decision making. Says David Spencer, Human Resources Director of Smiths Industries: 'Because people are well-informed, they feel the sense of urgency. It may take a while to turn the tanker around, but decisions taken on the bridge here are quickly understood by everyone else. We have had no problems with downsizing, for example. The trade unions have been involved in getting the size of the workforce right. It isn't always so easy in Continental Europe as in the UK and the US; people's understanding of the profit motive is not as great.'

Bob Lawson of Electrocomponents has also found that achieving strategic clarity helps make better decisions. He explains: 'We have not found it easy to develop a long-term strategy. It takes a lot of communication to get buy-in, not least because it may not be good news for everyone. We have tried to bring it down to simple essences. Where do we have to be in the long term and what do we have to do to get there? If you can't put it on six pages, you've not got it right. Once you have clarity about the long term, everything else is short steps. We struggle less than we used to.'

Clarity also helps speed up decisions on major investments. Says Bowthorpe CEO Nicholas Brookes: 'If you have a clear strategy and clear goals, the acquisition criteria become a lot simpler.'

In general, our high-performing companies do not perceive the standard kind of mission statement as being helpful to clarity. Says Martin Ellis,

General Manager of UK Healthcare at Rentokil Initial: 'We don't go in for highfalutin mission statements or anything like that. We believe in words of one syllable wherever possible.' And Electrocomponents' Bob Lawson states: 'I have a problem with mission statements. They are usually just statements of the obvious.' Our case study CEOs prefer to put the big goals and the strategic priorities across face to face. It may be much more time-consuming, but it is more credible, more effective and much more likely to result in positive action now.

INSTINCT PUTS THE URGENCY INTO STRATEGY

Although the boards of our high-performance companies all hold strategic retreats where they make six-monthly or annual appraisals of the strategic approach, strategy creation is in every case a continuous process. Explains Boots' Lord Blyth: '[Strategy] is a continuous discussion process with the board, rather than a great strategic presentation where the board agrees or disagrees. We talk to the heads of the individual businesses about their strategies all through the year.'

One of the reasons for continuous thinking about strategy is to develop rapid response at the tactical level: 'What are the implications of current events for the viability and delivery of our broad strategy?' Equally important, however, is developing 'feel' – the intuitive, instinctive understanding of the environment and the big goals that push people to act urgently almost automatically.

This instinctive behaviour is difficult to emulate, or explain. At Reuters, for example, says Director of Personnel and Quality Programmes Patrick Mannix: 'One of the things that underpinned our success was a complete absence of any formalised planning ability! If we had had a formalised planning process, we might never have done what we have done. If you look at the big projects we undertook (the original Reuter Monitor information system back in the 1970s, and the various transaction services for the Foreign Exchange market in the 1980s), if we had known at the beginning how big they were, we would not have done them. We thought they were smaller so we started on them. What we did have was an extraordinary ability to finish them.'

In general, the better the feel people have for the big game, the more urgency they apply to strategic objectives, and the less patience they have with formal planning procedures. Says SOL's Liisa Joronen: 'We do a one-year plan and it's too long. It must be shorter and constantly changing.'

For Jim Martin at N. Brown, close involvement in the detail is an essential part of strategic awareness, although he recognises the problems that occur when people focus only on the short term. He explains: 'As there is no "order book" to rely on in retailing, we have an intense interest in daily statistics of the business – namely sales. We expect every director and manager to have an intimate knowledge of activity and performance in their areas. It may seem a highly tactical approach but I find in the long term that really successful people, who are good at this, are also equally comfortable thinking strategically. They really understand their part of the business and I suppose seem to care that little bit more. We have little patience with woolly thinkers here.'

In general, high-performing companies don't do a lot of detailed long-term planning. They take the attitude that if you have a clear long-term vision and a sense of urgency about the present, you don't need many detailed plans. At IKEA, for example, says Vice President Sven-Olof Kulldorff: 'Our detailed long-term planning is very meagre. We do try to understand what things are influencing our business two to five years ahead. We don't do a lot of budgets, we skipped them some years ago. We follow up current changes. If you have 20 stores and some are increasing at 50 per cent and some are only doing eight or even zero, you don't have to have a lot of planning to know what to do.'

In summary...

High-performing companies focus their managers on both the long-term future and short-term action by having big goals and visions that inspire urgent action today and tomorrow. Group top management goes to considerable lengths to ensure that senior people in the divisions have a very clear understanding of the group big goals and robust strategies for their own businesses. Simplicity is, once again, an important criterion in both of these.

The last word on this subject goes to ABB's Percy Barnevik: 'Continuous change is not a threat, but a security. . . . If you stand still, you fall back.'

You will not be surprised, then, to find that the next chapter examines in more detail how high-performing companies manage the process of change, both in adapting to their external environment and in adapting their environment to facilitate the achievement of their dreams and ambitions.

5 | ACCELERATED EVOLUTION
Evolutionary versus revolutionary change

'I am a tortoise, and M&S is a tortoise. We don't do things unless we have thought them through very carefully.' *Sir Richard Greenbury, Chairman of the UK-based retailing giant.*

'If it can't be done in 12 months, why are you doing it?' *Bob Lawson, Chief Executive, Electrocomponents.*

'Change to us is fun. It's a way of life.' *Rob Rowley, Finance Director, Reuters.*

'If we were an organisation of revolution, we'd be having one every few seconds.' *Peter Job, Chief Executive, Reuters.*

Kill routine before it kills you.' *Liisa Joronen, Chief Executive, SOL.*

From the first quotation above, it would be easy to perceive Marks & Spencer as a dinosaur company, constantly in danger of being left behind by more agile competitors. In reality, behind the calm exterior of Marks & Spencer is a mass of continuous experimentation and modification, driven in large part by the carefully honed skill of listening to customers. The world-famous retailer is, in effect, a cautious but deliberate innovator, balancing the need for continuous change against the need to conserve core values.

Much the same is true of other high-performance companies. They have a very strong preference for evolutionary change, for a whole variety of reasons. It enables you to identify wrong turnings before too much damage is done; it gives time for both employees and customers to adapt; and it is less likely to disrupt people's attention to the core activities and values. They can, however, take rapid action when it is needed in response to unpredictable changes in their environment, because they usually have an in-built nimbleness.

Says Michael Treschow of Atlas Copco: 'Strategy? We haven't changed strategy. We fine-tune it, we become more clever in expressing it, but I cannot say we have changed strategy during my five years. I have a strong belief that drastic change is a disqualification of your way of operating because you should have known better so you didn't get to that situation. Unfortunately it happens, but every time you have to make a drastic change be aware that it takes a year to filter down each level. So if you have five levels in a corporation, don't change strategy more than every five years, or people will never have the chance to work it through.'

The two characteristics – evolutionary development and very fast change – may seem total opposites, but they are not. Two essential characteristics provide the bridge between them. One is a clear sense of direction, which provides an essential framework for guiding the path of change. The other is a determined emphasis to sustain the pace of change. By combining pace and direction, they build the capacity in both people and systems to handle a continuous stream of small changes. This enables the company, by and large, to avoid having to introduce large-scale change. When radical change is occasionally necessary, much of the disruptive impact is absorbed by the organisation's ability to decompose it into more manageable small changes.

Says Reuters' CEO Peter Job: 'On the face of it there seems to be a contradiction, but it isn't real. You have to free yourself from the detail of what's happening to step back, but you need to know the detail of what's happening to understand when something major in your environment changes. I think our board has a very clear understanding that every now and then changes occur which could be significant and that they have to watch out for those changes – what in the US they call a new paradigm. The Internet, for example, could be a new paradigm. At those times it's important to leave your strategy suitcase in the station and catch the train. Those changes may alter strategy in the long run.'

David Pearson, Managing Director of Sony UK, uses the analogy of safe driving to explain the combination of caution and fast pace that characterises both Sony and many other high-performing companies. Advanced drivers talk of *maximum controlled progress* – the ability to know where your journey is taking you, to look ahead to the next bend (and for clues to what is beyond it) and to adjust your speed and course to near the maximum that is safe for the road conditions. It takes a constant stream of accurate judgments and maximum alertness to drive in this way.

In SAP, says Henning Kagermann: 'We don't have two years or so of stable organisation and then radical change. Rather, we have lots of change every year.'

This combination of pace and direction also helps high-performance companies avoid getting tangled in the latest management fashions. 'I warn my managers to beware of -isms and fads,' says Singapore Airlines' Cheong. Instead, he looks for seamless change through long-sighted planning and, remarkably in a highly competitive and rapidly changing market, he usually gets it. 'For us, there haven't been any major upheavals. Changes have always been evolutionary rather than revolutionary. ... We have always insisted on having steady growth. The growth rate may change from one year to another, but over a period we stick to it. We don't try and anticipate the turns of the economic cycle. One of the woes of the industry has been that companies would become over-confident in the boom part of the cycle and order a lot of aircraft; then, just when the aircraft arrive, the cycle begins to turn and they cancel their orders, perhaps retrench staff. But if you plan ahead and stick to a stated growth rate, you are able to avoid a lot of these pitfalls.'

The benefits of evolutionary change

Cheong continues: 'Being in constant revolution is very disruptive. We prefer to plan changes way in advance, so that when they happen, they are seamless. For example, we decided that we had to contract out some of our more labour-intensive services to places outside Singapore, where the labour is more abundant and cheaper. We helped the Chinese in Beijing develop their own accounting system, trained their staff and then gave them a large part of our accounting work. As a result, 16 staff were not needed. However, because we had planned it long in advance, we were able to explain why it was necessary and that there wasn't going to be any retrenchment. We didn't have to fire anybody and we had the full co-operation of the unions. When the switch finally took place, it was not very noticeable.'

Although the changes that accompanied the privatisation of British Airways in the early 1980s were radical, BA too has concentrated on evolution, even through changes of Chief Executive. 'It's probably more difficult to take over a successful business than one that clearly needs something done to improve it ... so the change that has to be made has to be developmental,' says BA's current Chief Executive, Robert Ayling. Nonetheless, the plans he has unveiled for taking BA into the next century leave little room for complacency.

Adds Sir Colin Marshall: 'All of the changes we have made have been carefully planned and most were proactive, although some have been reactive, of necessity. The redefinition of the business has centred on the proposition that the company was no longer just an 'aircraft operator', but 'a provider of excellent customer service in the field of air travel'. BA is still working to achieve that goal, recognising both that it takes years to come about and that the goal itself is constantly moving as customer expectations rise and competitors catch up. The key, for both BA and Singapore Airlines, appears to be maintaining the pace of change just slightly ahead of both customer expectation and competitor effort.

Behind BA's preference for evolutionary change is a recognition of how difficult it can be to convince people of the need for radical change when the company is doing well. Says Sir Colin Marshall: 'There will inevitably be some inherent resistance, at all levels, to a lot of simultaneous change and the perceived 'initiative log-jam'. It has to be tackled through a carefully structured programme of dialogue, providing explanation, understanding and delivering employee "buy-in".'

Reuters, too, emphasises the evolutionary side of change. Says main board Director David Ure: 'In the real world, top management's job is about growing the business at a speed which is fast enough to avoid being interfered with, so you avoid any abrupt lurching of the culture. We have to ensure that a pendulum swing doesn't happen. At the same time, you have to be thorough. For us, arrogance and inflexibility are bad, but improvement is a slow, delicate process, which involves keeping the image of the company and not allowing it to deteriorate. When you reach our size, it's very easy to deteriorate.'

At IKEA, says Vice-President Sven-Olof Kulldorff: 'We work more with evolution than revolution. When we see that we're going in the wrong direction, or we're not performing optimally, we make a correction. The values give us the answer to a lot of these questions.'

Microsoft to an outsider might appear in a constant churn, but it nonetheless prefers an evolutionary approach – when it can. Says Mike Murray, Vice President Human Resources and Administration: 'Microsoft is constantly changing, both leading change and reacting to it. As a dominant supplier you will always prefer to evolve in a way that is predictable to your customers. But it isn't always possible, because your competitors are always trying to change the value equation.'

By taking the drama out of change, high-performance companies reduce turbulence and accustom people to a continuous stream of improvements. Over a period, those changes may add up to a radical transformation, but the disruption to both the operations and the employees' sense of security is minimal. The adage 'if it ain't broke, don't fix it' is one most of our high-performance companies ascribe to. 'We don't innovate for the sake of it,' remonstrates Thoeng Tjheon Onn, Director of Marketing Services at Singapore Airlines.

Evolutionary change also leads to greater predictability and therefore fewer swings in share price. Companies such as GKN keep external borrowing low by matching expansion and new initiatives to the cash available. The group rule of thumb, says Managing Director of Industrial

Services Marcus Beresford, is that 'a business is only cash hungry if it expands more than ten per cent. Below ten per cent growth, it generates cash.'

The benefits of revolutionary change

Occasionally, however, radical change is necessary. High-performance companies recognise that, like everyone else, they sometimes have to push through tough measures with urgency. They do so by sharing that urgency with all the people affected. Being used to managing constant change to meet challenging targets, the capability to handle change is already there. What has to be added is the commitment of people in the organisation to the purpose of the changes, what has to be done and how it is done.

One of the most remarkable stories of this kind of transformation is General Electric. The company was, on the face of it, doing well when Jack Welch became CEO. But there were underlying weaknesses that would have changed that, and so Welch launched a programme of radical change that is still continuing a decade later. He says: 'Incremental change doesn't work well in the type of transformation GE has gone through. If your change isn't revolutionary enough, the bureaucracy can beat you'.[1]

Companies such as GE and ABB appear to be in constant revolutionary change (GE's Welch was nicknamed 'Neutron Jack' because he had hacked away at the organisation so severely and ABB's Percy Barnevik has been happy to adopt a similar sobriquet). No sooner is one objective reached than another, potentially even more disruptive, arrives in its place. For example, having achieved the challenging goal of shifting a large part of production to Eastern Europe and improving productivity there to competitive levels, ABB rapidly switched attention to the developing countries of Asia–Pacific.

GE aims to revolutionise everything and has had to put massive effort into carrying people with it. Other companies seek revolutionary change in their core competencies, with a view to constantly wrong-footing the competition. For example, when Honda wins prizes for the quality of its products, its immediate reaction is to consider how it could do better. Said a company spokesperson: 'Our experience has taught us to believe that, no matter how good a product we have made, we can always make it better.' Honda forces revolution in product design by setting impossible goals. It starts with a definition of the ideal, then sets a design team the task of seeing how close it can get. That forces people to think of radical rather than evolutionary change in systems, components and manufacturing processes. To understand how the innovations they create will affect the customers, everyone in R&D at Honda Japan has to spend three months a year attending dealer shows, exhibitions and other events where they can talk direct to customers and agents.

At the same time, the mass of people in Honda are engaged in creating evolutionary change. Founder Soichiro Honda is quoted as saying: 'In a highly competitive race, only the width of the finishing line may decide whether you are a winner or loser. If you understand that, you cannot disregard even the smallest improvement.'

Balancing evolutionary and revolutionary change

Whether they favour evolutionary or revolutionary change, or a balance of both, the CEOs of high-performing companies all show an impatience with the pace of change. For example, says SOL CEO Liisa Joronen: 'To an outsider it's constant revolution, but I still find it too slow. We have constant change, a mixture of revolution and evolution. If nothing happens, we make it happen. The only steady things are our attitude and the sun.'

At ASDA, Archie Norman sees the balance between evolutionary and revolutionary change as a frequent cycle. He declares: 'The aspiration of all chairmen and chief executives is to create this process of continuous evolution and change. My experience is that very few companies can actually sustain that at a sufficient pace and that you need a combination of the two. Our approach tends to be to take an area of the business, to fracture it and to change every aspect of it and then put it back down again and expect it to evolve forward from there for a period of a couple of years and then reshape it again. If there is a model which creates a rapid enough pace of continual evolution to drive things forward, we haven't discovered it. Changing the mindset means rethinking and re-engineering every aspect of the unit, including the people. We've got terrific people here, who can move from one thing to another, and having some people movement is part of the process.'

Getting the right balance between evolutionary and revolutionary change for each company is a delicate matter. Almost all of our high-performance companies see it as an issue, although the solutions they apply can be very different. At one extreme are the innovation-obsessed companies such as Siebe, Sony and Honda, who know that their existence depends on staying ahead in the innovation game; at the other extreme is Rentokil Initial, where, says CEO Sir Clive Thompson: 'To be honest, we don't want a lot of innovation. As far as we're concerned this is how we want it done, go do it. We do encourage people to come up with ideas, but we don't allow them to implement them. We don't want branch managers with entrepreneurial ideas – you can all too easily end up with a business that is too diversified.'

The point here is that Rentokil Initial's competitive advantage is based at least in part on the ability to deliver consistency of service wherever it operates. When almost any change could have global rather than local impact, maintaining the balance towards caution and control in innovation makes sense.

Moreover, the focus on providing industrial services on a contract basis means that the company does not want to be dragged into less profitable activities that could dilute its core competencies. As Sir Clive explains: 'I can say our strategy is to develop industrial services in developed countries, using the Rentokil Initial brand. But why? We want to be in markets where the quality of service is very important to customers. We're very good at doing difficult things. Why industrial services? Because with domestic/residential services people want quality but aren't prepared to pay for it. Also, you can't get entry into their premises when you want it, but you can with industrial premises, which gives us the opportunity to get high productivity from our service people.

'We prefer service-based to one-off business as it give us better predictability of revenue. We can plan routes efficiently so our people don't spend so much time travelling between sites. Developed countries are best because of the hierarchy of needs. In other words, in developed countries they can afford our services.

'We didn't go into the utilities markets in the UK as they opened up – waste disposal, for example – as contracts were always going to be awarded based on price. The contracts would be won by clever accounting techniques, not quality of service delivery.'

A while ago, one of the authors was asked by a large European manufacturing company to look at its change-management processes. The first step was to interview the executive team about some of the major changes in the previous two years and how they had fared. The near-unanimous perception was that they had been introduced with remarkably few problems. A layer down, the factory managers were a bit more sanguine, but generally agreed that the changes had worked fairly well. Middle managers were rather less enthusiastic, pointing out that such successes as there were had only been achieved at the expense of other priorities. Junior managers and their teams reacted with intense frustration, explaining that none of the changes had been fully bedded in, and that they had delivered only what was essential to tick the boxes on the report forms before having to move on to the next initiative. And the operators were simply frustrated that they hadn't been given the training they needed to get the best out of the new technology. And yet top management continued to wonder why apparently successful changes stubbornly failed to deliver the expected productivity increases.

This is a scenario repeated time and again in large companies. The capacity to absorb change is over-estimated by top management and the payback from change rarely meets expectations. Recent studies by consultancy ODR illustrate how difficult it can be to push change through an organisation that is unused to it. ODR talks of 'enlarging the sponge' – increasing the organisation's capacity to absorb and manage change. A large part of this is placing in key positions people who have the special combination of drive, tenacity and adaptability to both accept change themselves and sell it on to others.

In order to maintain an emphasis on continuous rapid evolutionary change rather than spasmodic revolutionary change, companies have to enlarge the sponge. Our high-performance companies do this in a number of ways, including:

- doing different things or doing things differently;
- putting innovation centre-stage as the source of maintaining differentiation;
- giving bright people the space to drive change around them;
- using customers as change partners;
- recognising that well understood constraints can encourage rather than diminish creative innovation;
- experimenting widely but putting effort behind the chosen few ideas;
- demonstrating remarkable persistence;
- spreading innovation rapidly among operating units;
- making change happen fast; and
- staying nimble.

DOING DIFFERENT THINGS OR DOING THINGS DIFFERENTLY

A young Scottish entrepreneur, when asked at a recent conference how he had started his highly successful business, replied that he had spent six months and more studying how companies in the sector managed themselves. Then he sat down to work out how he could do each key process differently. It's an approach that our high-performance companies tend to empathise with immediately. Competition is not about doing the same as the competition, it is about doing things differently, or better still, doing different things.

Says Granada's Charles Allen: 'Unless you interrogate the things an industry has done for 20 years, you will get nowhere. To get ahead, in every sector, you have to break rules and make new rules.'[2]

In some cases, too, our companies have triggered a revolution in the markets they serve. For instance, when Reuters developed its first electronic dealing product in the 1980s, it did so in the knowledge that the concept was so new that there was no demand for it. When it was introduced, it meant that, for the first time, dealers could trade directly from their screens without relying on telephone conversations with intermediary banks. As such it actually changed the way that business was conducted, altering the market for ever. Since then, other Reuters products too have anticipated demand and even created it, rather than simply reacting to existing market conditions.

'Twenty years ago when we started out, housing was not product-led' says Tony Pidgley, Chief Executive of The Berkeley Group. 'We decided that it should be. Berkeley decided to concentrate on individually designed homes, with appealing elevations and floor layouts, together with specifications to suit all of today's needs. That was the niche we decided to enter. In that respect, we could lay claim to changing the housing market.' Berkeley continues to look for ways to be different, in particular by finding value in opportunities other housebuilders avoid. Says Pidgley: 'If you have the expertise, there's no shortage of land in the UK. OK, if you want to develop on greenfield sites with standard products, as the volume housebuilders do, then that is cost-led. The difference is that, with derelict and contaminated land, you have to meet many more challenges in terms of design, as the vast majority of these sites are located in city centres. The privatisation that has recently taken place with companies like Railtrack, Thames Water and British Gas has resulted in them being more commercially astute and working their assets much harder. The net result is that a number of their sites, which are classified as 'brown' land, which are not controversial in planning terms but that do have many difficulties to overcome, have become available. This is where Berkeley really has an edge over our competitors, given our breadth and depth of knowledge in operating on sites of this nature, which are difficult to develop and usually have to be developed as individual concept schemes.'

Similarly, at IKEA, founder Ingvar Kamprad regards being different as a core value of the business. He explains: 'If we from the start had consulted experts about building a company like IKEA in a small village like Almhult, we would certainly have been dissuaded from doing so. Nevertheless, one of the biggest establishments in the whole furniture business is situated today in Almhult. By daring to be different, we find new ways; by refusing to accept a pattern just because it is established we get further – not only concerning the big problems but also when we must solve the small daily problems.

'Our development must always be vigorous and dynamic. For this reason, for instance, I hope that we will never have two stores completely alike. We know that the latest store will always show several imperfections, but still, taken all in all, it will be the best. A healthy appetite for experimenting shall lead us forward all the time. "Why?" remains an important keyword.

'... Here are some examples: while other furniture retailers were selling manufacturers' models, IKEA started to design its own; while furniture dealers set up shop in the centre of town, IKEA was building large stores out of town; while others turned to furniture factories to help them make tables, IKEA got them made by door manufacturers; whereas others sell their furniture assembled, IKEA gets the customers to assemble it themselves.'[3]

Doing things different is essentially a mindset. It requires a degree of creativity, of course, but equally if not more important is being open-minded to ideas from any source. This can include things that didn't work before – after all, the reason they didn't work may have been the circumstances in which they were applied, rather than the soundness of the idea itself. It also requires an ability to think the unthinkable, to imagine how someone from a completely different industry and/or environment might tackle the same issues. Above all, it requires an attitude that says that common practice is always yesterday's best practice.

PUTTING INNOVATION CENTRE-STAGE AS THE SOURCE OF MAINTAINING DIFFERENTIATION

For some of our companies, innovation is so important to the success of the business that the culture is steeped in it. At Reuters, for example, looking for ways to turn the world on its head is a way of life. 'We are all latent revolutionaries in a way,' says Rob Rowley, Finance Director. 'We all like to change the way things are done. We are not comfortable with the way it is done today. We are always looking for new ways of doing things. When we see a new bit of technology coming along, we are always looking to see how it could be applied in different situations to change the status quo.'

Peter Job, Chief Executive at Reuters, expresses the same point slightly differently. Asked about the company's rather staid image, he says: 'It pays us to appear conservative because of the markets we are in. Just because we wear grey suits doesn't mean that our minds aren't constantly whirring. It's radical conservatism.'

For all the manufacturers and most of the service companies among our high performers, innovation is a critical source of strategic differentiation. For GKN, for example, R&D and product development are the only way to retain partnerships with automotive partners. 'Excelling at innovation is the basis of long-lasting relationships,' says CEO Sir David Lees.

Siebe's Allen Yurko takes the same view. The company spends an average of 4.5 per cent of turnover on R&D – ten per cent in the higher technology businesses. Like some of the leading American innovation companies (Emerson, GE, 3M) Siebe aims to have 50 per cent of sales over five years come from products developed in those five years. It focuses attention on this goal by requiring all operating companies to have at least five new product launches a year. They don't always have to develop the product. They can buy it in from another division and adapt it to the local markets, developing all the appropriate technical data locally; or buy and adapt a product from a company outside the group. 'We can't think of anybody that hasn't come up with at least five a year so far,' says Yurko. Adds his colleague, Financial Director Roger Mann: 'We treat R&D rather like capital, and monitor projects in the same way as capital expenditure.'

Boots appears to the outside world as a deeply traditional company, where innovation would be hard work. In fact, behind the scenes is a constant whirl of both technical and managerial innovation. Says Chief Executive Lord Blyth: 'Boots is a hugely innovative organisation. ... We do more genuine new product development on a much wider range of product than any other retailer in the UK by miles, across a huge technical range of products – cameras, film, toys, greeting cards, medical products, medical appliances, the list goes on. There's nobody in the world as genuinely innovative in over-the-counter medicine as we are.

'A second major area of innovation for us is the whole IT systems area. We were at the forefront of electronic point-of-sale in the 1980s and we leapfrogged the rest of the industry in terms of distributing processing to our stores. That will allow us to run our labour management systems and training programmes in store. ... We do store design where we can walk through computer models in 3D.

'I'm proud about the innovation we have in the business, even though there is nothing glamorous about most of it.' Boots restricts the amount of talks and conference speeches its managers and technical people give outside the company. Says Lord Blyth: If we let them, the guys doing IT, for example, would be talking at conferences every week. All that does is pass information to the competitors.'

Carrefour's growth and success have much to do with a single revolutionary innovation, on which it has subsequently managed continuous evolution. Explains Chief Executive Daniel Bernard: 'We invented the format of the hypermarket. We are the leader in the market and you have to improve constantly. The format is not yet fixed. For example, it is different in the US. The format is still moving every day. We are strong in innovation in merchandising, products and store layout.'

Top management's constant insistence on staying ahead through innovation has provided much of Singapore Airlines' competitive edge. Its aim always to be 'first in service' means what it says: the airline is determined to introduce innovations ahead of its route rivals, wherever the change is likely to increase customer loyalty. Says CEO Cheong: 'With us, good service is a religion, so we were the innovators of a lot of service features that are now industry standards, such as hot towels, free headsets, free drinks in economy class and so on. ... In the days when IATA was a protectionist cartel, it was easier for us. We could do a lot of things that were frowned upon by IATA, so we stole a huge march on everyone else. Now it's more liberalised, it's harder for us to stay ahead. We still succeed, both with the way we use our people and with technology. For example, we were the first airline to install satellite air-to-ground telephones that allow you to call from anywhere in the world.'

The airline also has another strong reason for innovating: its home market of Singapore has one of the most acute labour shortages in the world (Singapore Girl is more likely in reality on most flights to have been born in Malaysia). So innovation that replaces labour is in high demand. Explains Tan Hui Boon, Chief Executive of SATS Airport Services (the airline's ground services): 'With a tight labour market and our annual growth running at about eight per cent a year, we have to look for better ways of doing things. For us, the emphasis now is on how to automate service without losing quality. We're already looking at automatic check-ins, to cut down the labour element. We are also looking to reduce the time people spend waiting for their baggage. If a customer doesn't board the plane, then their luggage must be unloaded. It can take quite a while to find one suitcase in 400. We are looking at technology to help us stay ahead.'

Singapore Airlines moves the focus of its innovation effort in line with its strategic priorities. Over the years, attention has moved from cabin service to ground service to customer recovery. It does not stop innovating in the old areas; but it ensures that staff and senior managers understand and act in line with the current focus of innovation.

Housebuilder The Berkeley Group also puts innovation centre-stage, involving employees at all levels in thinking about design improvements.

For example, says Tony Pidgley: 'Everyone in the company is expected to have their cameras with them no matter where they are, on holiday or wherever. If you see a new feature, you take a picture and send it in. We're working on a Queen Anne house at the moment. I'm convinced there's a good new product in the idea but we haven't got it yet.'

GIVING BRIGHT PEOPLE THE SPACE TO DRIVE CHANGE AROUND THEM

As we shall see in the chapter on people issues (Chapter Ten), hiring the right kind of people is an important first step for sustaining an entrepreneurial culture. Brainpower is part of the answer. Says Boots' Chief Executive Lord Blyth: 'Apart from the professions, Boots takes in more graduates a year than any other organisation in the UK. . . . If you ram a lot of intellectual ability into an organisation, almost by definition, however much you waste, you increase its capacity to innovate.'

Similarly, Sir Gerald Whent at Vodafone: '[I] found the best man I could in each technical area. Both of them are managing directors now. . . . I have always believed you have to be the most technically competent and avant-garde and you've got to have great quality. All the other skills can be built on those.' By hiring people he could rely on and who could set the example, Sir Gerald was able to maintain the leading market share.

Having found bright, innovative people, all that remains is to give them space and resources to use their abilities. A few examples will suffice:

- At JCB, the ubiquitous yellow digger, the backhoe loader, is the product that the company is most usually associated with, though it manufactures a wide range of other products including excavators, wheeled loaders, skid steer loaders and telescopic handlers. The latter, together with the famous yellow diggers, are world market leaders. To meet continuing customer needs, the products are continually improved and developed. Seven years ago, JCB turned the farming community on its head when it introduced the JCB Fastrac, the world's first high-speed fully suspended heavy-draught tractor, capable of speeds of nearly 50 mph. But JCB is renowned for innovation and challenging the way things are done. The group set up a Special Products division to handle adaptations and staffed it with unusual people, the 'conceptors', as the Managing Director of Special Products Ltd, Jim Edwards, called them. He explains: 'We knew that it needed to be an unusual company, with people in it who would thrive on the unusual. We needed designers who could literally design off the back of a cigarette pack, and people who could just go and make it. We used to say to everybody "Whatever your question is, the answer is yes" and we've since had a hell of a good time. Here you have to be able to feel it, touch it, walk all the way around it and sit in it.'[4]

- As ABB's Percy Barnevik told *The Director* magazine: 'The fact that we have so many profit centres enables ideas to travel upwards. ... If you have 40 people, you can gather all their ideas. If you have 2,000, you get into committees and departmental managers.'[5]

- Bowthorpe CEO Nicholas Brookes tries to motivate bright technical people with their own career ladder: 'This is a technical company and a lot of the buzz comes from being in a technical community. What I am trying to do is also get the technical community together, to exchange ideas, and also get a technical ladder in place, rather like a managerial ladder, in parallel, so that an innovator who is not interested in managing people should be recognised and be able to progress away from line management. This has been very well received.'

- At Reuters, says Jean-Claude Marchand, Executive Director: 'You can really be the architect, you can create, come up with an idea and push it through. I tell newcomers that whatever they think the company should do, there is a possibility to achieve it. There is tremendous freedom. In my own career I don't think people ever stopped anything I thought we should do. Like any company, we have our frictions but one of the beauties is that you are your own boss. When I have an idea I don't try to impose it, I make sure that I bring people around me to think it was theirs. I have had no problem with people giving me tremendous ideas and telling the world that it was theirs. That's what helps us to go forward, never pinching anybody else's idea. Consensus is behind you at the end of the line, where you decide very important things, but through the ranks it's making sure that [for] the things you want to do, enough people around you think this is exactly what they would like to do too.'

- At IKEA, Sven-Olof Kulldorff sees the staff suggestion scheme as a sign of partial failure. He says: 'Because everybody should every day, every minute be working with improvements, in many parts of IKEA we don't have a suggestion scheme.'

- At Boots the Chemist, says Personnel Director David Kissman, 'there is a great diversity of opportunity. We are not just a retailer. There is Boots Healthcare, Halfords, Boots the Chemist, and so on. We leverage that diversity and people can choose to spread out across the group in order to build their career. We are more and more using competencies, which encourage this kind of cross-movement, rather than relying on qualifications, to assess people.'

- At SOL, says Liisa Joronen: 'We share innovations, excellent service practices and problem solving through the whole company by e-mail, during training sessions and meetings.'

USING CUSTOMERS AS CHANGE PARTNERS

Says BA's Sir Colin Marshall: 'Innovation is a vital competitive necessity. It is largely achieved by the constant customer dialogue which includes asking for their "wildest dreams" in an air travel service; and then using technology and service skills to translate these into practical reality. The First Class "flying bed" service; new Club World; new Club Europe; arrivals lounges; interactive in-flight information and entertainment systems are some examples. Breakthrough innovation is important for keeping ahead of the competition and maintaining customer loyalty. There is also need for incremental innovation, where useful and popular services require updating. Services and products cannot stand still – they have to be enhanced continually to provide the attraction of "shop window sparkle" for the customer.'[6]

Again, this is a theme we will develop in more detail later in the book (Chapter Nine), However, all our high-performance companies place great emphasis on developing service and product innovations with their customers and suppliers. They look, without exception, to create long-term relationships. And they welcome being challenged to meet new needs because these provide the stimulus for new products and services that deliver competitive advantage.

Among the examples of collaborative development that emerged from our interviews were:

- Smiths Industries and Boeing. Mutual long-term trust between the two companies persuaded Smiths to take a very large risk, in developing its ELMS (Electrical Load Management System) for aeroplanes. The system prioritises the use of electricity around a plane and saves hundreds of miles of cable. Smiths proposed the idea to Boeing, knowing it would have to invest $60 million of development money over three years before it received a penny back. 'Now,' says chairman Sir Roger Hurn, 'we have the best system in the world on the most modern airliner.'

- Says IKEA's Sven-Olof Kulldorff: 'We learn a lot on the factory floor and a lot from the customer. With our open structure and the flat organisation, and being out talking to suppliers and customers, a lot of ideas come up that result in changes.'

• For Reuters, working with key customers can also be an important way to ensure market acceptance for a new product. As Finance Director Rob Rowley points out: 'If you look at the financial markets, we've got the majority of demanding customers. When you are looking at new products, sometimes you are looking for key charter member customers to give new ideas impetus or to really be involved in the evolution of the product.'

RECOGNISING THAT WELL UNDERSTOOD CONSTRAINTS CAN ENCOURAGE RATHER THAN DIMINISH INNOVATION

Given total freedom to innovate however they like, most people find it very difficult. Asking 'How would you improve service to the customer?', for example, may provide some useful suggestions. But asking 'How would you improve service on Saturday mornings when there are five times as many customers and we can only afford twice as many staff?' provides a real challenge and will normally, in the end, provide more innovative and valuable solutions.

At Granada, as we shall see later in this chapter, placing financial restraints on the creative process has resulted in some highly innovative television productions. What counts, says Charles Allen, is how the challenge is presented.

Jim Martin, Chief Executive of N. Brown, talks of 'innovating within a framework'. He explains: 'Operational people do product development, extending the product range and also market innovation inasmuch as each year, on average, we come to the market with a new concept. This year it is a concept called "Shoe Tailor" which refers to detailed research on shoe fittings and provides a measuring device to help the customers with their correct shoe size and fittings. This minimises returns [of unsatisfactory purchases] and stimulates an interest in buying difficult products in their homes.' But the conditions under which each innovation occurs include very strict constraints on cost, maintenance of service levels, and so on.

How people perceive the constraints around them is an important part of how creatively they tackle them. Are they minor impediments to a big goal or major impediments to a small one? If our company and our competitors alike have to deal with the same constraints, can we turn some or all of those constraints into opportunities? Are we allowed to change the rules of the game? Whenever people feel positively about such questions, constraints seem to diminish in importance, and when they feel negatively, simple constraints take on insuperable proportions. Maintaining a positive, creative attitude depends to a large extent on the ability of managers to create and maintain sufficient challenges to oblige people to think outside the box.

EXPERIMENTING WIDELY, BUT PUTTING EFFORT BEHIND THE CHOSEN FEW IDEAS

High-performing companies enjoy experimentation. They encourage multiple approaches to multiple problems and opportunities, and happily abandon those that don't work. They can do this because they see experimentation as a blame-free activity and because they have so many ideas to try that it really doesn't matter when one doesn't work out.

Singapore Airlines has aborted at least as many innovations in its operations as it has eventually employed. Among those that didn't work, for example, were singing minstrels in the aisles. 'They didn't last long,' says CEO Cheong. 'We also tried old-style poker machines, where you pull the handle. Mercifully that didn't last long either.'

Reuters places great store on using its own staff as guinea pigs for new products. Says Martin Davids, Director of Staff Development and Efficiency Programmes: 'We are not afraid to experiment with technology internally until such time as it is robust.'

Experimenting widely has a number of dangers, however, not least that it is difficult to be sure which experiment brings positive results. Says Smiths Industries' Chairman Sir Roger Hurn: 'I was an apprentice at Rolls-Royce making cars in Crewe when I left school. One of the things I learned at that stage was that you never change more than one thing at a time on a development programme, because if you change more than one, you don't know which gives the good or bad effect. You change one thing at a time, then you run it to see what happens, then you change something else. I've taken the whole philosophy to running businesses. You don't want simultaneous change initiatives, because you will never know which was plus and which was minus in effect.'

Killing the sacred cow

When people have invested a great deal of time, energy and personal ego into an initiative, it is often hard for them to let go. They may feel that they are letting go a part of themselves. So they put more good effort into a bad project, as if throwing time and money at it will make it work. Knowing when to kill the sacred cow is a critical leadership skill that involves quite a lot of self-understanding and self-honesty. Our case-study companies, like those in the original *The Winning Streak*, seem to be remarkably adept at managing this situation. For Boots, for example, it would have been easy to continue to invest in ethical drugs after its main new product, Manoplax, fell foul of the US Food and Drug Administration. In practice, the problems with the FDA triggered a full-scale review of the options for that division. The analysis took 18 months, but then the decision to put the division on the market was rapid. Says Lord Blyth: 'We came out of that with the FDA thinking we were the most ethical organisation they had ever dealt with. We also got out of the business at a better price than people externally thought we could ever get for it.'

It helps, of course, if the decision to back out is not a 'bet the company' issue. Says Electrocomponents' Bob Lawson: 'Being successful gives you the financial room to deal with these problems. There's a cauldron of opportunities bubbling, so we move on to the next success. You avoid most of the emotional issues that way because you can easily redeploy. You are intolerant of failures because you have the resources to address and face up to the issues.'

Jack Welch at General Electric has probably built up the strongest reputation in the world as a slaughterer of sacred cows. For example, although GE's 400-strong strategic-planning department was the darling of the business schools, when he decided it was holding back decentralisation, out it went. Intentionally or unintentionally, some of the sacred cows Welch killed early in his career had major symbolic impact. When he disposed of GE Housewares, the business that put the GE name in every American household, it evoked howls of protest from within. But the sale – at $300 million a relatively small disposal – emphasised dramatically that GE was no longer in low-margin businesses and provided a clear and necessary break with the past.

DEMONSTRATING REMARKABLE PERSISTENCE

When our high-performance companies decide something is worth focusing on, they do so for the long term. They show remarkable patience when they are convinced that a move is essential to their long-term future. Michael Treschow, CEO of Atlas Copco declares: 'We are very very persistent. People know that once we have decided something, we are like a bulldozer. Even if the bulldozer moves slowly, it means we're getting there. Again, people understand that, so even if there's some resistance there's more support, because we all want to be part of a winning team. But you have to spend a lot of time to explain why we do it.'

Cadbury Schweppes, too, has been very patient and far-sighted in its approach to developing markets. Says Kevin Hayes, Managing Director of the Asia–Pacific region: 'People tend to examine Cadbury from a UK perspective. They often forget the benefits from the pioneering people in the company who came out to Asia–Pacific all those years ago and established themselves as market leaders in places such as Singapore. One day, Cadbury will reap the benefits when the tiger economies take over. He who gets in first and establishes the lead stays ahead. Cadbury is in there first in those Pacific Rim countries, and I think that will become apparent in time.

'In China we opened a $Aus 50 million operation last year in Beijing – the first Western-style manufacturing plant in our sector. Nestlé are building a plant; Mars are there too. But the strength of the Cadbury business is due to the entrepreneurial spirit of the company some 80 years ago. Back in the 1920s, Cadbury established itself in Australasia and is now market leader. We view China in that way, as a long-term involvement. It's a huge market. At present the Chinese consume an average of 28 g of chocolate a year each, compared to 12 kg in the UK and mature markets. My dream is to move Chinese consumption to 1.25 kg, in line with Hong Kong and Singapore, which would make it one of biggest markets in the world.

Reuters' persistence could almost be described as naive from an external viewpoint. The company has time and again taken on apparently impossible challenges and made them happen. Explains Patrick Mannix, Director of Personnel and Quality: 'We always used to push the boundaries so, for example, if we found the telecommunications regulations didn't permit us to run something like the Reuter Dealing Service in the 1980s, we went and got the regulations changed. In the regulations it doesn't actually say Reuters, but it was actually specifically changed after about three years of lobbying to allow us to do so.

'Another example was the early Reuter Monitor information service in the early 1970s. We could buy computers and operating systems and write some applications and we could do the same for terminals, but nobody in the world had a way of connecting hundreds of terminals to a central computer. It didn't exist. So we as a news agency had a technical group that actually built a communications interface – an extraordinary thing for a news agency to do. We never accepted the boundary. We decided what it was we wanted to do and bought as many pieces as we could. Then we developed the other pieces or pushed the boundaries of regulation or technology. By contrast, many much larger organisations came together, forming partnerships to try and do what we did and failed. They probably spent $100 million while we probably spent $10 million. The partnerships did not have enough in common, apart from short-term interest, to take them ahead. We tended to spend relatively little, not accept any boundaries and have a dogged determination. Eventually we would emerge and the thing would work.'

SPREADING INNOVATION RAPIDLY AMONG OPERATING UNITS

In Chapter Two, we referred in passing to the problem of sharing good practice in organisations that operate with a high degree of independence. Where there is a high degree of central control over an aspect of the business, it is fairly easy to roll out new ideas, whether as a centrally sponsored programme or as a strong 'suggestion'. For activities left largely to the operating units themselves, it is much more difficult. The answer for most of our case-study companies lies in largely informal networks driven by the operations themselves. Boots, says its chairman, is a mass of informal networks, which spread good practice rapidly.

At Cadbury Schweppes, as a further example, the technical network came about through the intervention of one manager, Richard Beardon, President of Cadbury's Latin American operations: 'We have technical people dotted all over the globe, who had little contact with each other. I came up with the idea that if we could empower these people to network with one another more, then development could be accelerated. We put together the first-ever global technical conference at the company. We pulled about 130 senior technical people together with the idea of trying to get that group to see itself as a network. It is typical of the culture here that, as I had the idea, I was free to get on and do it.

'Out of that conference the "Living Network" was created. We invested in a global e-mail system to put the technical people in touch with one another. It's not rocket science, of course, but the use of technology and up-to-date ideas for a particular community within the business. It means that people are no longer constantly re-inventing the wheel.'

One of the benefits of this kind of approach, says Beardon, is that, 'you're avoiding the trap of saying initiatives have to be driven from the centre. Over several days at the conference, people realised that this was something they could do that was in their own interests and the interests of the company. All we did at the centre was invest in the conference to bring people together and facilitate the idea.'

'Having created the networking initiative in one function – technical and operations – we realised the danger of doing this in isolation. Through a marketing group we initiated the idea that the technical functions and marketing should work more closely together. So we had a meeting [in 1996] with about 40 senior people from a mix of marketing and technical. That in itself is not revolutionary, of course, but when you do it for the first time it throws out a lot of new ideas.

'It's too early yet to see what will flow from that. But it is typical of the Cadbury Schweppes culture that initiatives are allowed to take off in this way. If you're wise, then you get the help and support of the centre. But it's not difficult; you just have to be prepared to have a go. My experience is that the ground is very fertile like that.'

Similar but longer-established networks are present in most of the other high-performance companies. For example, at Electrocomponents, says CEO Bob Lawson: 'Part of the secret of our success is learning what works in one market and launching rapidly in the rest. In the UK, we launched the first CD-rom catalogue in our industry. Now we are the only business in our sector with CD-rom catalogues across Europe. In the same way, our Italian operation invented a superb system for giving people information on-line. It means that an engineer can have access to technical information 24 hours a day. That's now being rolled out across the rest of our operating companies.'

MAKING CHANGE HAPPEN FAST

Once our high-performing companies have decided to make a change, they are impatient to get it over and done with. There are good and practical reasons for this. Says Electrocomponents' Bob Lawson: 'If it can't be done in 12 months, why are you doing it? The market will have moved on by then.' An executive of The Berkeley Group makes a similar point: 'A lot of it comes down to the fact that we're realists. We adapt to the changing market. We operate in a very cyclical market. We know we've got to sell houses in any market. If we sell our stock when the market is falling then we're able to re-invest in current prices. We adjust very quickly. Back when we turned everything into cash in 1989, we reviewed our land stock and what was going on. We moved it out one day and bought it back at half the price the next. I would say that was one of the finest commercial decisions ever taken in the UK.'

At Microsoft, says Mike Murray, Vice President Human Resources and Administration: 'Intranet is a good example of how we reacted in a revolutionary way to change. We realised we had to have an internal revolution in the summer of 1995. In December Bill Gates gave a speech announcing the scale of the changes. We had to turn on a dime to make sure we remained competitive. Within three months, 6,000 people were working differently and already beginning to bring in new products.'

Siebe's Allen Yurko encourages his businesses around the world to adopt rapid development approaches from software engineering. He explains: 'In technology, you don't have a lot of time to study, because you won't respond fast enough to customer needs. So the reality is that you get 70 per cent of the data you need to make the decision and you decide on that. Then you implement like crazy. If it's not perfect at the end of phase one of development, we never tack on another six months of development time. We finish phase one, gather up everything we don't like about it and use that knowledge in phase two. You apply that philosophy to even classic engineering businesses and all of a sudden you shorten the product development cycle dramatically. It's customer driven. We say to our engineers, "You have to design this thing concurrently with manufacturing. The customers are telling you what they want. As long as you deliver to cost with the promised benefits, the refinements can wait until version two."'

Another reason for getting on with change is that the discomfort and uncertainty are past all the sooner. Says Granada's Charles Allen: 'People don't like change, so they love the idea of it having a beginning and an ending. Then you aren't picking at scabs all the time. That's why I always brand the change programmes. Then people associate the negatives of the restructuring with that brand, and once you've made the reorganisation, you can shut the brand down. Constant restructuring is like dragging a plant up by the roots all the time to see if it is growing.'[7]

Adds Granada's Human Resources Director Stephanie Monk: 'Quite often it is easier for people to cope with revolution than evolution, particularly if they are quite clear in their mind about what the right objective is. They can become quite uncomfortable about you taking too long to get there. People have a high need for you to be clear, to be prompt, to deliver change.

'The first branded project we did was a major re-structuring at Granada Television, which was 'Fit for the Future'. The brand at Forte was 'Foundations for Change', which is a by-line we are still comfortable to use. By branding it, you give people a sense that you have a forward-looking objective It's a programme with a purpose, that it probably has a finite time-scale, and if you are able to segment it and say "stage 1 is about this" and "stage 4 ends up being about that", you give people a sense that they are moving through: an idea of the story, and a recognition of when you move out of change into a more steady state. If change is just going on around you without explanation and framework, it's quite difficult to assimilate. We try to compartmentalise various stages and explain what that phase is about. It was just as helpful in talking to the press as it was internally.'

The more painful the change, the more rapidly Granada tries to push it through. One of Charles Allen's changes was to shift people's perceptions and behaviours radically in the television production business. He recalls: 'The television company was making £5 million profit annually. The industry was going through massive change. We were facing large payments to the government in terms of franchises. For the first time, too, we were competing for air-time. This was a fundamental change, the impact of competition. The TV industry hadn't operated as a free market before.

'The key drivers which were starting to drive broadcasting were the move to become sales-oriented rather than simply order-takers, [and] the need to package and market our USPs (we had to promote the benefits of buying from us). At the same time we had to get across the message that we should be a business; we should make profits. That was a different way of thinking. We said, "Granada should be a supplier of programming not just to ITV but to competitors including the BBC."

'There was probably about a month of people being in shock. Here was this catering accountant running one of the doyens of British broadcasting. In the old culture, management was something that happened down here, it was a dirty activity that shouldn't get in the way of the creative process. To be fair, the shock didn't last as long as people thought. When you're dealing with very bright people, once you have re-positioned the game, they adjusted very quickly. Part of that involved understanding how to handle them.

'You have to challenge them creatively. An example of that was *Cracker*, which was made for two-thirds of previous production costs. What we tried to do was: as you take away in one area, you give more freedom in another. So, for example, costs have to be strictly controlled, but you challenge them to try new ways of making programmes.'

STAYING NIMBLE

Nimbleness is a much valued competence of high-performance companies. It links closely with the ability to act quickly once a change is decided upon, but it also involves being able to sense well in advance when a change is needed, being able to convince people to react quickly and positively, and having the dexterity to make the right response. Some of our case-study companies describe it in the language of guerrilla warfare – constantly watching out for danger and for any weaknesses in the competition, striking hard and fast and always moving on before the counter-attack comes.

For Cadbury Schweppes, part of staying nimble involves finding niches between Coca-Cola and Pepsi, where it can operate relatively freely. Says Group Finance Director David Kappler: 'Yes, we've had to be very quick on our feet, especially when we don't have a major cola brand. We don't really compete in the cola market to any great extent. The majors have non-cola interests of course, but their commitment is to their core product, which gives us some advantage here. We need people who are on their toes, and looking for new ways of partnering our bottling customers. I've just taken over one of the Latin American operations in a market where there are some interesting things going on right now. If we have slow-thinking managers, we'll miss out on the opportunities presented. In this market, windows open and close quite rapidly.'

Adds his colleague John Brock, President and CEO of Dr Pepper/Seven Up: 'What we do have is a portfolio of the best non-cola soft drink brands. We have people who are nimble, who can get in and out quickly when there's an opportunity. We don't have nearly as much money as Coke and Pepsi nor do we have the mega-brands which you can just turn on – although we do have Dr Pepper and Seven Up, two of the top-ten non-cola brands. But we do have to be nimble, we do have to be quick. It's part of our culture to be fast and flexible, and to always look for opportunistic moves. We don't try to compete head-on with cola brands.'

Unlike the soft drink giants, Cadbury Schweppes prefers not to own its own bottling plants and distribution companies because these would be capital-intensive and would lock it in, both in terms of asset management and constraints on how it thinks about its business. By focusing on brand development and working through independents (although it has had joint ventures with, and still retains some agreements with, Coca-Cola and PepsiCo), it leaves itself free to adjust strategy and tactics at relatively short notice.

The biggest of our high-performance companies were as vehement about the need to stay nimble as the smallest. Jack Welch, for example, says that 'We have to walk, talk, act and think like a small firm'. He uses the analogy of an American football team, where bulk is great for driving forward, but where the really fast defender can usually outrun his mistakes.

Boots has a built-in inflexibility in its shops. You can't just move them or change the layout without considerable time and cost. But the support systems, such as product development, can and do react quickly to change. For example, electronic data capture at the checkouts provides online evidence of changes in customer buying patterns, which leads to rapid changes in product ranges.

Reuters, says Jean-Claude Marchand is 'quick to identify opportunities, small enough to very quickly capitalise on them, and grow them in the dark at a time when all the big boys are busy looking at other things'.

Staying nimble is like being on a constant diet: it doesn't take long to get out of condition. High-performance companies keep in condition by staying lean and ensuring that managers have no chance to become too settled in their thinking – once again, in large part by creating constant challenge. Staying lean also involves avoiding carrying too much baggage – be it property, non-core functions, or concern with the past.

Liisa Joronen of SOL sums it up: 'To an outsider it looks like we are in constant revolution, but I find it too slow to my mentality. It's constant change, a mixture of revolution and evolution. If nothing happens, we make it happen.'

In summary...

High-performance companies ensure an effective balance between evolutionary and revolutionary change by aiming for a steady pace of rapid change. They have an impatience that prevents them ever 'taking time out' to recuperate from the last round of changes. They see the pace of change as the main guarantor against disruptive revolutionary change, but they are quick to embrace revolution when it is needed. They expend a lot of effort creating the kind of environment or climate where a fast pace of evolutionary change can flourish. The result is that they are trim, flexible and remarkably well able to adapt to changes in their environment by changing step. In short, getting the right pace of change is an essential part of their strategies for survival and growth.

Maintaining the pace of change also helps overcome the two biggest and most effective debilitators of company vitality – arrogance and complacency. But high-performing companies have a number of other ways in which they guard against those diseases, as we examine in Chapter Six.

6 UNDERWEENING PRIDE
Pride versus humility

'The better people think they are, the better they will be. Positive self-image creates success.' *Liisa Joronen at SOL.*

'I'm never satisfied. I'm always challenging. It's like a journey where you never arrive.' *Charles Allen of Granada.*

'Success is a lousy teacher. It seduces smart people into thinking they can't lose. And it's an unreliable guide to the future.' *Microsoft's Bill Gates.*

One of the phenomena we observed in our initial researches 12 years ago was the difference in the way employees of excellent companies and loser companies described themselves outside their working environments. When asked 'What do you do?', the excellent-company employees described themselves firstly in terms of who they worked for, then the type of work they did. They were clearly proud to be associated with their company. By contrast, many employees of our control group of relatively poor performers tended to respond by talking first about their occupation – accountant, salesman, manager and so on. Some described themselves as feeling diminished (in terms of social status) by association with their employer. It was hardly surprising that there was a corresponding difference in the level of motivation felt by these two groups of employees.

The benefits of pride
....

The relationship between financial performance and pride in company is unclear. Certainly, there are companies with strong financial results where cynicism is rife; and there are poor performers where employee commitment is high. The relationship between pride in company and other factors seems in fact more substantial – in particular, the factors of shared values, shared objectives, and the degree of excitement and challenge that companies introduce into everyday work. 'People like to identify with success,' says Sir Roger Hurn of Smiths Industries. 'It's hugely rewarding to be part of something successful. It's not the money that makes them feel that way, it's the image.'

The top teams of our high-performing companies set the tone. They feel and are passionate about the business. Of Sir Roger, for example, we were forewarned that he lived, ate and breathed Smiths Industries. At main board and subsidiary board level in The Berkeley Group, directors go into great detail to understand the finer points of each home they build, because they feel it is 'their' house.

Every chief executive we interviewed exuded an enthusiasm about the business that came from deep within. Although they were, by and large, professional managers, each had given themselves entirely to a dream built around the company that they led. They felt the successes and failures of the company personally; they believed to the core of their soul in its values; and they were fiercely jealous of its reputation. Most important of all, they were able to infect others with that same commitment and pride, and it was important to them that everyone in the company shared their pride.

So important is this innate sense of pride to Singapore Airlines, for example, that Mrs Lam Seet Mui, the Training Manager, who runs the company's management development centre, describes the initial training that all new recruits undertake as primarily aimed at 'making them proud to be part of SIA'. People who have pride in themselves and the organisation they work for, the airline argues, are more likely to have the self-respect and self-confidence essential to be spontaneously responsive to customers.

She explains: 'Underlying the core competencies are SIA's six core values which underpin the whole culture. When we formalised the core values about two years ago, we also produced a training video, *The SIA Spirit*. It's a two-and-a-half-hour training module to inculcate those values. The induction programme for new employees includes the core values in this way, so staff are imbued with them. Then we discuss with them how the values might manifest themselves in operational situations. Then they fill in a questionnaire about how they feel and relate to these values. The new-entrant programme is five-and-a-half-day course including outward-bound activities aimed at team building: we want to instil in them the pride of belonging to the organisation.'

Liisa Joronen at SOL sees pride and customer service as inextricably linked. She explains: 'Service is about good feelings. If you are not satisfied with yourself or with your company, how can you give anything to your customers? The right sense of pride is very important in low-profile businesses like ours in SOL.'

When we talk about pride in this context, of course, we mean pride in its most positive context – the sense of justifiable satisfaction from a job well done, and from the worth of the *task*. We do not mean hubris, the overweening pride that comes from an assumption about the excellence or worth of the *person or organisation*. Pride in task is what Sir Clive Thompson means when he says: 'We're arrogant; we expect to be the best. We get competitive advantage through being better than anyone else. In the service industry, Rentokil Initial is the model everyone tries to follow.' Adds Martin Ellis, General Manager for UK Healthcare at Rentokil Initial: 'We are arrogant up to a point, but we are also very pragmatic. I know that the only measure of me or the business is the trading account. If that slips, then the arrogance is soon removed. In fact, you do it yourself. You want to find any problems before someone else tells you you have a problem. You want to spot it before it gets out of hand. I'd say we are arrogant externally, but self-critical internally.'

So these companies recognise that high performance has to be continuously recreated to be sustained; and that the way to ensure pride does not lead to the complacency of hubris is to retain a strong sense of purposeful humility.

The benefits of humility

By humility, we do not mean being self-effacing or lacking confidence. Rather, we mean having the self-awareness and confidence constantly to seek out opportunities to improve. It is about recognising the value of ideas from elsewhere, about being honest with oneself, about welcoming constructive criticism as a gift from well-wishers.

Those companies from our original study who subsequently lost their way (*see* Chapter Fourteen) in most cases did so – at least in part – because they slipped from pride into hubris. Significantly, this is a characteristic shared by most failed companies. A study by one of the authors several years ago looked at the commonalities in leadership behaviour between companies that collapsed. One of the clearest indicators of a business in trouble was that it had stopped listening and learning, usually because top management assumed that they knew everything already. The mistake was frequently fatal.[1]

Perhaps the humblest of all our companies was Reuters, where top management was highly reluctant to boast about any of the company's considerable achievements. 'We haven't got that right yet'; 'We're still working on that'; and 'We have been very lucky' were typical comments from the interviews. Main board Director David Ure comments: 'We are in danger of overdoing the humility. You can't run an operation regarding everything in the future as uncertain and all your ideas as temporary.' To some extent, this is a defence against complacency, reflected in comments from companies such as The Berkeley Group, where the Chief Executive, Tony Pidgley, muses that he worries constantly that no one has ever beaten the market for so long before and that the unbroken success record is as much a cause for concern as for pride. He says: 'The danger is that our culture could become complacent. I keep looking at that. I worry that too much success could make us something else – the housebuilder that makes profits, maybe, instead of the house builder that cares, which we are now.'

Siebe chairman Barrie Stephens takes a similar view: 'Your organisation needs to be blessed and you need humility to attribute success in large part to good fortune.'

IKEA's founder Ingvar Kamprad was preaching the virtues of humility as long ago as 1976. He explained then: 'More than anything else, it really means respect. We are humble towards our competitors, respecting their proficiency and realising that we constantly have to be better than they are if we're not going to lose our market to them. Being humble isn't the same as keeping a low profile. If you have something important to say, say it. Being humble means admitting your weaknesses, and trying to put them right.'[2]

Taken to excess, of course, humility is as much a drag on the business as arrogant pride. If people set their sights too low, if they do not have boundless confidence in what they can accomplish together, if they are not motivated by the need to compete and achieve, then the company is unlikely to be a world-beater. We are indebted to Mike Murray, Vice President of Human Resources and Administration at Microsoft, for passing on the aphorism: 'Pride is concerned with who is right. Humility is concerned with what is right.'

Balancing pride and humility

So how do high-performing companies maintain a healthy balance between pride and humility? There are several common mechanisms, but the most prominent seem to be:

- choosing to compete and compare with the best;
- working with demanding customers;
- encouraging challenge within the core values;
- not letting the seat get too warm; and
- nothing is ever good enough.

CHOOSING TO COMPETE AND COMPARE AGAINST THE BEST

'Yeah, I think it's fair to say it's a bit daunting when you wake up every morning with a 17 per cent share of the market, knowing that the other two gorillas, Coke and Pepsi have 42 per cent and 31 per cent respectively, and they own pretty much all of their distribution chain, bottling and everything – which we don't. Our team has one of the most difficult challenges in the company,' says John Brock, Managing Director of Cadbury Schweppes' beverages stream and President of Cadbury subsidiary Dr Pepper/Seven Up. Daunting it may be, but it promotes a high degree of alertness among Dr Pepper/Seven Up employees, who are constantly looking for ways to leverage a little more advantage in the spaces between the two giants. 'One of the secrets of our success has been to use their bottling and distribution operations,' says Brock. 'If you put Dr Pepper/Seven Up and Coke on the same shelves there's an incremental gain for both. The customer doesn't buy one instead of the other; he buys a six-pack of coke and a six-pack of Dr Pepper/Seven Up.'

Adds Chairman Dominic Cadbury: 'When you are competing with Coca-Cola, Mars and Nestlé, there isn't a lot of room for arrogance for very long because you can very frequently be looking at levels of performance which keep you right on your toes, if not humble. I don't think we would like to feel that we were humbled in any way by comparison with them, but certainly a realistic sense of our vulnerabilities and the intensity of the competition.'

'In television, we meet our competitors on a daily basis, so our success against the competition is tested every day,' says Granada's Charles Allen. 'One important measure of success in that business is the ratings. I am constantly asking: "Did we win on Friday night?" If Granada didn't, senior managers will want to know why not and what will be done about it.'

Similarly, at Electrocomponents, says Bob Lawson: 'We try never to compromise our standards. Our differentiation is customer service, so if someone beats us on an aspect of service, everyone is in here all weekend if necessary until we decide how to deal with the challenge. You have to impose a level of discomfort, including for yourself.'

At Siebe, competitive benchmarking is built into the technical culture. Allen Yurko describes the process: 'We bring in our competitors' products and benchmark against them any way we can. We talk to our customers and benchmark against them. We also ask our customers to give us simple, written reports on where and how the competitors' products are better. We also hire industry consultants to benchmark for us.'

So what do you do if you *are* the best in the areas where you want to compare? You look beyond your competitors to find broader benchmarks.

Says Colin Marshall: 'We do not necessarily compare ourselves with other major airlines, although that is necessary from an operational/customer service point of view. In general, we compare our performance with that of major international companies of all sectors. The long-term incentive scheme for managers is based on stock market performance against other blue-chip firms, not on how well it meets air transport competition.'

Says Boots' Lord Blyth: 'We benchmark ourselves against bigger companies, such as Coca-Cola or Procter & Gamble, because there is part of their pursuit of excellence that seems to us worthwhile our aspiring to.' Boots also benchmarks its financial performance – total return to shareholders, comprising gross dividends paid and growth in share price – against a basket of ten leading UK companies. The composition of the top ten changes with their performance and with major events within Boots itself. So, for example, the disposal of Boots Pharmaceticals led to the removal of Glaxo Wellcome and Fisons from the list and the inclusion of two retailers.

At Electrocomponents too, says Bob Lawson: 'We benchmark ourselves outside the industry. On distribution, against retailers; on customer service, against retailers and some of the American high-service catalogue retail companies. Our mission is to differentiate ourselves, so why benchmark against competitors? We learn from successes in unrelated businesses.

'We have borrowed a lot of customer-knowledge processing activities from the retail and direct marketing sector, particularly from Marks & Spencer in how it went into food and housewares. We copied our organisation structure from M&S and Nordstrom, for example, to make sure that people in product teams and customer-facing operating companies can see clearly how they make a contribution.' Electrocomponents resists, however, thinking that it has to be like these companies, preferring to adapt the ideas in its own way. At Smiths Industries, too, says Chairman Sir Roger Hurn: 'We compare ourselves with the best, but we are not necessarily a miniature of them.'

At Carrefour, taking ideas from elsewhere is built into the culture. Says Chief Executive Daniel Bernard: 'We are never arrogant. We check the format constantly. We take ideas between the countries in which we are operating. We also take ideas from others. To say we are leaders has no significance. We must constantly be satisfying our customers – just becoming the leading player tells you very little. Everybody takes ideas. Wal-Mart took ideas from us and we took ideas from them.'

Alternatively, you look internally, as Rentokil Initial does. Says Group Finance Director of Rentokil Initial, Chris Pearce: 'The only purpose of benchmarking for us would be to improve. In our case we're so profitable compared with other companies that benchmarking with them would probably make us complacent. Our margins are so high that, if we compare ourselves with other companies, they will be worse, which doesn't help.

'We try to benchmark internally. Sir Clive has a saying that the only purpose of management is to improve the business. If managers are not doing that, then you might as well leave it to the service people.

'We benchmark across the business, so we might say to pest control in France, "Why don't you look at what they're doing in Germany as they're obviously doing something that works?" So in that sense we're always looking sideways.'

At SAP, says Henning Kagermann, internal companies are benchmarked against each other on 20–25 key ratios. 'It helps us see the contribution of the business from an all-round perspective,' he says. Similarly, at SOL, says Liisa Joronen: 'We use internal benchmarking, finding out the best practices between our 15 independent districts in SOL and especially between our 140 supervisor areas. At first it was very difficult to create internal benchmarking as a significant method of constant improvement, because everyone was jealous of their good practices. Now people realise that they all benefit from it.'

One thing high-performing companies in general avoid doing is taking over their competitors. All that achieves is to remove some of the pressure to perform on behalf of the customer – at least till someone else seizes the opportunity to fill the vacuum. Says Reuters' Peter Job: 'You need strong challenges all the time. Anybody who says you should buy your competitors is overlooking the fact that you should beat them.'

WORKING WITH DEMANDING CUSTOMERS

High-performance companies value positively demanding customers, because they force the pace of improvement. They are able to discriminate between those customers who are demanding because they set and achieve high standards themselves, and those who are demanding simply because they dump the problems of their own inadequate practices on their suppliers. High-performing companies seek to develop strong partnerships with the former and to educate the latter.

Singapore Airlines' policy of staying ahead on customer service has actively encouraged the development of positively demanding customers. Says CEO Cheong: 'Singaporeans are our sternest critics. The slightest lapse and they tell us about it. The more awards we win, the greater people's expectations of us, so I get letters that say: "I'm a frequent flyer on your airline, and I've always been very satisfied with it. However, the last time I flew with you ..." They just won't let us become complacent.'

Positively demanding customers don't grow on trees. They need to be cultivated, encouraged, nurtured. To find and keep them, companies need to:

- be very clear about the value of such customers, at all levels and particularly among customer-facing employees;
- seek to build value with and through them – so both parties acquire leading-edge knowledge, skills and capability; and
- make them aware of how highly their 'demandingness' is valued.

What happens in most companies is that staff are trained to mollify demanding customers. While this may be appropriate to negatively demanding customers, to the positively demanding it can appear highly patronising, even if the interaction has been handled very professionally – especially when the customer is dissatisfied with some aspect of the product or service. To take a mundane example, one of the authors recently took a package holiday. While pleased with every other aspect of the accommodation, he was unimpressed by what had been promoted in the brochure as a 'quality restaurant'. A complaint to the tour rep was handled very politely and resulted in a refund without quibble during the holiday. However, the rep insisted on pointing out that no one else had complained when she had asked them. An offer to help think through her questioning technique, given that these same customers were complaining among themselves, went unanswered. The unspoken assumption that anyone who expects high standards must be a pain in the neck cannot easily be addressed by customer-care training. It requires a systematic approach to using demanding customers as the driving force for raising the standards of service. It means placing less emphasis on customer surveys and much more on using frontline staff proactively to gather ideas and opportunities for improvement direct from the customers themselves.

We weren't able to measure how systematic our high-performance companies were in managing this issue. But example after example suggests that their frontline staff do often use their most demanding customers in such a constructive manner.

ENCOURAGING CHALLENGE WITHIN THE CORE VALUES

Says GE's Jack Welch: 'One of the hardest things is to get the maximum out of a rising business. The worst sins are committed in boom times, when everybody feels satisfied. That's when managers get fat and arrogant.'

It is also the time when constructive challenge can be most valuable. Our high-performance companies want people to speak out when they see something they don't agree with. They encourage people to ask both naive and challenging questions. Says Electrocomponents' Bob Lawson:

'It's OK here not to understand something. We expect people to challenge things they don't understand, because they are probably not alone.'

Singapore Airlines has a biennial event aimed at combating complacency. Called TOP, for To Optimum Productivity, it takes between four and five months to complete. Explains CEO Cheong: 'It involves everyone at every level of the company and in every division of the group. It's a bottom-up process where we encourage people to come up with ideas: how to change the way we do things, how to automate and how even not to do things that aren't needed any more. We do this every two years, no matter whether we are making a lot of money or profits are declining. In fact, we tell our staff that it is when we are doing well that this exercise is most important, because it's then that you tend to become a bit sloppy. The most recent TOP exercise saved over $30 million Singapore. That's a small sum, but the spirit of the exercise is what is important. We explain that, if we keep doing this, if it becomes part of our culture to question continuously, then we will never need to have a re-engineering exercise. Re-engineering might save a lot more money, but it is much more traumatic and you may retrench thousands of staff.'

M&S branch managers, far from resenting visits from head office as an unnecessary intrusion, welcome the opportunity to influence thinking at the centre. Collecting constructive criticism is everyone's job, including senior management's. People are encouraged to speak up by a folklore that emphasises the success of people whose careers took off once they impressed top management with their criticisms. For example, Derek (now Lord) Rayner came to the then chairman's notice by complaining about the excessive volume of manuals and paperwork in the company. He went on to become chairman himself.

At Reuters, says Director Rob Rowley, constant positive challenge comes from 'strong leadership, a lot of travelling, people having a tremendous breadth of interest, by being willing to work around the system as well as through it, and having a situation where we are all comfortable about other people talking to our subordinates. It is really an absence of boundaries in many ways. There's a relatively high confidence level of people in what they are doing, and we have an open and debating – maybe even slightly cynical – organisation on occasions.'

NOT LETTING THE SEAT GET TOO WARM

The high-performance companies go to great lengths to ensure that people don't get too settled in their jobs. At The Berkeley Group, for example, Chief Executive Tony Pidgley prevents people becoming too comfortable by giving them new challenges. He explains: 'With most organisations, you rise to the top and then relax. We don't do that. There's nothing better for the managing director of a successful company than to be moved to one that is not performing well. It's hard to be arrogant or complacent if your own company is bottom of the pile.'

Charles Allen at Granada takes a similar view: 'We keep people fresh by moving them around quite a bit. Recently, for example, the head of leisure moved to the rental business and the head of rentals went to leisure.'

Singapore Airlines constantly rotates people into unfamiliar areas, so they can both learn and provide a fresh perspective. Explains CEO Cheong: 'The incumbents in jobs always say that their job needs a specialist. We broke that in finance eight years ago. Up to that time the chief finance director was always an accountant. It was in their interest to tell us that the person had to be an accountant to understand what the accountants were talking about. Then we put an engineer in there and he had no trouble. In fact he ran the department much better than all his predecessors. The nitty-gritty you can leave to your lieutenants, but the broad financial decisions, the financial management, that's not difficult to grasp. Before I became managing director, I was put in charge of the computer department and I'd never touched a computer before.'

Some more examples of this approach can be found in Chapter Ten.

NOTHING IS EVER GOOD ENOUGH

One of the few personal characteristics our high-performing CEOs and chairmen all share is an inability to accept that anything is good enough. At N. Brown, for example, says one of the senior managers: 'David Alliance, the Chairman, is restless and never satisfied. . . .'

'I'm never satisfied. I'm always challenging. It's like a journey; you never arrive,' says Charles Allen of Granada.

So restless and concerned to question everything was Joe Bamford, founder of JCB, that he earned the nickname from a French business partner of *'Jamais Content'* Bamford. The name stuck, not least because Bamford felt it described exactly the value he wanted to instil in the business.[3]

It is difficult to over-emphasise how seriously the CEOs of high-performing companies take the issue of preventing complacency. The following comments give a flavour of their passion for seeking out and preventing complacency within their organisations.

• When managers at Siebe or Rentokil Initial meet their targets, they know that that is no more than a foundation for achieving more. 'We set targets for everything,' says Siebe's Allen Yurko. 'We don't accept failure.

If you sat through one of our performance-review meetings, you would not only see a target for sales growth, profit growth, return on capital and cash flow, but you'd also see a target for improvement in quality, warranty, safety, productivity and so on. There is a budget and a target – and they are different. Budget is the commitment that they say they are going to improve productivity from, say, 74 per cent to 78 per cent this year or sales from $110,000 to $120,000. But there is also a stretch target, which is, if we really do it right we could hit $130,000 this year. That's what we'd really like to do. By the time we think we're getting really good, we set a higher target.'

- 'Complacency: we root it out,' says Boots' Lord Blyth. 'It's a mindset. Whenever we find ourselves saying we can't do better than that, we will go round it 20 times before we accept that we can't. Then we invite people to prove us wrong.' Changing the mindset, he says, is about changing people's perception of how much can be achieved. 'Once we provide people with a belief that they can stretch much more than they thought possible, everyone does,' he maintains.

- At Granada, says Human Resources Director Stephanie Monk: 'There is a very high level of self-criticism within the organisation. We present a very positive front but there's a continuous requirement to keep thinking about improving and changing. A steady state is not a likely state round here.'

- 'Bill Gates and Steve Bellman constantly feel the competition is going to catch them up. They never let up,' says Mike Murray, Vice President of Human Resources and Administration at Microsoft. 'I have often thought that if Microsoft were a car, we'd have a very large gas pedal and a very small brake. There'd be a very large windscreen at the front, to see where we were going, but no rear-view mirror – we know the competition is right on our tail, so we don't need to look back.'

- Says Roberto C Goizueta, Chairman and Chief Executive of Coca-Cola: 'Don't wrap the flag of Coca-Cola around you to prevent change taking place. It is extremely important that you show some insensitivity to your past in order to show proper respect to the future.'[4]

- 'Restless discontent' is a phrase coined by Marks & Spencer CEO Simon Marks in the 1930s. 'He was never satisfied, never. He was driving all the time,' says the current Chairman, Sir Richard Greenbury. 'From the top down you have to be pushing people all the time to do better. It's easy to say that we're the most profitable retailer in Europe, that no one's within miles of us. But that could so easily change: we could drop, our competitors could get better, and we've got to keep striving. That's a management thing: it's me pushing, the board pushing, the senior management of the business pushing down, and a restless discontent with everything the business is doing.'[5]

- The mythology around IKEA founder Ingvar Kamprad includes an occasion when the top team was considering the figures from a record year of sales and profit. Recalls Sven-Olof Kulldorff: 'Ingvar said: "It's difficult to find anything to complain about. Let's take a minute of satisfaction. . . . Right, now let's get back to work." ' Sixty seconds of self-congratulation was all he would allow them.

- A similar attitude occurs at Reuters, says Rob Rowley: 'It's always been there. One of the great strengths of the company is never believing anything. Even when we are successful we are always looking to see where we could go wrong. Its something we are trying to breed into people, self-doubt. Its schizophrenic because we are actually at the same time telling people we are going to succeed, because people have to be confident in what we are doing, but we are also asking them to examine where we are not good enough.'

- Says Graham Thomson, Chairman of Berkeley Homes (North London) Ltd: 'We always want to get better. I want my business to be the best in the group. My opposite numbers feel the same, I'm sure. So we always want to improve the product. No matter how well a development goes you can always do something a little better next time. The pride is in the job. Our people are proud of what they do.

  'If a single-plot site becomes "just a single-plot site" and the business doesn't take the same trouble with it as a bigger plot, then you could lose that passion. I've spent the whole day sometimes reviewing the pre-plan for a single-plot development and made our people re-design it if it's not good enough. That's the way we are and our people are proud of that.'

  Adds his colleague Geoff Hutchinson, Chairman of Crosby Homes: 'Let me give you an example. Say we bought a single plot of land and said we will sell it for £100,000. We plan it all out and develop it, then we sell it and get £120,000. Some boards would just say good, this one would say, "Hang on a minute – why? Could we have got more? Could we have improved the product in any way?" Optimisation is the key.

  'So although we could start to think we can walk on water, you have to be self-critical to avoid complacency. We will sell a successful house and still take it apart to look at whether we could have done it better, right down to saying, "OK, the airing cupboard was a bit cramped;

could we have found a way to put in more shelves to make more space?"'

'Restless discontent' at the top becomes reflected in our high performance companies at all levels. It is perhaps the most significant aspect of being a role model at top management level – an infectious compulsion that shapes the behaviour of people across the organisation.

Rooting out complacency

Occasionally, a high-performing company loses its grip on the balance between pride and humility. That certainly seemed to be the case with British Airways for a period between 1993 and 1995, for example. The airline was involved in a series of scandals concerning its competitive behaviour and, at the same time, many of its staff began to demonstrate an arrogance that was sharply reminiscent of the airline's public sector days. It was unfortunate that, a week before a laudatory article about British Airways in *Harvard Business Review*, one of the authors of this book experienced a classic case of disastrously poor service right the way through from check-in to complaint response from top management. It appeared that top management, in chasing global expansion through acquisition and merger, had taken its eye off the ball long enough for pride to set in.

In British Airways' case, the reaction to that burgeoning hubris has been a fierce reinforcement of core values, along with radical plans to restructure the airline so that it retains its competitive advantage. Few of the original *The Winning Streak* companies that slipped into hubris managed to claw their way out again. That BA should do so is a tribute to its determination and also to the manner in which it has managed succession at the top (*see* Chapter Twelve).

One source of complacency in organisations is simply getting too comfortable. When Sir Clive Thompson at Rentokil Initial says he would be disappointed if he didn't engender some tension when he visits operations, it is this he has in mind. A similar view has been expressed by Andrew Grove, the CEO of Intel, the US-based semiconductor giant. He believes that some fear is healthy in organisations that have a long history of success, because it forces people to keep looking for ways to stay on top. Grove's motto 'Only the paranoid survive' encapsulates this thinking. He spends much of his time acting as the role model for constructive paranoia. Say Brandenburger and Nelbuff in *Harvard Business Review*: 'Grove is remarkably good at not letting pride or ego get in the way. He recognises the need to step outside Intel, so to speak, and analyse a situation from the perspective of someone who doesn't have vested interest in the status quo. He regularly tries to prove himself wrong by looking for counter-examples to his current thinking.'[6]

Intel did become complacent at one point, when it forgot to take an outsider's perspective of what was essentially a minor fault on its Pentium chips. Instead of announcing that there was a fault and it was being fixed, it kept quiet. A public relations catastrophe ensued, when knowledge of the fault leaked and Intel ended up with a write-off of over $400 million and a substantial loss of goodwill. The experience has had some benefits, however: it reinforced the message about constructive paranoia across the organisation.

Reuters had a close brush with complacency a decade or more ago, but instinctively recognised the dangers. Says Peter Job: 'In the 1980s, we were like a lot of other companies. We put up our prices every year and believed in a product-driven style, making products and saying to customers, "You want these, don't you?" These two factors led to our reputation for arrogance. Since then we haven't put up our prices much and we've tried to be more market-led.'

IKEA, too, got the balance between pride and humility wrong a few years ago. Its rapid international expansion ran into difficulties in the United States when it failed to adapt to local market conditions. Chief Executive Anders Moberg says the company 'had become a little like a stuffed tiger'. Complacency led IKEA to assume that North American customers would have the same tastes as Europeans. Puzzled by poor sales of beds and kitchen units, it eventually realised that Americans preferred larger beds and bed linen than Swedes, and that kitchen units had to be big enough to store pizza plates.

In its other markets too, IKEA had begun to get a little soft. Overheads (non-goods costs) increased from 30 per cent to 37.5 per cent in the early 1990s. The company reacted swiftly when the danger became clear, revising all of its key business processes, especially the supply chain, to restore margins. 'We learned a lot from that experience,' says Vice President Sven-Olof Kulldorff. 'We learned that we had to make adaptations – of sizes, for example – but not in style or expression. We used to focus on having large-scale production efficiency, but now we also have to have different versions for each country.'

To ensure the company doesn't slip into complacency again, IKEA created internal competition. Wherever IKEA intends to set up in a new market, the local operating company may find itself competing against a separate franchising operation, Inter IKEA.[7]

In summary...

Getting the pride–humility balance wrong is so very easy. Complacency is always waiting around the corner. Getting it right needs constant attention from top to bottom of the organisation. A long-dead and possibly apocryphal founder/chief executive of an engineering company in the North-East of England held biennial "umble' weeks, where everyone in the organisation was expected to examine critically everything the company did, by putting themselves in the roles of customer, colleagues, suppliers and competitors. A New England insurance company invites selected customers to audit its policies and processes, to provide a different perspective. There is no shortage of ways to test the pride–humility balance, but it has to be done constantly, because it doesn't take long for this particular plate to start to wobble.

For Sir Roger Hurn at Smiths Industries, preventing complacency has become almost a mission. 'It's a very real risk, in a high-performing company like this, that managers will get complacent and occasionally we find some who do. We do what's necessary to shake them out of it or change them. I'm acutely aware that complacency is probably the biggest single risk to the continuation of our performance, so I make everyone around me aware of it, too, at every opportunity. We talk about it a lot, because not to do so would be complacent in itself. I say: "We've got to keep stoking the fires."'

Preventing complacency is largely about maintaining a healthy balance between legitimate pride in achievement and the introspective humility that comes from a sensitivity to the ephemerality of good fortune. Top management has to provide the initial energy – the spark in the cylinder head – to set the organisation's pistons moving and to help to maintain and increase momentum. Throughout a company with underweening pride, people search for new challenges – external benchmarks, stretching demands from customers, opportunities to increase differentiation from the competition. They are, indeed, *restless*.

In Chapter Eight, we look at an important ingredient in sustaining both constructive pride and humility – the values system of an organisation. If the values are appropriate and well-managed, then a drift into arrogance will quickly become apparent to people at all levels of the organisation. Before we do so, however, we examine another key element in preventing excessive pride – the ability to maintain a clear focus around what business the company is in.

7 | BIFOCAL PERSPECTIVE
Focus versus breadth of vision

'The core business is jealous of our attention and well worthy of it.' *Peter Job, Chief Executive, Reuters.*

'If people are more focused, they are more likely to be watching the pluses and minuses [of alternative courses of action]. You get the picture faster, the more focused you are.' *Sir Gerald Whent, Chief Executive, Vodafone.*

'We are the world's most diversified integrated company. Like a bumble bee, we shouldn't be able to fly, but we do.' *Jack Welch, Chairman and Chief Executive, General Electric.*

Just as bifocal spectacles are primarily an accessory for the middle-aged and older, so the need to take a bifocal view of the world becomes greater as businesses achieve size. The bigger the business becomes, the more choices it has to make about where to focus its efforts. For example, does a successful California-based software company elect to expand by taking the same products internationally to new customers, or by developing or acquiring new product lines for its existing customers and focusing on the home market? The temptation is to do both at the same time, yet very few companies manage to pull off such a trick successfully.

Our high-performance companies perceive this issue in terms of *how do we focus on the core business and new opportunities at the same time?* And they defuse the conflict, by and large, by asking *how will each change affect the core business?* Will it support it, or will it draw effort and attention away from it?

They are, in effect, using bifocal vision, looking at themselves alternately through concave and convex lenses. A convex perspective leads to a very high degree of perspective, doing a few things exceedingly well and ignoring opportunities to slip into other markets. A concave perspective views the business as a jumping-off point for all sorts of potential ventures. While the convex perspective acts to narrow down the options for growth, the concave opens them out. The greater the concave curve, the broader the horizon of opportunity the company perceives.

Almost all of the high-performing businesses are built around a central core business or businesses, in which the core competencies and business values are nurtured and safeguarded. Around the core(s) are a number of other businesses that feed off the core competencies and business values and – equally importantly – give back to the core business by reinforcing them. So none of our high-performing businesses could truthfully be called a conglomerate, nor would they appreciate being described in those terms.

Peter Job, Chief Executive of Reuters, makes the point plainly: 'We are already under tremendous pressure to move fast. We only have time for investments which bring real synergy to this process. Rather than seeking growth through the purchase of mature businesses at a big premium, we would prefer to return unneeded cash to shareholders. The core business is jealous of our attention, and well worthy of it.' At Boots, too, Chairman Sir Michael Angus told shareholders: 'It is our policy that if, in the medium term, we cannot forecast an investment opportunity which will create returns greater than the cost of capital, then we will return surplus cash to shareholders in the most efficient manner.' In other words, diversification just to achieve greater size isn't an option.

Singapore Airlines, for example, consists of one of the world's largest passenger airlines, with some hundred or so smaller subsidiaries around it, responsible for everything from engineering to airport management. The core competencies the airline brings relate to service quality and innovation, along with prudent financial management.

On the ground, the subsidiary that manages Changi airport acts as the front line for passenger encounters. It *has* to maintain similar values and core competencies to the airline (for example, very good customer recovery skills), but it also has to have special competencies of its own (for example, in rapid movement of baggage). The same is true of every other subsidiary, from cargo handling to engineering, even when they become relatively large operations in their own right.

This introduces another potential difficulty into the equation. When faced with a conflict of interest between Singapore Airlines and their own customers, what do the subsidiaries do? The issue is defused by reference to the values: *what would the customer want us to do?* Preserving customer goodwill is in the long-term interest of the group, so the conflict never becomes anything but potential. Boots' concept of 'dual citizenship' (*see* Chapter Three) has many similarities as a process for deciding such conflicts of interest.

Bifocal vision also applies to how the high-performing company views what is important. British Airways promotes to its staff the concept of 'nothing too big, nothing too small', by which it means that the business should at the same time be striving after big, global goals and paying close attention to all the little things that make the difference in the impression gained by the customer. So, for example, a minor change in customer comfort or an employee's response to an individual customer's problem is just as important as the discussions around a major merger or acquisition. Getting that message through is a major preoccupation for BA's top management.

The argument for a convex perspective

The high performers, which have stayed firmly within their niche, share a common view that it is hard enough to stay ahead in the business you know well; learning new businesses would simply divert attention from the main game. Intensity of effort and concentration are what provide their competitive edge. It is simply too dangerous to be diverted by attractive but unsynergistic opportunities in other markets. For example:

- Sir Gerald Whent at Vodafone maintains: 'If people are more focused, they are more likely to be watching the pluses and minuses [of alternative courses of action]. You get the picture faster, the more focused you are. ... In the early formation period of a company, when you are putting a lot of resources in, it's particular important to be focused.'

  Vodafone, says Julian Horn-Smith, Managing Director of Vodafone Group International, is in 'mobile telecommunications, pure and simple. We are not diversified, we are not into other forms of tele-communications – not in fixed telecoms, cable television, trunk PMR, or any other form of telecoms. This was a conscious decision. We thought it was the best way of enhancing shareholder value. It was the fastest way to achieve growth and give value to shareholders.'

  Indeed, the creation of Vodafone – carved out of electronics group, Racal – was a recognition of the importance of a convex perspective for a young company. Says Sir Gerald: 'Vodafone is different from Racal. Racal is a series of entirely different businesses; it's a conglomerate of small businesses, so it makes some sense to split into little companies. This is a single business; it has a lot of small companies to it, but they are all in the same orchestra.'

- Southwest Airlines is one of the most focused of high-performance businesses. It has a very simple service concept built around low-cost one-class flights of about one hour between US cities. It does not provide meals, does not belong to any of the airline reservation systems (so customers or their agents have to call the airline direct). This keeps its costs per seat-mile at about two-thirds the industry average, enabling it to sustain lower fares. It constrains its ambitions to North America, where there is still great scope for growth, and prefers to open up more flights to the same destinations than to cover the map with red lines.

- SOL's Liisa Joronen declares: 'I used to think that it is good for a company to have many pillars to rest on. If one business has difficulties, the others would help. Now I have realised that this is self-deception.'

- When the *Financial Times* suggested to ABB's Percy Barnevik that the company was a diversified group (it has five business segments: power generation, power transmission and distribution, industrial and building systems, transportation equipment and financial services), he rejected the idea completely, explaining: 'We regard ourselves as highly focused and we strive to be the leaders in what we focus on.'[1] ABB has a much narrower spread of markets than its global electronics competitors (it isn't in telecommunications, computers, medical equipment or defence, for example). And, says Barnevik, there are very real synergies between the businesses, with sales to one customer often requiring products from several business areas.

- At SAP, says Henning Kagermann: 'The focus is the development and sale of standardised enterprise software. It is a very clear focus. There are many opportunities in this area and we are expanding the business a great deal in it. Analysts sometimes think we are doing too much – we are in consultancy, we are in many different things. But the focus is not to transfer skills outside this area; we need to maintain the focus to continue our success.

- At ASDA, says Chairman Archie Norman: 'This sort of business, because it's pace-driven and because it's about understanding and managing and a load of detail and responding fast, benefits from being mono-focused. It's a word we use: we want mono-focus management. We're only driven by competing in large-volume stores and selling to ordinary working people and their families who want value – that is our business, and it's complicated enough to do that. The more we diversify, or the more complexity we add, the slower we move. An enormous amount of the effectiveness of the business is a function of how far the top management can get close to the stores – and really close, really listening and really involved. If your top management group is worrying about complex new systems or fancy new ways of marketing, then you will lose something in the stores; that can't be avoided. It's a trade-off you have to make.'

- IKEA, too, is heavily biased in favour of focus. Says Sven-Olof Kulldorff: 'The competition in this market is so hard that you can't spread out, because then you will never be very good at one thing.'

If there is a key lesson here, it is expressed by Reuters' Peter Job: 'A colleague said something that I think is very significant – "there's always more in your core businesses than you think." It's true, you can always find another layer of activities you can do, and another.'

In short, a convex perspective helps a company to:

- focus on doing one thing or a few things really well;
- present a very clear image to both internal and external audiences about what it stands for;
- know its customers better and respond more rapidly to their needs; and
- keep a close eye on what is happening in the market.

The arguments for a concave perspective

Those high performers who have spread outside their niche – taking a concave perspective – have nonetheless been careful to ensure that they retain a focus on the core competencies and values. For the retailers, for example, a convex perspective would argue for taking their skills international before seeking to move into other areas of retail. In practice, many of them have been cautious about the viability of transplanting a retail formula from one country to another, and have opted first to expand into other areas of retail. Some had little choice – IKEA's home market in Scandinavia was so small that it *had* to make the convex–concave choice early in its development.

There is little pattern in the approaches our retailers have taken. Marks & Spencer, Carrefour and Boots have all internationalised and see the global market as a logical next step. Carrefour, for example, is 'at the top of the consumption curve' in the French market, says Chief Executive Daniel Bernard; but they have mostly also taken a concave perspective and moved into related sectors. Carrefour innovates through incremental additions of new products. Says Daniel Bernard: 'A good example of innovation is that we are now number one in Europe in sending cut flowers. In this market, we guarantee fresh flowers within one week. Within three years we're number one in Europe. We have developed parapharmacy, private labels and banking.'

Marks & Spencer, as a second example, has launched a number of financial services products. The rationale was very clear: the M&S brand was a guarantee of probity and integrity in a market that had a dubious reputation, so the company's core competencies of value for money, quality and customer service provided a distinct competitive advantage. The new products, although sold in a different manner and a long way from clothes retail, were not so far away from the store's own credit card, and supported the core business in the sense that they provided another route to reach existing and potential customers, to bring them into the store.

Among the most concave businesses in our study, on the face of it, are GKN and Granada, both of which are in two or more apparently unconnected markets. Close to them is Cadbury Schweppes, where, although there are obvious links between soft drinks and confectionery (not least that they are sold at much the same outlets and through the same intermediaries), the two business streams are treated as independent entities. 'Cadbury has moved from being a diversified consumer products company vulnerable to takeover, to a focused confectionery and beverages group, which is more likely to be predator than prey,' comments Andrew Lorenz for *Management Today*.[2]

Although some financiers have promoted the notion that Cadbury should demerge its two business streams into two separate companies, top management argues that the core competencies of the two businesses are the same: brand management (at both local and global levels) and niche operation in markets dominated by global giants.

GKN's triple businesses are automotive parts, industrial pallets and defence – three apparently very different markets and types of operation. The rationale for this structure goes back to the company's move out of steel and steel bashing. It recognised in the 1980s that it could not provide the level of shareholder return of a world-class company unless it switched industries. This was a radical and bold step, yet it was made remarkably smoothly. The industry it chose was automotive parts, but that had its own weaknesses, being highly profitable in the good times, but all too dependent on the global automobile industry, which is notorious for its boom–bust cycles. The pallet business was acquired and developed as an alternative source of income, to ensure that it can continue to invest during the downturns. So the pallet business supports the core competence of continuing research and development during automotive industry downturns. The automotive business, in turn, provides a global presence and the cash flow to expand the pallet business into new areas during its good times. David Lees explained the strategy in the 1995 Report and Accounts: to reduce the cyclical imbalance of the group by concentrating on three core businesses, which are influenced by different economic cycles but which all have the potential for growth in international markets.[3] He adds in our interview: 'We have in the portfolio one big business which is quite cash demanding and another which throws off cash; that is quite a nice balance. The third one is geographic balance. The defence business is important to us because one of the by-products of the 1980s was that almost all our profits were coming from overseas. All the defence profits are in the UK, so that gave us quite neat fiscal balance. I would rather build on those three than have four or six, because there is a limit to what I think is manageable.'

Bowthorpe is the nearest thing to an old-fashioned conglomerate among our high-performing companies. Chief Executive Nicholas Brookes explains: 'The way it was driven in the past was not based on seeking significant synergies across businesses. Some niche acquisition opportunities came along that looked good, so we acquired them with the aim of growing them individually.

'The basic underlying business philosophy is to concentrate on selected, targeted markets so we are not over-reliant on any one customer or industry, but not to be so unfocused that there are not synergistic benefits to be gained. We want to be a truly global business – we already have over 30 per cent of our business in the US and over 80 per cent outside the UK, but we need to concentrate more on the Far East, aggressively marketing our products as well as manufacturing more there.'

Selecting where to focus involves more than simply choosing a different set of markets. Explains GKN's Head of Corporate Planning, David Pulling: 'GKN has been honest enough to step back and look at what it's good at and not good at. It was a painful process. GKN tends to be quite good at running businesses that are capital-intensive, large, international market positions, with generally not that many people involved in them in relation to the size of the operation. Those businesses tend to require decisions that are quite large and affect the business for a long time. Therefore they need to be deeply analysed and properly thought through. GKN does that quite well. What it's not been good at has been running the sort of businesses where you need to be fast on your feet, often with large distributive workforces, working in markets where there are large numbers of customers, where decisions are required more rapidly, close to the ground. The sorts of decision-making processes we have don't equate very well to them. We realised that and concentrated on businesses with the characteristics we could play to.'

From the outside, Reuters appears to be a many-faceted business, although it is fairly highly integrated. Its expansion from an international supplier of news to an international supplier of mainly financial information involved a gigantic broadening of focus, although its original journalistic values remain vital to its market position.

The most concave company, by far, that we encountered in our initial trawl of possible cases is Virgin, where the only core competencies seem to be the strength of the corporate brand and the ability of the founder, Richard Branson, to select and empower very able people to manage entrepreneurial ventures. Branson establishes ventures apparently at random, with some major successes and some less well publicised failures. Central to the brand is the public's trust in Richard Branson to deliver value for money and quality. There are many similarities between the Virgin brand and the M&S brand in this way.

In short, a concave perspective helps a company to:

- dilute the impact of natural industry cycles;
- support cash-hungry growth businesses;
- avoid or postpone the dangers of going international; and
- develop a broader awareness of market trends than can normally be observed within a single market sector.

Balancing convex and concave perspective

For the successful company, there is never a shortage of opportunities. It's not just that people within the business keep coming up with potential new ventures and products; most of our high-performing companies have a constant stream of other companies approaching them with ideas to pursue. People like to be associated with success; they also hope that some of that success can rub off on them. So an important part of the role of senior managers in our case-study companies, at both group and operating company level, is knowing when and how to say 'no' to an opportunity.

They manage the delicate balance between convex and concave activity in several ways:

- being very clear about the boundaries of the business they are in;
- ensuring that core competencies are the organisational glue;
- being intolerant of dog businesses; and
- investing in success not failure.

WHAT BUSINESS ARE WE IN?

High-performing companies are very clear about what business they are in – and what they are not in.

- At The Berkeley Group, Tony Pidgley maintains a very sharp focus on what is and isn't the company's business. Berkeley concentrates on the core business of the operating companies, and is predominantly a residential housebuilder, but has diversified its activities both in product mix and geographical location to spread the risk of the inevitable downturn. He explains: 'The housing market in this country is cyclical by its very nature and it is therefore vital to maintain cash flows extremely tightly and watch for the 'Indian signs' for any changed sales patterns. We manage to buck the trend a bit better than our competitors due to our wide variety of product. However, what I love about the residential housing market is that there's always someone looking for a bargain. You can always recover your cash, although the selling price might not be showing a profit. What we don't like about the commercial property market is the speculative nature, insomuch as you might give £5 million for a development site, spend £10 million building on it and then you have to hope you find a tenant. Even if you do, the yield might change. That is why we are very aware of speculative commercial development.

  'We don't need any more divisions. If someone suggests putting £300,000 into a playground because a deal looks attractive, I'd say no, because we're not in playgrounds. If we want to be in playgrounds, let's be in playgrounds, not with the odd £300,000.' The company has never had any inclination to step outside its niche of high-quality housing, nor to pursue market share. 'We don't concern ourselves with the competition. We are just interested in our market share, which is about one per cent of the total market.'

  Within its niche, however, Berkeley is prepared to be very concave in its thinking: 'The housing market is about demand and supply of land. We do a lot of research before we buy land, so we know the market. It always surprises me how many companies don't. Because of the nature of the market – feast and famine – you have to have a diverse portfolio. We have a diverse operation; for example, we do everything from refurbishing a Grade I listed building into a £2 million home, to starter homes.'

- 'My people quite often come to me with new business ideas and companies to be bought because they know I am greedy for growth and we have cash' says SOL's Liisa Joronen. 'I always say that their duty is to find new services in the cleaning business, not find new businesses.'

- At Electrocomponents, everyone is very clear about the business niche. It is a secondary electronics parts-supplier to engineers around the world. It does that one thing very well, using catalogues rather than a direct sales force. Says CEO Bob Lawson: 'Clarity is the key, clarity of what we are and are not. We are not a mainstream supplier to our customers; we are a vitally important secondary supplier. We are not in retail; we are only good at communicating with supporting engineers. Our love, in the product sense, is technical things; we are not good at supporting non-technical people. Our marketing is focused on people who can use our products. Our business is very replicable: engineers understand the same language of physics everywhere.'

Once again, however, at the detailed level there is often fierce debate about how focused the company should be in, for example, the products it offers. Says Lawson: 'It's the most active area of debate for us. We don't know how broad we can go and not damage the brand. We haven't got a good answer except to expand in a low-risk way.

'Our view is to experiment to learn, so we keep pushing. We've had our fair share of failures both ways: we've narrowed down too much and missed opportunities, or gone too broad and not created sufficient momentum to be viable. On the narrow front, we thought the primary driver of this business was technical innovation. We totally missed the impact of legislation, so we were late in getting into health and safety. Conversely, we put out a catalogue with a large product offering equivalent to 80 per cent of the total UK range. People couldn't see who it related to; it just confused them, because it wasn't focused enough.'

- Says Chris Pearce, Group Finance Director of Rentokil Initial: 'The strategy has been to diversify the business base. Sir Clive [Thompson, Chief Executive] has deliberately driven the business to be in a wider range of services and to be in 40 different countries including all the major developed economies of Europe, North America and Asia–Pacific. If you have our objective of growing the business year in and year out then you need that spread, otherwise you are bound to be quite cyclical. We also concentrate on contract-based business rather than one-off business. That way you go into each year with a portfolio of customers and you know that as long as you satisfy them you'll keep them and you can keep adding more contracts.'

- At Reuters, says Peter Job: 'We provide people with information and related technology for the purpose of letting people do their work more effectively. We don't supply information directly to consumers as such, but to people in work situations.'

- One of the first steps taken by Archie Norman, when he took over as CEO of ASDA, was to refocus the group on its core. Allied Carpets and Maples, a furnishing retailer, were slimmed down and sold off as quickly as practical. He also disposed of the company's 25 per cent interest in another troubled furniture group, MFI, and the food production business, Lofthouse Foods. Mike Killoran, now Head of Customer Services at ASDA, recalls the environment at that time: 'Just before Archie and Allen [Leighton] arrived, we lost our way. I remember the very early days of the company. It was founded by two Northern entrepreneurs in 1965 as Queen's Supermarkets – named after the old music hall where the first store was sited. But we diversified into other areas with the Allied Carpets deal and others. We really lost our focus on the core business. Prices increased and margins drifted up. Our customers started to fall off. Morale wasn't very good at that time. The general managers [GMs] like myself could see what was happening. Our business formula is not a difficult one: keep prices keen, look after colleagues and customers, and profits take care of themselves. But we moved away from that. The company had become very hierarchical. The GMs were just administrators with no way to influence the business. Archie and Allen brought us back to grass roots.'

• Although Bowthorpe has eight business sectors, it still regards clarity of business as a critical element of its success. Explains CEO Nicholas Brookes: 'We have a team of eight senior managers plus the Chief Executive and Financial Director which meets each month to review the strategy of one of our sectors with the senior executive (global business manager) responsible and some of his key managers. The whole team knows what the aim is for any business. Any member can ask the naive question which sparks off ideas, or input some market knowledge from elsewhere. However, this end strategy is then reflected in hard numbers for the three-to-five-year timeframe, and particularly in the budget process.'

Being clear about the boundaries of the business you are in pre-empts a great deal of debate about opportunities at or beyond the margin. By and large, our high-performing companies are very good at saying 'no' to opportunities that don't fit within the range of their business vision.

CORE COMPETENCIES ARE THE ORGANISATIONAL GLUE

As all of these examples illustrate, high-performing companies constantly check for both convex and concave perspective and adjust the balance as needed, and also ensure that any diversification both draws on and reinforces the core competencies and values of the company.

It is hardly surprising, then, that they regard culture fit as an important element of any acquisition they make. Says Cadbury Schweppes' Group Human Resources Director Bob Stack: 'We acquire only businesses that fit within our culture. ... People sell to us more cheaply because we are compatible.'

Those high-performance companies, such as Granada and Rentokil Initial, that are prepared to follow the hostile acquisition route do so in the knowledge that they will have to change key elements of the culture of their acquisitions. Doing so is part of the cost–benefit equation, and they are for the most part ruthless about installing new core values where they believe it to be necessary. Says Rentokil Initial's Sir Clive Thompson: 'In acquiring BET I'm sure there will be some excellent people, but we probably won't allow ourselves the luxury of finding out how good the managers are. We will put in Rentokil Initial people, so we know how they will do.'

High-performance companies are also effective at separating glamour from profit potential. Explains Granada's Charles Allen: 'One of the first things with the Forte acquisition was to put the less glamorous businesses on the agenda at a very senior level and put some passion into them. Forte management had turned so much of their attention towards the famous luxury hotels like the George V – even though they didn't make that much profit – that they had neglected the budget hotels like Travelodges, which are where the real opportunity to build a profitable brand lay. We had to make Forte managers understand that, at Granada, it's not the chandeliers that make a hotel glamorous, it is the profit potential.'

Boots sees its core competencies as adding value 'by concentrating on the key elements – focused product ranges, competitive prices, customer service and the right shopping environment', says Chief Executive Lord Blyth. In diversifying into other areas of retail, it is these competencies that have defined whether Boots can add value to the acquired businesses. More than once, Boots has been criticised for its acquisitions, but Lord Blyth presents a very positive rationale, explaining that, based on the data available then, he would still have bought into do-it-yourself in the late 1980s. Boots paid £900 million for A.G. Stanley, of which it has since recouped £200 million in sales of unwanted subsidiaries. But, says Lord Blyth, 'We now have one of the businesses we acquired in that sale, Halfords, which we could sell tomorrow for what we paid for the whole business.' The turn-around in the Halford's business has largely been due to that investment in developing the same competencies that drive the core business.

Rentokil Initial's strategy, says Sir Clive Thompson, 'is to develop industrial services in developed countries, using the Rentokil Initial brand. We want to be in markets where the quality of service is very important to customers. We're very good at doing difficult things. Why industrial services? Because with domestic/residential services people want quality but aren't prepared to pay for it. Also, you can't get entry into their premises when you want it, but you can with industrial premises, which gives us the opportunity to get high productivity from our service people.'

For IKEA, a core competence is its global sourcing network of some 2,300 suppliers in 67 countries. It nurtures that competence by giving its suppliers long-term contracts, by providing technical advice, and by leasing them equipment. In return, they have to agree not to supply IKEA's competitors and to keep driving prices down, with help from IKEA.

Being clear about the organisation's core competencies is the starting point for deciding when to take a convex or concave perspective. The retailers that have successfully diversified, for example, have by and large done so by acquiring businesses with different products but very similar logistics. The management skills are therefore highly transferable and so are the group values. The more different a new business is in its logistics and core processes from the initial business, the more difficult such transfers will be, and the more the group is obliged to behave like a conglomerate.

However, our high-performing companies rarely delude themselves that they can transform poorly performing acquisitions simply by inserting their own managers. They first look for a reasonable degree of culture fit – of shared values – that will allow the new company to feel comfortable as part of the group. And they look for a complementarity in the core competencies of the two organisations. Where they replace top managers, it is as often as not to restore and reinforce core values and competences, rather than change them.

AN INTOLERANCE FOR DOG BUSINESSES

'We don't believe in throwing money at companies that aren't performing,' says Roger Mann, Finance Director of Siebe. He is supported by Sir David Lees, Chairman of GKN: 'I don't think businesses that can't reliably make 20 per cent [return on capital], taking one year with another, have a place in our portfolio.' Like most other high-performance companies, GKN will not allow its attention to be diverted by businesses that do not have the potential to be high performers. All high-performing companies are made up of high-performing subsidiaries. Those that aren't high-performing aren't wanted.

GKN had adopted a strategic classification in the early 90s dividing the various operations into core, performance and divest. The core businesses are the largest in the group. They are very international, have strong market positions and are the highest priority in terms of the allocation of investment funds. The performance businesses are smaller in scale, less international but are capable of generating returns on capital in excess of 20 per cent. They are retained in the group more because of their financial performance than their strategic significance. The divestment description is self-evident, but after the strategic refocusing that has taken place since 1990, little now remains in this category. Determining the strategic classification was not always easy, says Trevor Bonner, Managing Director of the Automotive and Agritechnical Products Division: 'We didn't get it right at every step of the process. When we went through the searching process of taking a hard look at our portfolio and deciding which businesses to define as performance and which to divest, for example, we originally defined some as performance businesses, which didn't make it. They migrated to the divestment category.'

His colleague Marcus Beresford, Managing Director of Industrial Services, adds another dimension, explaining that it was critical to 'identify the three cores and ruthlessly focus down to those and to do so at a time when economic progress was not that great. We were generating cash selling businesses, so not earning quite the profits that we earned before. Nobody outside was prepared to believe in what we were doing till the company actually got there. When three to four years ago the economy began to turn around, the core businesses were there and the company started to grow.'

Boots also follows the practice of defining performance businesses and others. The sale of its Pharmaceuticals division was a direct result of a reassessment of the potential of the business in the light of problems licensing its heart drug Manoplax. Says Lord Blyth: 'We never spend good money on dross.'

For US semiconductor giant Intel, it was the core business that became the dog. Recognising that was both painful and difficult, to say the least. Fierce attacks by Japanese rivals on its core business – memory chips – led a great deal of soul searching at the top. After some months of trying to match the Japanese price cut for price cut, top management stepped outside the box and asked itself, 'What would a new CEO do?' When the answer came back, 'Abandon the memory chip business and concentrate on microprocessors,' that became the logical though very painful course to take. Had Intel waited and debated, the resources would not have been diverted early enough into microprocessors to allow the company to seize a distinctive competitive advantage there.[4]

INVEST IN SUCCESS RATHER THAN FAILURE

The Intel decision highlights the importance of looking to the future rather than the past; of being prepared to take a detached view, while retaining a passion for the business.

At Boots, says Lord Blyth, for a while, the company had allowed itself to be fascinated by the businesses into which it had diversified, relegating Boots The Chemist to the role of cash cow. 'We now recognise Boots the Chemist as the core of the business,' he says. Now the company ensures that the core business is protected by giving it the management attention and resources it deserves to stay ahead. 'We said not only is it not a cash cow, but it has the capacity to outstrip the performance of the other parts of the business. We must make sure that it never hiccups. We have kept driving that business forward by putting new people in there, by really stressing innovative marketing. We have continued to gain tremendous growth from the biggest, most successful part of the business. We are determined never to lose sight of how important Boots the Chemist is to the business.'

General Electric's Jack Welch was stimulated to think about business focus by a question from a veteran commentator on management, Peter Drucker, who asked: 'If you weren't already in the business, would you enter it today?' Answering that question released a torrent of disposals and acquisitions that shifted GE into businesses where it could meet very tight criteria. In particular, where it could be number-one or number-two in the market, where it could make above-average margins, ... and where it could bring to bear its core competence of managing large, complex projects.[5]

In summary...

IKEA's founder, Ingvar Kamprad speaks of 'concentrating for maximum effect'. Staying focused clearly does help companies put maximum effort into being very good at the things that matter in their business and to their customers. But business focus is rather like operating a beam of light. The further the beam goes, the wider it becomes. Keeping the focus relatively narrow demands very accurate definition at the start point and, for some applications, carefully placed lenses to refocus the beam. In the same way, businesses need frequent reassessments of their focus, to ensure that they have the right balance between narrowness and breadth.

Recognising when the focus is wrong – when it is too close on the core business or on new opportunities, or not sufficiently focused on either – is not a matter of applying mechanical analysis or some kind of strategic formula. 'Those kinds of approaches can help,' says one executive, 'but in the end you *feel* whether the balance is right or wrong.' How do companies develop that kind of feel? By relying on the sense of rightness that comes from their values, as Chapter Eight will investigate.

8 | LIVING THE VALUES
Values versus rules

'This is a company steered more by vision than by figures.' *Anders Moberg, CEO, IKEA.*

'In Carrefour, you have to rely not on recipes and policies but on values. This ensures we have entrepreneurs who can go anywhere with a suitcase.' *Daniel Bernard, Chief Executive, Carrefour.*

When top managers start talking about 'values', the cynics immediately start wondering what unpalatable change they are being sold. So often, values are wheeled out at times of tension, in the same way that politicians appeal to deep-held prejudices whenever an election nears. While a great deal has been written about the values-driven company, the reality is that very few use shared values as an effective tool for driving performance.

Running a business *entirely* on values has its attractions but isn't really practical. Values are essentially a limbic brain, emotion-derived way of dealing with the events and circumstances that we encounter. They enable individuals to relate their perception of the world – and in particular, how they feel about issues – to how their colleagues and the company as a whole perceive them. Values are powerful, because they draw upon our sense of personal identity.

Values also allow people to react faster to events around them. They may not have to be consciously aware of those events before the instinctive reaction cuts in. But while speed of response may be an effective survival mechanism in most cases, if the instinctive response is inappropriate it can lead to serious problems (for example, the instinct to run from a wild and dangerous animal might actually encourage its aggression). So effective values need to be applied appropriately to a wide range of circumstances, so that instinctive responses do not lose in appropriateness what they gain in speed.

To overcome the negative potential of instinctive, emotion-driven responses, effective behaviour and decision making – indeed, every way in which we respond to our environment – demand intellect too. An analogy can be made with different parts of the human brain. The neocortex, the seat of rational analysis, provides us with the ability to establish and respond to rules. Many times slower in reaction time than the limbic system, the neo-cortex ponders, sieves, analyses, and provides a more reasoned response to events. On its own, however, it is useless. People who are unfortunate enough to lose access to their limbic brain and have to rely on their neo-cortex prove unable to make even simple decisions. It seems that we need an overlay of emotional context to make rational judgments.

The ability to balance intellect and emotion appears to be the anchor of functional intelligence in people. The same principles seem to apply equally strongly to organisations. The balance of emotional and rational decision making is what produces organisational intelligence. Like people, some organisations are better at managing that balance than others.

The value of values

All of our case-study companies place great store on the development and dissemination of *core values*, namely the relatively few values that establish the cultural identity of the company and with which they expect all key people in the organisation to have an instinctive empathy. Almost without exception, these values are very long-lived. At Reuters, Chief Executive Peter Job takes a modest view of the company's success in balancing its core values. 'If you go back to the core values', he says, 'you're going back to 1851 when the company was founded. Basically, those core values are speed and accuracy, and given that these are mutually exclusive propositions it's not surprising it's taken us 150-odd years to try to bring them together.'

Values provide a short-cut to effective decision making. They are also a great help in establishing relationships – with customers, suppliers, advisers and even acquisition candidates. At Cadbury Schweppes, for example, says Finance Director David Kappler: 'I was talking to [an acquisition candidate] this morning. I won't say where. On the day he sold his business to us, I know he had another offer that was as high if not higher than ours. One of the reasons he sold to Cadbury Schweppes was our reputation for treating employees well. It isn't that we are soft. We take hard decisions when we have to, closing factories and that sort of thing. It's that we don't take hasty decisions and we treat people with respect, explaining the reasons. This is definitely beneficial to the company when making acquisitions. In another recent case, the former owner of a family business we bought was worried about rumours that Unilever was going to buy Cadbury Schweppes. He said if it was true, then he wanted to buy his company back.' Culture fit is so important that Cadbury will walk away from an acquisition prospect that has a radically different culture.

Values provide a cohesion of identity for distant operations. Says Kevin Hayes, Managing Director of Cadbury's Asia–Pacific operations: 'Values don't lose their power. They're handed down in an almost legendary way from one generation of managers to the next. They hold good in Australia as they do in the UK. From the outside perspective, because of those values we are seen as nice people to do business with. The odd thing is that if you asked an Australian, he'd probably think Cadbury is an Australian brand – I think that relates to the values. It's true throughout the old Commonwealth.'

Values can also be a means of assessing whether people fit the organisation. For example, at Southwest Airlines Herb Kelleher is adamant that employees who compromise on the values don't last long.[1]

A clear sense of values can be very useful in helping a company get back on track. For example, looking at where Honda had lost touch with its customers, President/CEO Kawamoto told *Fortune*: 'The traditions that guided this company weren't functioning properly. Our focus on the customer was vague.'[2]

'One of the purposes of a strong sense of values with a strong sense of involvement is not that it'll stop you making mistakes, but that you'll as sure as hell find out when you do, because you feel it,' says ASDA Chairman Archie Norman. For example, a well meant plan to confine Christmas bonuses to people who were continuously at work before Christmas went sour because 'we got ourselves into difficulties distinguishing between people who were off sick and people who simply decided not to come to work. But I don't think it clashed with the values, because I think people believe in fairness as a value.'

One company, which successfully turned over a new leaf a few years back, was the US motorcycle legend Harley Davidson. A management buy-out in the early 1980s saved the company from bankruptcy after an ill-judged strategy led to a decline in the quality of its products. The changes instigated at that time restored the company's reputation and fortunes. More recently, Harley Davidson has worked to clarify and communicate its values. The aim? To ensure the company doesn't make the same mistake again. So, for example, one value the company holds dear is 'keeping its promises' to customers and employees. Another is that it 'encourages intellectual curiosity'. Those values, the company believes, will underpin the integrity of its products in the future.

Our high-performance companies tend to have very good antennae for emotive issues that arise within the company. They are also well attuned to feelings among stakeholders, and especially among customers. They harness emotion, through values, to direct it positively. They use values as a means of motivating people to act on their own initiative. And they are very good at projecting those values at stakeholders as a means of building positive goodwill and lasting relationships.

All of these characteristics require a combination of sensitivity to both the inner and external worlds, and ability to temper emotion with rationality. The same is true of the debate between values and rules. While there can be continuing discussion about whether to change the rules, or how to apply the values, throughout the organisation, there are almost always a number of relatively clear guidelines that, in effect, arbitrate between the two. For want of a better phrase, we have called these 'operating principles'.

So what kind of values do our high-performing companies hold? Most have some form of written values, which reflect the type of industry, the nature of their ambitions and the kind of behaviours they wish to be known for – although some, such as SAP, prefer to rely on showing the values by example and central monitoring. Says Henning Kagerman: 'We don't have one or two pages of written company values. Nevertheless, people do have the same values, which is very important for success.'

The table below illustrates just how varied the companies' values are:

Table 1: Company values

Company	Values
Boots	*building shareholder value, well managed, ethical, socially responsible.*
GKN	*high work ethic, painstaking attention to detail, close financial control, extremely careful risk-taking.*
IKEA	*humbleness, will-power, simplicity, thinking differently, avoiding bureaucracy, common sense, looking after the interests of the majority (of ordinary people).*
Reuters	*accuracy, freedom from bias, be open and accountable, innovation, speed, focus on customers, think global/local.*
SAP	*reliability, innovation, partnership.*
SOL	*sunny customers, sunny employees, best at what we do.*

Of course, we have encountered many companies across the years, whose value statements are of very little real impact. And our case-study CEOs are almost universally dismissive of the standard mission statement.

In general, however, value statements by the high-performing companies give the following.

- They genuinely represent the 'gut feelings' of the people in the business. They are not just the thoughts of a top management team, pulled together in an away weekend in a comfortable hotel. They are an evolved set of instinctive understandings about what is fitting and right.

- They portray the way things by and large are, rather than a set of pious hopes. Values can't be created by speeches or exhortation, no matter how charismatic; they can only be created by action and managed instinct. Only then are they credible enough to be written down. For most of Singapore Airlines' history, its values were unwritten. Says CEO Cheong: 'We tell our people at training courses that our values didn't come about because a group of us just sat down together and made a list. We asked ourselves, "How did we get where we are?" and, "What are the things that have been important to us – the things we have always abided by, all these years?".'

- They are part of the everyday language of decision making. 'It isn't that people refer to the values every day,' says Richard Beardon, Mexico-based President of Cadbury Beverages, Latin America, 'of course they don't. But the values provide basic building blocks, which are secure. People in Cadbury, wherever they are in the world, don't have to wonder where we stand on business ethics, for example. They know. It's fair to say that there are a number of people in the US operation who have spent enough time in the UK to appreciate and respect the values. We appreciate and practise those values. But, to be candid, the US operation is an amalgam of cultures. In 15 years we've gone from a 20 million case a year Schweppes business, which is all we were, to a billion case business in the US. We've done that largely by acquisitions. We have adopted values from the UK but you also have to build in values from all the companies you acquire to reach a best practice culture.'

Another common factor to the values statements of our high-performance companies is that their values tend to be both few in number and powerfully emotive. The largest number of any company in our study is seven (at Reuters). This fits well with the conclusions of the insightful analysis of the dynamics of vision within successful organisations by James C. Collins and Jerry I. Porras, in their book *Built to Last: Successful Habits of Visionary Companies*. They maintain that: 'Companies that enjoy enduring success have core values and a core purpose that remain fixed, while their business strategies and practices endlessly adapt to a changing world.' Our own studies broadly support this view, although it is clear that values *do* sometimes evolve in their interpretation and meaning. Collins and Porras say that the companies they have studied have 'outperformed the general stock market by a factor of 12 since 1925'. They describe core values and core purpose as the key constituents of core ideology: 'the enduring character of the organisation – a consistent identity that transcends product or market life cycles, technical breakthroughs, management fads and individual leaders'.[3]

Core values, according to Collins and Porras, are few but powerful, rarely numbering more than five. They represent beliefs that will stand the test of time. Core purpose is 'the organisation's reasons for being ... people's idealistic motivations for doing the company's work'. Larger than life, core purposes cannot normally be achieved in one persons lifetime, if ever. They stimulate organisational change as successive generations of managers strive to find new ways to get closer to the ideal.

Most of our high-performing companies take care not to confuse core purpose or vision with 'mission statements' – especially the kind that are full of exalted philosophy and grand prose. For example, at Vodafone, says Julian Horn-Smith, Managing Director of International Operations: 'We don't have a mission statement. We don't need to do that – we all know what business we are in. I'm personally sceptical about the fad of mission statements.'

What our companies do have is relatively simple and straightforward statements of purpose. Southwest Airlines' mission is to deliver 'positively outrageous service at unbelievably low prices'. IKEA's (lengthier) is 'to contribute to a better everyday life for the majority of people, by offering a wide range of home furnishing items of good design and function, at prices so low that the majority of people can afford to buy them'. The Berkeley Group's is simple: 'A passion for building'.

One of the most interesting sets of values (referred to as key success factors) came from Microsoft. The six were:

- a long-term approach (including strategic thinking and developing our people);
- results ('We drive for immediate results');
- teamwork ('We get things done in a complex environment');
- a demand for individual excellence;
- a passion for our products; and
- continuous customer feedback.

These make up three pairs of natural tensions or balances. Long-term thinking and immediate results are apparent opposites; so are teamwork and individualism; so are technology push and market pull. These values were not derived as a wish-list; they come from a detailed analysis of what had led to business success in the past. Managing balances has therefore been an overt part of Microsoft's competitive edge from its early days. More recently, Microsoft has revised its six values to four, combining two sets to read 'teamwork and individual drive' and 'a passion for our products and customers', to emphasise that these balances must be maintained.

Articulating the values

One of the companies focused on by Collins and Porras is Sony. Sony's remarkable growth over 40 years has been underpinned by a set of values that have evolved only slowly over the years. The three core values expressed in the 1950s were:

• Elevation of the Japanese culture and national status. By this, the company meant, in particular, that it was important to change the global perception of 'Made in Japan' from 'poor quality' to 'high quality'.

• Being a pioneer, not following others; doing the impossible. David Pearson, Managing Director of Sony UK, explains: 'It wasn't about being arrogant, it was about survival. Sony had to break free from the Japanese herd mentality; it had to do what others didn't. A good example was in colour television. We didn't invent it, and RCA led the market with its Shadowmask technology. But we knew that being first wasn't as important as being the best. So top management bet the company on Trinitron, which we launched a few years later in 1968.' Trinitron is still, 30 years later, the industry standard.

• Encouraging individual ability and creativity. 'That's about being different in people terms,' says Pearson. 'Respecting individuality is very unusual in the Japanese culture. Sony, along with other post-war companies such as Honda and Canon, are regarded as mavericks by their peers in Japan.'

The first value was adapted by Akio Morita, Chairman of Sony in the late 1980s, because it had largely been fulfilled. 'Made in Japan' was now synonymous with high quality. Morita coined the term 'glocalisation' to cover more than just 'think global, act local'. He intended, says Pearson, 'taking the standards achieved in Japan and making them global, so – insofar as Sony goods are concerned – "Made in Wales" would be as good as "Made in Japan".' The change was inspired in part by the need to manufacture close to developed world markets and in part by the need to export production from Japan to the developing countries.

A fourth value, customer value, was added later by Morita's successor Ohga. 'The reason it wasn't there before,' says Pearson, 'was that no one thought it necessary, it was so obvious. Only when the company was very big and successful did it start to have significant numbers of people who never met customers.' Ohga called the new value CS100. 1 stands for treating each customer as an individual; 0 for zero defects; the final 0 for zero complaints.

Sony's current president, Nobuyuki Idei has begun to shift the core value of being different. The intention is not to abandon it, but to redefine it in a manner more relevant to an age where competitive advantage comes from establishing the technical standard that others must adhere to. He explains: 'Sony used to make things that were different from everyone else. That is what made a product a Sony. We ourselves may have come to think that being Sony meant doing something different. But I think this is wrong. I think it is possible to make the same things as everyone else and still make something uniquely Sony. For users, what makes something a Sony is that it is good. It is a perception of reliability, good design, sophistication and something slightly unique. In the age of the network, we have to continue to redefine what makes something a Sony.'[4]

At Boots, formalising the values has been an uphill task, says Lord Blyth. 'We have had a huge internal debate about whether and how to define the core values, by which we run the business. About two years ago, we set out to write them down. Then we ran into huge conflicts between individual businesses or between businesses and the centre. Getting the whole organisation to sign up became incredibly difficult, so we ended up with just three paragraphs.'

Those three paragraphs contain just four values: well-managed, ethical, socially responsible and building shareholder value. Indeed, says Blyth, the first three are simply the way to achieve the fourth. 'The fundamentals of how this organisation thinks is the continuing delivery of long-term value to the shareholders. That's it. We start and end there. We don't want to trammel individual parts of the business with declarations of intent that are so imprecise they are meaningless. Instead, the individual businesses have taken on the issue and added their own values, relating to the things they want their people to be clear about.'

Ingvar Kamprad, the founder and Chairman of IKEA, refers to the values he tries to create in the organisation as his 'testament'. Developed in 1976, they are unchanged today. One of the core values is that IKEA must always offer a substantially lower price than its competitors. CEO Anders Moberg told the *Financial Times*: 'It puts a lot of pressure on us. Our people cannot compensate [for increased costs] with price increases. They have to get volume growth and better efficiency in our stores.'[5]

In the United States, Wal-Mart's aggressive growth has been supported by two core values: customers should be provided with what they want, when they want it, all at a value; and team spirit, that is 'treating each other as we would hope to be treated, acknowledging our total dependency on our Associate-partners to sustain our success'.

Marks and Spencer's core values – quality, value and customer service – were established in 1886 by the company's two founders. They run, says Chairman Sir Richard Greenbury, 'through the business like blood through veins, from sales assistant to chairman. We forget them sometimes, but we pay a price when we do.'[6]

At Reuters, the company's seven core values (as listed in the foregoing table) are written down. Says Chief Executive Peter Job: 'There are all sorts of vulnerabilities – if we get the information wrong, or we upset the authorities in a certain country. We have to rely on what we've relied on since 1851. We don't make judgments. We're fast and we're accurate. That is the best safeguard. That editorial philosophy is so embedded here that no one would have to consult about it, it is just a given. Reuters is risk-averse. We're not writing highly opinioned pieces, we're objective.'

Two values in particular emerge from all the interviews we conducted with Reuters people – impartiality and valuing change. Both are part of the journalistic legacy. Explains Executive Director David Ure: 'Neutrality, in terms of not siding with one bit of the market against another, of dealing with all-comers in an equal way, runs through the organisation and all its commercial approaches. It's almost invariably an asset to be neutral as opposed to a disadvantage. There's an illusion occasionally that it is a disadvantage, because it would be very nice to cosy up to one particular group or segment of the market. People who have been around in this building a long time recognise that that would be fatal.

'Change to us is fun. Change is a way of life. We would all just shrivel up and die if things stopped. We are driven by when the sun comes out every day, having something new to do. It's a value people who have been through or near to journalism have picked up. But you don't have to be a journalist to have this value system. Ironically those values are probably more shared now by non-journalists than journalists.'

Reuters people, wherever they are, share the same basic values, says Executive Director Jean-Claude Marchand, responsible for Europe, the Middle East and Africa. 'There's a huge Reuters proudness ... a Reuters culture backed up by strong local cultures.'

SOL hasn't written down its values. CEO Liisa Joronen explains that they are so simple, everyone recognises them: 'a sunny customer [one who is more than satisfied] with a sunny service cleaner; and being the best in all we do. The values are in people's minds.' People are reminded of the values by the strong symbolic presence of sunny yellow everywhere in the company. Says Joronen: 'When SOL people attend external or internal training sessions they always use yellow. That also happens when we have our own parties or we attend customers' parties. During SOL days, which we have three times a year always during the weekend, everyone is dressed in yellow. Yellow is a big part of the company culture.'

When rules rule

Although our case-study companies emphasise values, they also recognise that rules can be useful, too. In a regulated industry, for example, rules help prevent employees from landing the company in trouble with the authorities. Rules are also helpful for new employees, providing them with guidance on what to do, while they figure out or absorb why. Rules provide a logic for dealing with crises, when there is no time to sit down and work out the best approach to a problem.

Rules don't have to be written down. In fact, they may be more powerful if they are not written down. SOL, for example, has few – if any – written rules, but lots of unwritten ones. Says CEO Liisa Joronen: 'The cleaners must wear their uniforms when they are cleaning, and when we go to customers, we wear yellow.' Call it peer pressure, or alignment with the values, or simply pride in being part of the SOL team, but people expect to behave according to the rules and expect their colleagues to do the same. People don't *have* to turn up to weekend staff meetings in the company uniform, but by and large they do because it's what their colleagues would expect.

But rules written or unwritten are what make organisations inflexible. They can inhibit customer responsiveness, innovation and the development of both individual and team competence. When rules rule, people carry out tasks for their own sake, rather than to achieve specific objectives; people find it difficult to feel part of a goal greater than themselves; and opportunities to delight customers or seize competitive advantage pass by unnoticed.

Our high-performance companies all work on the principle of having the minimum rules possible. So, for example, Southwest Airlines spends considerable time and effort encouraging staff to make up their own minds about the right thing to do. CEO Herbert Kelleher talks of 'giving people the opportunity to expand beyond the horizons the organisation tries to define for them'.

At ASDA, says Archie Norman: 'We're not big on rules. The way we look at it is that rules never motivate anybody. You do have to have rules in any business and form of human enterprise because there are some things which are unacceptable – there are some performance criteria which, if we didn't meet, we should not open the shop in the morning. If the floor is dirty, we're not meeting basic hygiene or health and safety requirements, for example. So there are rules and people have to be aware of them, but once you've established those at that basic level, everything else is to do with achievement. You can't control exactly what people will do but if you give them levels of achievement to aspire to then they will strive to do better. If you give them rules, they'll strive to avoid failure and striving to avoid failure is not very motivating.

'The other problem with rules, is that all rules have to be enforced. A rule unenforced is not a rule. In fact, it's even worse; it's actually saying that what the management say round here doesn't matter. So, if you have an organisation run by rules, you have to have enforcement mechanisms, which lead on to checking and controlling and punishing and that's a very short step away from a fear culture. A very high proportion of retailers are driven by that – checking, controlling, punishing and a fear culture. It can work, it does work so long as behaviour in the retail store and in serving customers is driven by highly simplified, lowest common denominator behaviour. You fill shelves this way, then I can measure that and I can control how you do it, and therefore I don't have to worry about higher productivity, about any particular skill, about learning to bake a loaf of bread or make a cake or smiling at customers.'

At IKEA, says Sven-Olof Kulldorff: 'We don't like rules. We agree about this and we like that – but when it comes down to rules about small things, we are not an easily led or guided organisation.'

The principle of operating principles
....

As the arbiters between values and rules, operating principles are how the organisation sustains its flexibility. They are in the middle of the scale of mutability. Core values are set in stone. 'They may evolve, but they don't change' says Electrocomponents' Bob Lawson. Evolving usually means a reassessment or redefinition of meaning, in order to match the social and economic environment better. So evolution is unlikely to take less than 10 or 20 years.

Rules change frequently. They are a tool for instant response to events in the environment. They may be radically overhauled by a new manager, at any level, or shifted *pro tem* to meet a sudden need for, say, a freeze on recruitment or capital investment. In theory, rules should operate in line with the core values, but it is fairly easy for the two to become misaligned. For example, several years ago an airport authority launched a comprehensive and expensive campaign to promote customer service among ground staff. At the same time, a handful of security and cleaning staff were caught helping an illegal immigration ring. The manager responsible for these staff issued a new rule – no talking to anyone not in uniform. So when customers approached security or cleaning staff to ask for directions, they just turned away. Had the manager acted within the values, a more sensible solution would have been found!

Operating principles can be any generally accepted behaviour that bridges values and rules. Collins and Porras quote in their book[7] an anonymous company, where the top team debated whether quality was a core value. Could they be sure that customers would still insist on quality in 20 years time? The answer was no; so it was not a core value. We would say that, in that case, quality was an operating principle.

Operating principles are reasonably long-lived, but not immutable. They simultaneously interpret the values and draw general conclusions from rules. They can be (and often are) replaced or adapted as the strategy changes and different behaviours need to be emphasised. They are typically far more numerous than core values (with which they are often confused), but much fewer than rules.

Operating principles also provide a means of customising the culture in the operating units, without compromising the core values. Says Electrocomponents' CEO Bob Lawson: 'We have no Brits overseas, except on short-term assignment. Our culture is to bring non-UK top management here for a year to absorb the culture and way we do things. At the end of that time they've got the 'fundamental gold'. One of the jobs of the CEO is to build and protect that. The moment he sells it short, you're finished.'

Some examples of operating principles include:

- The Berkeley Group's Graham Thomson, Chairman of Berkeley Homes (North London) Ltd: 'One of the principles of the philosophy they gave me when I joined the company 14 years ago was "Never confuse effort with achievement." '

Then there were a number of points around:

  → acting properly towards employees, customers and shareholders;
  → long-term gain rather than short-term;
  → aiming to provide customers with superior products; and

> → using our endeavours to employ the best people at every level in the company.

- 'There is no such thing as an average customer' – N. Brown.

- Marks & Spencer had six guiding principles, established in the 1930s by Simon Marks and Israel Sieff:[8]

> → To offer customers a selective range of high-quality, well designed and attractive merchandise at reasonable prices under the brand name 'St Michael'.
> → To foster good human relations with customers, suppliers and staff, and the communities in which we trade.
> → To encourage our suppliers to use the most modern and efficient techniques of production and quality control dictated by the latest discoveries in science and technology.
> → With the co-operation of our suppliers, to ensure the highest standards of quality control.
> → To plan the expansion of our stores for the better display of a widening range of goods (and) for the convenience of our customers.
> → To simplify operating procedures so that the business is carried out in the most efficient manner.

Revised from time to time, these have been the basis of the company's approach to people, products, property and suppliers ever since.

- General Electric's Jack Welch promoted six basic operating principles (he called them rules, but it's clear what he meant) when he started his revolution at the US business giant.[9] These were (and still are):

> → Control your destiny, or someone else will.
> → Face reality as it is, not as it was or you wish it were.
> → Be candid with everyone.
> → Don't manage, lead.
> → Change before you have to.
> → If you don't have a competitive advantage, don't compete.

- Electrocomponents has four basic operating principles, says CEO Bob Lawson:

> → get clarity about what to control
> → communicate it
> → put in the systems you need
> → be open that they will change over time

'It's all about meeting objectives,' he adds. 'I was amazed at how many rules we had, that I and the people round me didn't know about. What actually runs our business is the operating principles.'

- SAP's operating principles include maintaining as flat a hierarchy as the local culture will allow; and taking the long-term view.

- Although Boots struggled to articulate core values at the group level, it has always placed great importance on its operating principles as the practical manifestation of its values. Says David Kissman, Director of Personnel for Boots the Chemist: 'For example, we were practising equal opportunities long before it became the issue it is today. We would rather practise it than write about it.'

So how do our high-performing companies get to the point where their values become part of the genetic make-up of the organisation? We found several common factors:

- having the right role models where they will make a difference;
- does the furniture fit the house? – managing the unconscious messages;
- continuously looking for opportunities to reinforce the values; and
- managing the operating principles, keeping the rules at bay.

HAVING THE RIGHT ROLE MODELS WHERE THEY WILL MAKE A DIFFERENCE

We will explore this issue in more depth in Chapter Eleven, which concentrates on how leaders make use of the values to drive performance. However, a couple of examples illustrate the point:

- 'Trust comes back to the character, behaviour and values of the company' says Dominic Cadbury. 'You only achieve trust and retain it if you behave in a way which inspires trust. You can easily destroy and undermine trust if the behaviour is not consistent. I think it's largely built on behaviour. Lots of noble sentiments can be expressed in writing but they don't add up to a row of beans if your behaviour is not consistent with them. People judge you on your behaviour. Trust is living the values essentially.

   'Values like honesty, openness, and fairness are not going to change because the competitive arena changes. As the company becomes more international or global, so you are going to have new parts of the company where local values can be different. Yet this company will not have used bribery to establish itself in Russia, where life is very difficult, capitalism has only just got started, and there's a huge amount of lawlessness. It's extraordinarily difficult to get a building put up in time. There's much more red tape and bureaucracy and difficulties. Nevertheless, the core value of dealing in an even-handed and honest way continues to be what is practised. If we get the factory built on time, we got there through continuing to behave in the same way that we try to behave all the time.'

- Adds Atlas Copco's Hans Ola Meyer: 'I would say that certain individuals exemplify the culture. In particular, there are non-Swedes who carry the Atlas Copco culture more than any of the Swedes I can think of. They have seen that culture in many parts of the world.'

- At Electrocomponents, says CEO Bob Lawson: 'We were one of the first businesses to publish our salaries. I discuss it with people on the shop floor. No one gives a damn when it is out in the open. But if I didn't follow the rules on holidays, they wouldn't see it as right and fair.

  'Rightness has to come from the top; then everyone else looks after it for you. You can't say to people on the warehouse floor, "it's too danger-ous for you to drink at lunchtime," if you have a couple of glasses of wine over lunch.' [That applies to lunch away from the office as well, where he studiously sticks to sparkling water.] 'It's infinitely more power-ful to act it, than to say it,' Bob Lawson insists.

- At SOL too, Liisa Joronen sees her job in large part as providing a role model. Because the yellow colour symbolises the positive sunny service culture, Liisa Joronen always wears yellow. Even her swimsuit and evening dress are yellow. Joronen also sets the example in being self-sufficient. She explains: 'We do not have secretaries or other service people in SOL. Everyone writes his/her letters, sends faxes, takes copies, makes the coffee for customers, answers the phone etc. I must be the role model for everyone, and always do everything myself.'

MANAGING THE UNCONSCIOUS MESSAGES

A while ago, one of the authors of this work visited the training centre of a company that had been a high performer for many years, but was showing a distinct plateauing in its results (and has since undergone severe con-vulsions in an as-yet unsuccessful attempt to return to its previous levels of performance). At one side of the door to the converted stately home was a sign directing participants in a course on employee involvement and empowerment. On the other was a slightly larger notice, reminding people that parking at that spot was 'for directors and management grade 1 only'.

While the incongruity of these two messages was not lost on most of the participants, the managers only saw it when it was pointed out to them.

Living the values demands not just reinforcing behaviour on the part of senior managers; it also requires close attention to the unconscious messages that are sent out by what Harvard academic Ed Schein calls 'artifacts' – structures or tangible manifestations of the culture. The more strongly and widely values are shared, the more likely incongruities are to be identified and remedied.

So, for Rentokil Initial, for example, the core value of cost consciousness is reflected in the style of branch offices. Says CEO Sir Clive Thompson: 'Our costs are low. We see no reason why our premises should be lavish. You won't find Rentokil Initial in the most expensive buildings in a town. We go for small, low-cost premises because our customers don't come to our premises; we go to theirs.'

At SOL, the values of equality and concern for employees are emphasised by the quality of facilities such as the children's playground at company headquarters. Cost consciousness is also an important operating principle, which Joronen role models. She rides a yellow bike, travels tourist class and has the smallest car in SOL with a big sun on the car's bonnet and huge SOL logos on each side. At Bowthorpe, the existence of a dual career ladder (management and technical) reinforces the value the company places on its technical people. Few, if any, of these examples are deliberate demonstrations of the values in action; they are simply natural outcomes of the beliefs and sense of rightness that people in these businesses share.

An interesting example of how artifacts can demonstrate differences in values can be seen by comparing the annual reports of Sainsbury (*see* Chapter Fifteen) and ASDA. Sainsbury provides a picture of the board together in an office, presumably at headquarters. ASDA's directors are all pictured where the action is, on the shop floor.

Archie Norman at ASDA deliberately changed many of the artifacts to emphasise the change of culture he desired. For example, says Mike Killoran, Head of Customer Services: 'I remember before Archie and Allen arrived, we used to walk around the stores in pin-stripe suits with a name badge that said "Mr Killoran", and people used to call me that. I'd go to inspect the produce department in a store and the store manager – also in a suit with "Mr Smith" or whatever on his badge – would come along with me. I'd ask the store manager if there were any problems with produce, and he'd turn to the produce manager who was standing next to me and ask him. It was like hearing an echo. Archie and Allen introduced a "No Jacket Required" policy. My badge no longer says "Mr Killoran", it says "Mike, Happy to help". At the same time, the management structure was flattened.'

CONTINUOUSLY LOOKING FOR OPPORTUNITIES TO REINFORCE THE VALUES

At Singapore Airlines, the six core values are made part of everyone's induction training, where people are encouraged to discuss how the values should be applied and interpreted in their work. They also have to fill in a questionnaire about how they feel about and relate to the values. The values theme is then echoed and re-echoed in training thereafter, to ensure that new ideas and skills are always set within the values framework. Says a company spokesperson: 'All employees are reminded of the values frequently by their department managers. If they make a mistake, they can expect to be reminded how that affects a core value. For example, customer focus applies to both external and internal customers, so if someone takes a week to respond to a memo, they could expect to be reminded of the customer focus value.'

The main agents for communicating the values are the managers, but they are supported by wide publicity in the company newsletter and other materials. The unions also help. Says Managing Director Cheong: 'They will always let us know, especially in areas about concern for staff. We bring the unions into our management courses to make sure they discuss the values too.'

Southwest Airlines constantly reinforces its values through a hundred-person 'culture committee'. The committee meets out of normal work hours to discuss how to sustain 'the Southwest spirit'. The members take back the discussions to their own workplaces, to share with colleagues. In this way, the values are constantly discussed and made relevant to the work people do.

At GE, says Steven Kerr, Vice President for Corporate Leadership Development: 'We are very concerned that values should not be just a three-inch-by-four laminated card. With our students at Crotonville, we do a lot of backward imagining. "You are at the end of the year, celebrating success in inculcating the values of the business into your organisation. What are you doing now to make that picture a reality?"'

'The IKEA spirit' is similarly introduced to all new recruits and discussed with employees frequently. Based on founder Ingvar Kamprad's testament – an explanation of his fundamental beliefs about furniture retail – it provides a values framework that substitutes for rules and guidelines. Says Vice President Sven-Olof Kulldorff: 'We have a very strong company culture and everyone who comes into the company says "here is something very special." And you accept it and you like it – or you dislike it and then you walk away.' Senior managers are expected to set an example on all aspects of the culture. So, for example, says Kulldorff: 'I was in Asia last week and then Sunday evening I flew to Singapore and Monday morning there was a board meeting. One could say that from a very theoretical point of view it would have been better for me to fly business class, but we don't do that. Everybody flies economy.'

Changing the physical environment can have a significant effect on reinforcing values. At SOL, for example, CEO Liisa Joronen wanted to break managers out of the mindset that they were somehow more important than the people that worked for them. She explains: 'I meet a lot of managers socially and I am less and less able to understand why in the morning and evening they are able to make the coffee and take the dog out, yet when they come to work, they are not normal any more. They can't make the coffee, do their own letters, order a taxi – they use secretaries to do all the things they do themselves at home. The bigger they are, the more helpless they become. Why do offices have to look like offices and factories look dull? Why should you have a bigger and better office, the more important you are? These models are in our heads and they make us behave in stupid ways.' Wiping out the obvious trappings of power – secretaries, drivers, personal office space and so on – was a bold move. But it stimulated people to think creatively about a whole range of work issues. Most importantly, it allowed managers to step back from controlling behaviours and the cleaning staff to take personal responsibility for doing the job.

Taking a public stand on issues reinforces internal values powerfully. SOL, for example, believes strongly that people should be responsible for managing their own time; that recording and monitoring people's hours of work is an intrusion on trust and autonomy. Yet Finland – 'probably the most unionised country in the world' according to Joronen – has strict legislation requiring employees to record working hours, to prevent employees being made to work above the legal maximum each month. She says: 'We are the only company in the country that doesn't measure working time for many of our people, such as supervisors and office workers. I'd go to jail before I start to measure my people's time!'

Jack Welch at GE reinforces the value of 'boundarylessness' by rewarding employees who speak up. In one recent incident, after he and other executives had made a presentation to salespeople from the medical systems division, a young salesperson complained that the compensation system meant that he and his colleague didn't get paid on time and that it was causing hardship to their families. Welch used the opportunity to emphasise that this was just the kind of message top management should be getting. Once he had heard a few days later from the Vice President of Sales that the problem was fixed, he wrote to the salesperson, sending 'a modest CEO's award' of $1,000.

As these examples illustrate, management by values doesn't just happen. It is a process that demands continuous attention and an ability to take advantage of every opportunity for reinforcement. Put another way, every opportunity for reinforcement that is missed has the potential to become a negation of the values.

MANAGING THE OPERATING PRINCIPLES, KEEPING THE RULES AT BAY

A practical example of managing the operating principles is provided by Lord Blyth at Boots. He explains: 'You can put the values out front and say they are the overriding goal to aim for, but you also need to be obsessed by other things that are critically important. I went to see the Healthcare business some months ago and got a bee in my bonnet about the way in which we were packaging vitamin capsules. It was difficult to tell from the labels which product class they were in. We had some with 100 capsules, for two daily doses; some 60 capsules, one per day. They said, "That's not a problem." I said, "Do the research and tell me how many should be in those packs and I bet it should be a multiple of 30. I bet you need to colour code the packages to describe the type of vitamins in them. If you do that, consumers will welcome it."

'I went back three months ago. They said, "You were right." You have to be very determined in pursuing things that you believe are important; then the message gets compounded throughout the organisation. What Blyth had done was to establish a clear operating principle, relating to the core value of ethicality – the company has a responsibility to make over-the-counter medicine as clear for the consumer as it possibly can and doing so is an important part of the relationship with the customer. The rules, largely defined by the economics of the packaging machinery, could then be modified in terms of the core values.

IKEA's experience in the United States caused it to re-examine several of its operating principles. While the values of low price and high quality were retained, the operating principle of 'always the same, everywhere' had to be drastically adapted to make the US business profitable. So out-of-touch were some of the products with American tastes that customers were buying flower vases as drinking glasses, because they found Swedish glasses far too small for drinks filled with ice. The US operation was given a lot more freedom to redesign products to meet local market needs and has had strong growth ever since.

Relying more on values and operating principles than rules to get things done takes courage and trust in people's innate ability to empathise with and reinforce shared beliefs. Getting this balance right makes it easier to manage all of the other, internally focused, balances. It also makes it easier to place the initiative for customer service largely in the hands of ordinary people, as we shall explore in Chapter Nine.

In summary...

High performing companies get people to do the right thing with the minimum of rules, by having a few, powerful values that drive decision-making and thinking. But values on their own are like a fly-wheel without a shaft – they need to be attached to the engine of the organisation for their power to be released. Clearly stated, often repeated operating principles provide the link. By managing the operating principles diligently and consistently, high-performing companies find that the values largely take care of themselves – and rules frequently are not required.

9 CUSTOMER FOCUS

Customer care versus customer count

'If there is one key lesson for us, it's that we have to stay with the customer. In fact, it's not one lesson but a whole series of lessons. Whenever we forget that we get a solid whack and we are brought back to reality.' *Cheong Choong Kong, Managing Director of Singapore Airlines*

'We have always been obsessed by our customers.' *Lord Blyth, Chief Executive of Boots.*

Is there a business anywhere that doesn't think it is customer-focused? Probably not. The past 15 years have ensured that most managers have been imbued with at least some of the language of customer care and quality. Asking top managers if their organisations are customer-focused is akin to questioning their intelligence. We have yet to see a company of any size or longevity that readily admits 'we really don't care about our customers'.

Nonetheless, there is something special about the relationships between high-performing companies and their customers. It isn't necessarily that they spend more on customer care than other companies, nor that they have more sophisticated systems of relationship management than their competitors (although both would be true in many cases). What makes them special is the fact that genuinely *do* make customer service a source of competitive advantage.

This is much harder than it seems. Although many companies aspire to achieving competitive advantage through service, very few succeed. There are several reasons for this. Firstly, it is hard to make customers notice the difference between service providers, unless one is *consistently* better than its rivals in the same market over a significant period. One or two experiences of excellent service by one company may be easily balanced by occasional bursts of excellent service from another; and vice versa. To really notice the difference in service quality – to the extent that they are conscious of it and act as goodwill ambassadors for the company – customers need to feel that several of the criteria (conscious or unconscious) on which they judge service are routinely dealt with substantially better by that company. You don't achieve that kind of differentiation unless it is either built into the fabric of the organisation or unless the leadership structure, from top to bottom, is obsessed with creating a difference customers will notice.[1]

Secondly, competitive advantage can only be sustained through constant evolution. Both the front-line systems and the behaviours of customer service are becoming increasingly easy to copy, at least superficially. So staying ahead demands more than just watching the competition's latest move. It requires a company to establish a sufficient lead in the service race that it can frequently climb trees and take a broad, long-term perspective on how to stay ahead. Again, you don't establish that kind of lead by keeping pace with the pack.

Thirdly, there is a perpetual conflict between the need for achieving the required volume of customers and the need to make each customer feel uniquely served. This conflict becomes most obvious when companies fail to match capacity to demand, allowing long queues to form. If long queues are not part of the customer expectation (the psychological contract) then frustration and customer dissatisfaction rapidly set in. The more customers a business acquires, the more difficult it becomes to treat them as individuals, to retain their interest and loyalty. Yet business growth usually demands increasing numbers of customers.

Fourthly, customer expectations don't stand still. What was yesterday's delightful surprise is today's norm. Companies have to calculate carefully the cost of new service features against what the customer will pay. Yet it takes a great deal of courage and commitment to balance the question 'Would our customers appreciate this?' not against 'Can we get sufficient immediate return on the investment in the short term?' but against 'Will it provide sufficient long-term competitive advantage?'.

Fifthly, it's more important to be aware of what your customers are thinking than what your competitors are thinking. Says Dr Claus Heinrich, member of the board of SAP AG: 'We focus all the time on our customers. We cannot get too bogged down with analysing competitors because we have different competitors from three years ago and they will be different again in three years time. There are a whole myriad of competitors and we don't focus too much on them. They can make mistakes, and if we follow them too closely, that may happen to us. We have a very large customer base and we concentrate on this.'

Our high-performance companies have met all these challenges and drawn the sting from them. They do so in a variety of ways, but in particular:

- recognising that the best customer is usually an existing customer;
- focusing on the customers they really want to keep;

- building both relationships and databases; and
- putting competitive advantage before cost.

The best customer is usually an existing customer

'Market share issues have never been important to me at all,' says Sir Roger Hurn of Smiths Industries. Far more important is maximising the value of the customers the company has, most of whom are long-term partners. 'We are not pursuing volume; we are pursuing high-value niches with technology and marketing pluses. It's a deliberate choice that enables us to maintain a high margin, a high market profile in terms of brand, and to introduce products under that brand that have a Jaguar type of image.'

Smith's Industries represents one end of the spectrum of solutions to balancing volume against service quality. By sticking firmly to the quality end of the spectrum, it is able to achieve the margins it needs to stay ahead on innovation. Its customers pay, because they perceive significant additional value in dealing with Smiths Industries companies compared with cheaper competitors. For instance, says Sir Roger: 'Anaesthetists insist that their hospital supplies departments specify Portex single-use tubes, which command a premium over the commodity items, because they know they will be getting a product with a higher performance. After all, it is a product which has been developed by paying very close attention to their particular requirements.'

Rentokil Initial takes a similar approach. It sees service quality as the main hook to retain customers and is unashamed about being more expensive than its competitors. 'We have got to be better than our competitors because, to people in our industry, Rentokil Initial is the model. So people who set out to be like us use us as the price benchmark, against which they have to discount. The reason our margins are higher is that our prices are 15–20 per cent higher than those of our competitors and our costs are 10 per cent lower. We are not embarrassed by that!'

And at the other end of the spectrum that ranges from a quality niche and high price to the volume market and a low price, Vodafone and its competitors are perforce engaged in a fierce battle for share in a market where economies of scale are essential both to the bottom line and to achieving the margins that finance service improvements.

Reuters, too, is well aware that the success of new products depends on market acceptance, which in turn requires a critical mass of subscribers to the service. In the case of dealing products, for example, take-up by key players in the markets makes it easier to sell the service to other customers.

At the same time, the usefulness of the product or service is often determined by the number of computer terminals using it. The issue, then, is a combination of customer care and customer count.

As Finance Director Rob Rowley explains: 'Transaction products are contingent on a number of key players being willing to accept the concept and run with it. In the rating of the financial markets, you have got to see who the shakers and movers are and you have got to work with them in areas where you want to introduce change. You can't usually impose these changes on the markets. The reason we are able to roll out new products into these marketplaces is because customers – typically in the trading areas – are always looking for new ways of doing things, for new sources of profit.'

In between on the spectrum sit the airlines, where the scale of competition makes niche picking largely untenable yet where customers will pay for consistent quality of service. A handful of airlines – in particular, British Airways, Southwest Airlines, Singapore Airlines and Swissair – have successfully distanced themselves from the pack and shown the benefits in terms of profitability and growth in passenger numbers. Singapore Airlines, for example, although based in one of the smallest countries in the world, is one of the largest airlines in the world by market value (50 per cent higher than British Airways and only slightly behind Nippon Airways).

The keys here seem to be to maintain a constant pace of service innovation (*see* Chapter Four) and to invest heavily in quality of both customer impression management and, in particular, customer recovery. Singapore Airlines exemplifies both. In terms of innovation, it has always been at the leading edge, from complimentary hot towels to high technology. Says Director of Marketing Services Theong Tjhoen Onn: 'We have a long tradition of innovation dating back to the 1970s. We were the first to put in additional crew, to provide a more personal service, choice of meals and complimentary drinks. More recently, we were the first to introduce a global in-flight fax/telephone service for business passengers, and our in-flight entertainment is the most comprehensive in the industry at the moment.'

A CONSTANT PACE OF SERVICE INNOVATION

'We don't innovate for its own sake. We do so to improve the service and comfort of customers, so they come back. We have to be the innovation leader in our industry,' says Singapore Airlines' MD Cheong. Adds a senior colleague: 'Two years ago, we started our "Outstanding Service on the Ground" programme to expand our excellent service standards in the air to the ground operation. We wanted to ensure that, from the moment a customer makes contact with us to the moment they leave us, they experience excellent service. So, from ticketing to check-in, through boarding, in flight and at the other end with baggage handling, we provide excellent service. We see a baggage problem as an opportunity to impress the customer. We try to turn a negative experience around. Say a flight can't take off because of technical reasons. A delay is a financial disaster for an airline, but we train our staff to respond very quickly, to ensure hotel accommodation is arranged and an apology made. All staff are trained in this sort of crisis management. Every problem is an opportunity to impress and satisfy customers. It's amazing the number of letters of praise we receive in such situations. The reason is that we ensure that problems such as delays are very carefully managed.'

'Reuters too builds customer relationships through constant updating of its existing products and introduction of new products,' says director David Ure. The company does this through high levels of account management with customer help desks around the world, and the fact that it is global and local with service in 24 languages. As a result it maintains an ongoing dialogue with customers all over the world.

IMPRESSION MANAGEMENT

The phrase 'orchestrating the customer experience' comes from BA's Chairman Sir Colin Marshall. His vision of competitive advantage was that it would come through BA providing a better experience across the five basic services the company delivered: 'Get passengers where they want to go, do it safely, go when they want to go, provide some nourishment and let them accrue frequent-flyer miles.' On their own, none of these services could create long-term customer loyalty – it was easy for rivals to duplicate or exceed them individually, for example, by offering more air miles. Linked together into a seamless experience, however, with excellence in each, they became a powerful engine for differentiation. The mission of the airline's customer services department is 'to ensure that British Airways is the customer's first choice through the delivery of an unbeatable travel experience'. That doesn't sound too different from many other aspiring service deliverers; the difference is that BA by and large seems to have made it work.

Daniel Bernard at Carrefour also subscribes to the notion of customer experience. He explains: 'The store must be a place where people can be happy and go and get everything they need. There has to be some spectacle. For example, our fish counters are like theatrical experiences, beautifully arranged and dramatic.'

An interesting aside on how high-performance companies sustain employee commitment to managing customer impression is the way they use negative stories. Managers don't just explain what behaviours they do want; they also draw on a fund of anecdotes about customer service failures to dramatise the issues when they discuss them with employees. So, for example, John Rugman, Head of Human Resources Services of GKN recalls: 'I remember, about 1976, I was sitting in the PA's office of a senior manager who ran a large chunk of the automotive components business. She was on the phone to a customer who was trying to speak to the senior executive and she was refusing to let him speak. He had obviously got part of his line stopped because of a problem we had, yet she was giving him a hard time, as if it was his fault and her boss was much too important.' Such accounts often bring customer service issues to life far more vividly than any amount of demonstrated good practice.

CUSTOMER RECOVERY

An innovation in British Airways has been to recognise that customers whose luggage has been damaged rarely relish the thought of having to go out, in their own time, to buy a new suitcase, make a claim to the airline and then argue the value of the damaged item. The standard airline process elongates the period of distress and frustration felt by the customer. Far better to maintain a stock of the most common luggage (bought at hefty discount from the manufacturers) and replace damaged items on the spot.

One of the most effective customer-recovery processes is operated by The Berkeley Group, where, says Chief Executive Tony Pidgley: 'If we find we've built a bad house, we'll buy it back immediately, or do whatever work is necessary to put it right. If there's a problem, I or the Chairman, whoever is necessary, will arrive immediately and we're always very honest with the purchaser. We've only ever had four bad houses and the owners are all personal friends of ours now.

'If a client moves into a house and something's not quite right, that can lead to a lot of irritation even if it's only a small thing that's wrong. We expect a director to get on the phone to the customer or jump in a car and go see them. It's our reputation that's at stake. It's often not the size of the problem, it's the speed of response that counts.'

At Granada, too, the emphasis on customer recovery has been an important part of increasing profit performance. Says Roger Mavity, Managing Director of the company's rental division: 'I don't agree that customers only give you one chance. They'll give you a second, but not a third. If you bend over backwards to put things right, you can actually seal the relationship. That problem is a window of opportunity which can go either way. The mistake is to miss that chance to cement the relationship.'

One lesson Mavity and his colleagues have learned from listening to customers sympathetically is the importance of rapid response. 'We used to investigate every individual complaint with almost masochistic thoroughness. That might easily take two weeks. So by the time we got back to the customer, even though our response was technically very correct, it was so late that the sheer delay confirmed their bad impression of our service standards. We realised we had to speed things up. As most customer complaints fall into one of a small number of categories, we developed a simple, standard procedure for dealing with each of these main categories. That gives us the tools to answer virtually every customer complaint, not only well, *but very quickly.* The pace of response is crucial if you are going to win back the customer's confidence, because it is the pace of response which proves that you have taken the issue seriously.'

Customer recovery has been an issue of continuous interest to us since the original *Winning Streak.* One of the conclusions that emerges from subsequent, largely unpublished research is that the customer's self-esteem is more important in the recovery process than any other factor. The level of compensation, the degree of satisfaction (or mollification), the sense of having been fairly or unfairly treated all have at their roots the extent to which the customer feels respected and valued. The fact that so many of our high-performing companies talk about friendship – a very soft value – with their customers says a great deal. Customer recovery is at root about finding ways to build a great relationship out of a shared problem.

Focusing on the customers you want to keep

Even those high-performance companies competing for volume have a clear identity of the customers upon whom they wish to focus and why. For example, Rentokil Initial's Sir Clive Thompson is vehement that the company only 'wants to be in markets where the quality of service is important to customers'. So, when major opportunities for expansion into the public sector appeared in the late 1980s, Rentokil Initial was content to let them slip by. 'We didn't go into UK utilities markets such as waste disposal as they opened up, because contracts were always going to be awarded based on price. They would be won by clever accounting techniques, not quality of service delivery,' he explains. So Rentokil Initial focused its efforts on international expansion in markets that could deliver the kind of margins the company demanded.

British Airways looks for customers who are 'willing to pay a slight premium for superior service'. By 'slight' it means about five per cent. 'On our revenues of £5 billion,' Sir Colin Marshall told *Harvard Business Review*, 'that five per cent translates into an extra £250 million'.[2]

He went on to explain: 'Even in a mass-market business, you don't want to attract and retain everyone. The key is first to identify and attract those who will value your service and then to retain them as customers and win the largest share of their lifetime business. We know that 35 per cent of our customers account for more than 60 per cent of our sales. Commitment to customer service, innovation and quality has enabled British Airways to hold on to its margins, at times when serious cut-price competition has broken out in the air travel market. This has brought profitable growth and the ability to re-invest in products and services, so keeping us a step ahead of the competition.'

N. Brown's detailed segmentation allows it to identify the customers it most wants to keep against its criteria of recency, frequency and speed. Says Bob Cunningham, IT Director: 'As we add more and more information about a customer's preferences, the more we can predict offers that will interest them. So the longer we have someone on file, the higher the value and the more marketing costs go down. The worst sort of customer for us is the one who we recruit, orders once and then returns the goods. Frankly, they are a disaster, because we've had all the cost of recruiting them with no profit. The ultimate goal would be to be able to predict behaviour at almost an individual customer level. Our goal is to attract sales with minimum costs. The ideal would be to know you were making an offer that the customer could not refuse.'

However, Bob Lawson of Electrocomponents takes a different line: 'We want to keep all our customers, but we service them all differently. If you let a customer go, that strengthens a competitor. The easy answer is to get rid of difficult customers. A better question is "How should I serve them?" It hurts when we lose a customer.'

In practice, because Electrocomponents has chosen to focus on a very specific market niche, there is little real conflict between his view and N. Brown's. At heart, the dilemma for companies here is how to define their target customers sufficiently narrowly to maximise unit profitability, yet sufficiently widely enough to achieve numbers and shut out competitors – in other words, quality versus volume. This will never be an easy choice, not least because the ground is constantly shifting. But the more convex the business focus, the easier it becomes.

Building both relationships and databases
....

Our case-study companies are fiercely protective of the relationships they have with their customers. For example, at Electrocomponents, says CEO Bob Lawson: 'We get very upset if any of our competitors outserve us with a customer. It's a personal affront if anyone else serves them better. We have three ground rules for customer service: we will be the provider of innovation to our customers; we will always provide the customer with an innovative solution; and we will always be their first choice.'

High-performing companies also seem to be remarkably adept at building relationships that go well beyond the transactional. The 'character' or 'personality' of the company colours its customer relationships. It is about more than just showing they care; it involves many of the elements of a personal friendship.

'Our customers want *us*,' says Smiths Industries' Chairman Sir Roger Hurn. 'Boeing want us on the programme because they know we deliver, we are prepared to invest, have the technology and the people both to back a programme and sort out any problems that might occur. That's the key. Do the customers actually want you to be part of the programme? It makes for very long-term relationships.'

In the automotive industry, GKN has developed close relationships with the customers it wants to be alongside by being very proactive. Explains Chairman Sir David Lees: 'Our whole approach is not to sit on our butts waiting for the customer to issue drawings to half-a-dozen manufacturers, but to get in at the early stages when a car is being designed. We say: "We have the technology, particularly in the driveline area, such that if you give us the specification, we will tailor a solution that will give you optimum cost and drive characteristics." Our strength is in having technical expertise that will add value to the customer.'

It has also accepted that, to be truly customer responsive, it has to be prepared 'to go anywhere in the world where our customers go, provided that there is sufficient scale there,' says Sir David. 'So Toyota, for example, knows that wherever they go in the world, we will have a supply capability there for them.'

Allen Yurko at Siebe regards customers as the main driving force behind the company's remarkable pace of technical innovation. 'What makes us different from most of our competitors is how closely we listen to our customers.' Yurko himself attends the big trade fairs and makes sure he has an opportunity to listen to the top 12 or 15 customers talking about their industry, their plans and their views of technical needs. 'Last year at our Foxboro Division, 39 out of 40 new products that we launched at the process automation trade show were customer-driven. Only one did the customers miss, a new software system based on Microsoft Windows. We did a survey and only 35 per cent of our customers thought it was a good idea. Before we dropped it, however, we changed the question and asked whether they thought it would be a good idea in five years' time. 78 per cent said yes. So we developed the product, at a total cost of $50 million.' Now it's selling like hot cakes.

Southwest Airlines makes a policy of involving the customers in its fun. Calls to make a reservation (the airline doesn't belong to any booking networks, so customers or travel agents have to dial direct) may be answered with: 'If you have been on hold for more than five minutes, push 8.' Then, a few seconds later: 'This didn't speed your call, but don't you feel better? You can push 8 as often as you like until an operator is free to take your call.' Staff have been known to surprise customers by hiding in the overhead lockers and the pilots and cabin crew go out of their way to create opportunities to laugh with the customers.[3]

JCB builds special relationships with customers by treating them all with great respect, on many occasions even providing an air taxi service to ferry them to the factory and back again. This means that a potential customer on the continent could visit the factory in Rocester near Uttoxeter, discuss any special requirements, and be back home in his own country in time for an evening meal. The setting of the factory in the middle of rural Staffordshire is an exercise in environmental sensitivity. The JCB factory is often cited as being a planners' role model of how industry can be merged successfully into a rural setting.

Home Depot spends heavily on training so that staff will always be knowledgeable about the products they sell. The term 'customer cultivation' was developed to describe the way in which store staff help a customer think through a home improvement, giving encouragement and advice until the customer has the confidence he or she can tackle it. Where appropriate, they will demonstrate building and repair techniques for the customer's benefit. If customers wish, they can come to evening workshops in the store, to learn skills and techniques from qualified craftsmen.

IKEA bases its customer relationships on a mix of price and value, and the shopping experience itself. Explains Vice President Sven-Olof Kulldorff: 'IKEA should be a day out. That started in the first store here in Almhult. In the old days, to come to our store they had to leave early in the morning. For an average customer, the journey would take a couple of hours and many of our customers had small children. So we have had crèches for a very long time, and facilities for children, and we have restaurants. We believe that the restaurant prices should be very low, so that customers with young families should be able to afford to eat there and not have to bring sandwiches. They shouldn't have to leave IKEA just because they are hungry. We don't have entertainers every day, but very often on Saturdays and Sundays we will have a clown for example.'

The special relationship that N. Brown establishes with its customers includes a number of service issues, but among the most important is stock availability. Says Chief Executive Jim Martin: 'Our researchers have shown that our customers require deliveries to be made consistently, and also expect a high level of goods to be in stock when they place their order, particularly when they are ordering a co-ordinating set, which requires matching. We pride ourselves on having one of the highest service levels for goods in stock. Initially this is between 90 and 92 per cent and the ultimate level of service, after 2 or 3 weeks when delayed goods have been received into our warehouse, takes that up to about 97 per cent.'

At Bowthorpe, CEO Nicholas Brookes expects every managing director and senior member of operational management to spend at least 40 per cent of their time directly with customers.

At The Berkeley Group, says Chief Executive Tony Pidgley: 'The passion we have feeds from the centre. If you aren't passionate about what you do, then you don't last in this business. Call a customer a punter in this organisation and you're in big trouble.'

It's the little things that make the relationship, believes The Berkeley Group. It constantly looks for new ways of making customers recognise that it cares. Says Tony Pidgley: 'We give all our customers a moving-in pack – all the documentation they need about their house in a leather binder. They cost us £80 each. When you buy a new car or fridge, for example, you expect that; but when you buy a house, which in all reality is probably your biggest expenditure, you don't. Most people have a dream. We try to sell them that dream. We advertise in *The Sunday Times*, we take the back page, because we want to appeal to people's lifestyle aspirations.'

Detail is also of critical importance to Reuters' customer relationships. Says Chief Executive Peter Job: 'Reuters has 15,000 people spread around the world in units which are not always very large. Those people have clients who have particular demands. When you buy a car, you just buy the car. It might have the steering wheel on the right or the left, but all the other essential characteristics will be pretty much the same. When you buy a Reuters service, if it doesn't have the local stock market on or doesn't have news in your local language, it may be of no use to you. So the local unit has a mission to make sure the features of the product are suitable for that particular market. That motivates and gives a lot of strength to that unit and also hopefully satisfies the customers. At the same time, each of the people in each of these units is made to feel part of a global nexus. More than 12,000 employees have access to an e-mail screen around the world, so electronically you can be in touch. We have a daily bulletin, a company forum. So, on the one hand we encourage people to be Russian in Russia, on the other they are plugged into a global network.'

At ASDA, says Archie Norman: 'If you have people who are competent and you hire the right people in the first place, people who are service-oriented, naturally positive in disposition, then you will create personality. Rather than inhibiting personality, you're freeing personality because they express themselves. An expressive store is a store which delivers service with personality. That's a much, much harder thing to do than simply making sure that you don't have checkout queues. If you can do it, then you've created a different kind of place to shop. Shopping is a chore and it can become a boring chore. And if you can make it a human exercise in which there is a personality, a bit of fun, some recognition that I'm part of a community, I'm valued in the store, then you've achieved something truly different.' Among many innovations ASDA has introduced to add sparkle to shopping are 'singles evenings', where customers can make new friends while picking up their week's grocery.

For Vodafone, customers were initially seen to be mobile phone service-providers. Carrier networks such as Vodafone were not encouraged to seek contact with service consumers. All that changed as new networks appeared. Having initially been wrong-footed, says Sir Gerald Whent, Vodafone needed to establish an identity with its ultimate customers. 'We have now swung our advertising around to umbrella advertising, as a brand. We re-established ourselves as number-one within 18 months.'

In general, the high-performing companies are effective at establishing relationships early on. They are also good at seeking out small customers who have the potential to develop into big ones. This is particularly true of the way they approach the developing world. For example, says Trevor Bonner, CEO of GKN's Automotive and Agritechnical Products Division: 'We went into Mexico in 1981, whereas a lot of other companies waited until the NAFTA agreement. Again, we went into the Chinese market in 1988 ahead of a lot of other companies.'

Corporate personality is a much deeper phenomenon than the corporate brand. The brand is the projected image – what I want the world to see about me – modified by what they actually do see. Personality is a combination of beliefs, values, foibles, traits and ways of looking at the world that can only be appreciated by those who get sufficiently close to see beyond the projected image and their own surface observations. Though strongly associated with culture, it is more than culture, just as an individual's cultural background is only part of their mental make-up.

When we say that someone has no personality, we are really saying that they are bland, dull and unexciting to be with. It would be hard to justify that statement insofar as our high-performance companies are concerned. They do not stand out just because they are consistently highly profitable, but equally because they are recognisably different from other companies in their personality. Some, such as SOL and Southwest are 'whacky'; others, such as Granada or Smiths Industries more straightlaced. Yet all the high-performing companies manage to imprint people to the extent that the perceptive observer can identify that they must have been a GE or Siebe or Carrefour person at some stage in their career – because the corporate personality is expressed most strongly through its people. For the customer, therefore, there is always something special about a relationship with the high-performance company, and with the people who are its front-line representatives.

It must also be said that personality doesn't have to be 'nice' to succeed, though it does have to be honest. A simple example makes the point: a free house (an English pub independent of any particular brewer) not far from London was run by a dragon of a landlady, who had never been known to smile in living memory. Scarcely a night went past without her insulting a customer deeply. Yet the pub was always packed with people who appreciated good food and beer from a genuine character. The down-turned mouth and insults were all part of the experience. When she retired at a ripe old age, some customers cried. As we saw in Chapter Five, it pays to be different. And one of the reasons why it pays is that customers prefer to associate with an organisation that is interesting, rather than one that is bland.

USING CUSTOMER KNOWLEDGE TO TARGET SERVICE

British Airways' advertising budget, though large, is proportionately less than many of its biggest competitors. The reason, says Sir Colin Marshall, is the effectiveness of its database marketing. BA tracks and records customers' flying patterns, any complaints they might make, their lifestyles and what they value from the service. It all helps the airline focus improvements and build repeat custom.

Electrocomponents builds and maintains a similar level of customer information, captured from the users of its catalogues. Says CEO Bob Lawson: 'We applied the principles behind the Tesco loyalty card. We capture by individual customer everything we do with them. We used to track companies, but then we missed valuable data.' Identifying and tracking several customers within a business increases sales because Electrocomponents can vary the catalogues it sends them. The ultimate aim is 'to have an offer directed to a market of one – to serve you among all the others uniquely.'

Clothing catalogue company N. Brown 'is probably the most complex mail order operation in the world,' says Marketing Director Nigel Green. That complexity in the back room allows it to deliver simple offers at the customer interface through a wide range of leaflets and catalogues targeted at specific 'files' – groups of customers with similar characteristics. In many cases, the 'file' has its own brand name. For each customer the company records recency, frequency and value of purchase, in other words the three key measurements that predict whether and what they will buy in the future. Knowledge about the customers allows N. Brown to develop highly targeted catalogues. Says CEO Jim Martin: 'To differentiate us from the competition and from the high street, we try to identify small groups of people who have particular needs. Some of our catalogues have products that run from the average of size 12 right up to size 26, and 32 in some cases. So we cater for the large lady in the way that a high street shop couldn't economically do – it couldn't display that many items. We've also identified that people who are short, less than 5'2", have a lack of choice in the shops too. We have the most comprehensive range of footwear in Europe. Clearly footwear shops only sell a limited range, and they tend to stock only average widths. We have a range of 3,500 with many widths.

'Our database has every customer transaction over the last three years, from monthly payments to all of the products she's bought from us, including the size, fitting and colour, the catalogue or promotion details, and the date of purchase, and any goods she has returned. We can build up an interesting picture of her behaviour, which helps us to tailor the catalogue to her particular needs and interests.'

IKEA has had a 'family club' from its early days, as a means of both rewarding customers and tracking their expenditure and tastes.

BUILDING RELATIONSHIPS THROUGH CUSTOMER LISTENING

'We have to end up with a large market share, to set the standards so people use our products. The only way to obtain and retain large market share is to get continual feedback from your customers,' says Mike Murray, Vice President Human Resources and Administration at Microsoft. Building relationships requires exceptional listening skills, combined with the willingness to 'unlearn' common knowledge. Singapore Airlines also uses a vast amount of customer research. Says Director of Marketing Services Theong Tjheon Onn: 'We don't try to second-guess what customers want; we ask them. We use focus group lunches with frequent flyers, customer surveys, letters and feedback gathered by staff, alongside media and industry surveys. It's very dangerous to guess what they want.'

A dual attention – both strategic and tactical – to complaints and customer perception throws up unexpected opportunities to adjust the services in line with customer needs. For example, says the company: 'Recently we've been receiving complaints about how elaborate the service is in First Class. We serve lots of courses and passengers suggested it was taking too long. Now we have a team researching how to speed things up without lowering quality. Ten years ago, this wasn't an issue; now, it's important to save time for our passengers.'

N. Brown carries out regular surveys of customers. It analyses these along with customer complaints in great detail, and publishes the results internally. In addition, it collates service failure down to fine details, such as a mechanical failure in the mailroom, to illustrate to staff the impact on customer service. Says Chief Executive Jim Martin: 'We are trying to develop a service quality culture and have been given some help to realise this from Manchester Business School. Clearly the merchandise level of service is important, but the time taken to deliver, the quality of customer communication, and the whole range of other activities relating to our management of this relationship are considered.

'We've managed to reduce this wide range of issues to a Quality Service Index, where we have identified 50 critical issues in the relationship between us and the customer. Each of these has a different weighting according to its importance as seen by the customer, and is calibrated to a maximum score of 1,000. This has become our real measure of success, rather than the previously simplistic measure of how many complaints we had received. The Quality Service Index is a more balanced attempt to arrive at the true level of service.

'I get that information on my desk weekly. We then cascade it down to the managers, who can then influence their own areas through regular team meetings.' Last year the company score averaged 738 out of 1,000. Martin doesn't think it's good enough.

Most of the high-performance companies carry out a great deal of customer research. Says Lord Blyth: 'Boots has always had a very strong tradition of doing exit surveys and finding out what customers thought of it. It has always been obsessed by its customers.' Putting that information to effective use in improving service has significantly benefited its positioning with customers, to the extent that Boots' reputation is not far behind that of Marks & Spencer. 'We regard that as a major source of competitive advantage,' Lord Blyth affirms.

It can be powerful medicine, if not particularly palatable, says Siebe Chairman Barrie Stephens: 'It's got to be a painful system. Regularly in all our companies we have an independent assessment of how their top one-hundred customers see them in terms of service, response to complaints, delivery capability and so on. Some of the answers are going to be very upsetting. But they get to the heart of what we have to do. Going through this kind of pain is part of our culture.'

IKEA bucks the trend among high-performance companies by carrying out relatively little *formal* customer research into new products. Jan Kjellman, head of its Swedish division, where the international design team is located, told the *Financial Times*: 'We don't ask so many questions before we start up things. Last year [1994] we launched the "Swedish Cottage" range without any market research, but the customer liked it very much.'[4] But IKEA does listen closely to its customers by carrying out continuous dialogue with them in its stores. Explains Sven-Olof Kulldorff: 'Being close to the customer means you know their needs. By being close to the factory as well, you also understand the construction processes, so you know how to get good value for money. This combination is important. We knew the customer wanted the Swedish Cottage range, for example. It's a lot of pine, and back-to-natural materials, and that is a trend. We knew it. A lot of products are developed that way. We know that there are opportunities to get good value-for-money products. That was no guess. But then we don't go on the product level and ask customers; we let people see it and react to it in the stores.'

Herb Kelleher of Southwest Airlines recalls: 'We had a little experiment here at Southwest recently, which we thought was terrific. We had a new programme that was really going to please our customers. And our people were very imaginative, very ingenious in coming up with it. They knew it would work. But our customers didn't like it. So everyone is sitting around and saying that our customers should like this idea. I said: "Well, they ... don't ... like it. So ... we're ... going ... to ... stop ... doing ... it."' Once the laughter had died down, the decision was taken and the lesson learned.[5]

Pat Farrah, a co-founder of Home Depot, doesn't have a title. He does have a job, however, criss-crossing the United States visiting stores to observe, teach and listen. Among the lessons he tries to inculcate into buyers is that they should always meet suppliers in the stores, where the customers (and instant opinions on any merchandise) are.[6]

At SOL, customer listening is the responsibility of the person who does the work – the cleaner. Each month, he or she asks the customer to fill in a comment form, which instead of numbers has laughs, smiles, frowns and tears. The company's goal is to have 90 per cent laughs or smiles across the board. Says Juuka Suuniitty: 'There have to be some kind of rewards for achieving goals. It could be that they made coffee together and had cake, or if a goal has been bigger they could go out together to have dinner. If they miss the target there is no reward.'

Each SOL cleaner has a 'quality passport' where they collect smiles and laughs. If they do not get the two highest scores, the unwritten rule is that they immediately discuss with the customer to find out why: no one is satisfied with the lower scores. Some supervisors have set the target with their cleaners to get 100 per cent – the highest score – every time through the year. And these people very often meet the target.

SOL has joint quality groups with its big customers. The members of the quality groups are representatives of the customer, the SOL supervisor and some cleaners. The purpose of the quality group is to develop the service together with the customer. 'It is very important that the cleaners are members of these quality groups,' says Joronen.

Putting competitive advantage before cost

Probably the most enduring example in our study of putting competitive advantage before cost is Boots the Chemist. The pharmacy business inside Boots stores has never been a startling profit performer. There are many other profitable uses to which the same store space could be put. But it has, till now, been a valuable differentiation between Boots and other high street retailers. Customers come into the store to spend a small amount of money on prescription drugs, but they usually leave with other, more profitable items as well. It is a trade-off that Boots has been more than happy to make.

Boots has also been happy to make the trade-off against stock availability and cost, to ensure that people find the goods they want when they are in the store. It currently achieves 95 per cent availability, a substantial improvement over the past decade. (In *The Winning Streak* we reported that, at one time, customers on average only spent 74 pence of each pound they had intended when they visited Boots stores, because they could not find the other products.)

At N. Brown, the trade-offs are mainly around stock availability and the vexed question of how much time telesales staff should spend talking with customers. 'Our staff will say, "It's a sunny day in Manchester, what's the weather like where you are?" If customers want to chat I won't rush them. We deal with a lot of elderly customers so that aspect is important,' says Director of Administration Iain Macfarlane. Time spent with the customer is an investment that pays off in increased sales.

Chief Executive Jim Martin talks of wanting to create 'a personal relationship ... an illusion of being a friend. If the customer would like to talk about a private situation at home, then the operator is encouraged to spend a little time with her, talking through that particular issue.'

Another difficult trade-off was whether to accept the costs of returned goods – about one per cent of total turnover. Says Jim Martin: 'We carried out a lot of research with our customers to identify their negative feelings about us. On many of the earlier surveys, the fact that they had paid postage for returned merchandise was in the top two or three issues. It is not necessarily our fault if the product doesn't match the rest of their wardrobe or they have ordered the wrong size, but it is an issue of concern to the customer. The rates of returns are high in our industry at more than 30 per cent of all goods despatched. As the profit impact of any change of policy in these areas would be significant, we carried out a test with two identical groups of customers. For the control-group customers we continued the current practice and the test group had their postage paid. Over the 12 months we discovered that the test group customers, although they returned more, did increase their net sales and the profit in the end, after payment for postage, was higher than on the control group. We have since also found that this test group of customers stayed with us longer. They had a greater bond with the business.'

It helps greatly to have discussions like this actively promoted, as well as supported from the top. Says Iain Beveridge, Distribution Director at the company's J.D. Williams operation: 'Our chairman is well known for his belief in satisfying the customer but also for running a tight ship. Having a customer champion at the top of the company is very important. Production numbers are all too easily associated with costs, so it's very helpful to have someone always attaching value to customer satisfaction, otherwise it would be too easy not to make it a priority.'

'Delivering the optimum level of service such that we make the optimum level of profit is a difficult balance,' says Rentokil Initial's Sir Clive Thompson. Underpinning that balance is, for Rentokil Initial, a clear operating principle: 'We do not compromise on price.' He explains: 'We don't market price; we cost price. Price is based on a formula, which takes account of how much the service will cost us and then builds in the margins we want ... Our view is that once you start negotiating on price, you end up negotiating anything and everything.'

For Granada, says Don Davenport, Group Managing Director of Granada Hospitality, the key is not just to taking costs out. It is also about improving quality at the same time. 'We start with what the customer wants and work back to see what we don't need, to reduce costs. You can keep taking costs out, but you have to find new ways to improve quality to compensate.

At Singapore Airlines, says Theong Tjheon Onn: 'How do we weigh the costs versus the benefits of a service improvement? Once we find out what passengers would like, we set up a task-force to evaluate the feasibility. We don't want to do something we can't support properly or sustain – you can fall flat on your face too easily. If there's a major cost, the issue is brought to the Executive Committee, which makes the final decision. We certainly look at the cost–benefit analysis, but where service is concerned it is often very difficult to attach the value of a new feature to the customer. We go by what the customers tell us and a certain amount of gut feel, especially in situations where we can't simply pass the cost on.'

'Where there is any doubt about operational ability or whether passengers really want the change, we test first. For example, at the moment we're looking at noise-reduction headphones for First Class customers. We've put in a trial because we are not sure customers would like the added weight and tightness, especially for long periods. So we put the new headphones on board for a month or so and collected feedback. As a result, we are now trying to modify the equipment to meet customer needs.'

At Electrocomponents, says Bob Lawson, 'Last year, we made a conscious decision to throw a lot of money into inventory, because of some supply problems. So we took the controls off: customer service was paramount. This year, we put the controls back on again and inventory has fallen again. But, boy, did we win in the marketplace.' Competitors who had focused on inventory cost made a short-term saving but paid for it in terms of customer goodwill.

Marks & Spencer sees staffing levels as a critical component of customer service, and one on which it must not compromise. So, rather than add another £50 million to the bottom line in the short term, says Chairman Sir Richard Greenbury, it took the longer view: 'We could certainly have made more money this year, and much more money last year, if we hadn't put 3,000 more staff in the stores over that period. With 300 stores, that works out at ten people per store, and I don't suppose anyone would have noticed in the short term – we employ 700 or 800 in the bigger stores. But I think *we* would have noticed it, in the fullness of time. More people would have criticised the service.'[7]

PASSION ABOUT QUALITY

'Driving a bottom line,' says Granada's Charles Allen, 'is easier where you are passionate about quality. It's also easier, if people are passionate about your products. You can put the foot down on both the profit and the passion pedal at the same time.'

Most of our high-performing companies share this passion for quality, and particularly for service quality. Finland's SOL, for example, is regarded by quality guru Dr Joseph Juran as a shining example of the future of quality. It cannot enter the Finnish Quality Award again because it has already won it twice in five years. It still scores more highly on the competition's criteria than the other companies that have won. Likewise, almost all of our high-performing companies have cupboards full of quality trophies. Where those are won and kept depends in large part on the company's attitude to control and autonomy in quality issues. The centralists, such as Marks & Spencer, tend to win awards centrally; the decentralists, such as The Berkeley Group or Granada, in the operating businesses.

The link between quality, autonomy (or empowerment) and financial results has been extensively explored in recent years by professor Ed Lawlor at the University of Michigan. Lawlor found that on all but one of a basket of measures:

- companies with a high emphasis on quality outperformed their less quality-passionate competitors and peers;
- companies with a high emphasis on empowerment outperformed their less empowering competitors and peers; and
- companies with a high emphasis on both quality and empowerment outperformed virtually everyone.

In a previous study by one of the authors,[8] companies were categorised in terms of their service quality approach as

- *naturals*: companies that have institutionalised service quality from their earliest days and have so inculcated service values that employees would not consider operating in any other way;
- *aspirants*: companies which have very strong ambitions towards achieving an in-built customer orientation and are determined to become service quality leaders within their own market niches;
- *followers*: companies which have been forced into service quality largely against their inclination; or
- *laggards*: companies that have developed such poor reputations for service that they would have to work twice as hard as aspirants to gain customer trust – but are unlikely to expend the effort without a major crisis.

In seeking common themes in our high-performing companies' approaches to quality, we found only one: the high performing companies all fall into either the 'naturals' or the 'aspirants' camps. The value of quality is deeply ingrained in their organisations. They may not use the language of Total Quality Management, however – particularly the naturals, whose own terminology often predates the TQM movement. Some, such as Siebe and General Electric, espouse even more demanding quality criteria, such as the Sigma Six standard pioneered by Motorola and equivalent to near-zero product defects per million units produced. And, without exception, they have a very clear understanding of the gap between quality potential and where they actually are – sufficient, at the very least, to prevent them being in any way complacent about their quality performance. For example, Liisa Joronen of SOL says: 'We are far, far from perfect. We have so much to do.'

At Singapore Airlines, front-line service is allowed to drive all the back-room processes. So, for example, says a senior SIA manager: 'Customer focus . . . was our original philosophy when the business was started. Other airlines focused on, for example, tiptop engineering of their aircraft. Of course, we require that too, but the logic for excellent engineering and maintenance links back to customer service, which is our *raison d'être*.'

CUSTOMER FOCUS + EMPLOYEE FOCUS = SHAREHOLDER VALUE

With few exceptions, our high-performance company CEOs don't watch shareholder value too closely. They reserve their attention for customers and employees, in the belief that shareholder value will then take care of itself. Says ASDA's Archie Norman: 'I've seen companies where people are very explicitly concerned about shareholders and share prices, and in my experience in customer businesses that attitude tends to be corrosive. It's like concentrating on the scoreboard instead of concentrating on the goal. Instead we have a very simple attitude that people can relate to, which is that if you work with colleagues in the stores – who are very close to the customers and are the same type of people – and if you make sure that they're motivated, make sure that they have an input and influence on the way the business is run, then you will meet the requirements of the customers.

'If you are close to the colleagues and customers, then shareholder value will follow automatically. We try to make our business simple. Our basic beliefs are all interlocked, and they're all built around a clear idea of the type of store we run for customers. It's all about volume, value for ordinary working people and their families, large stores, wide range, service with personality – they all fit together.

'In more complex organisations, which have diverse objectives and a lot of ambiguity and are trying to face three or four different ways at once, then you have to remind people from time to time that the purpose is to generate return to shareholders.'

No company we have met has ever got the balance between customer care and customer count 100 per cent right, if only because no company has ever satisfied 100 per cent of its customers. But the closer you can get to an effective balance, the better for both the company and its customers.

A large part of achieving that balance lies in the attitudes and behaviours of the people inside the organisation. In our previous study, we found that high-performing companies recognised a strong correlation between the sense of being respected and valued that was felt by employees and the respect and value they exhibited towards their customers. Chapter Ten looks at how the companies in the current study make that connection a reality.

In summary . . .

High-performing companies, by and large, don't experience much conflict between the need for gaining customer volume and the need to make every customer feel uniquely served. Their determination to achieve both is so great that minor obstacles are not allowed to get in the way. It has long been recognised that superior customer service leads to customer growth, because satisfied customers recommend others. However, that phenomenon can be greatly leveraged by a clear focus on acquiring those customers who are most likely to appreciate what the company does for them.

10 TOUGH BUT FUN
Challenging people versus nurturing people

'My aim is to make working for Bowthorpe interesting, challenging, and satisfying.' *Nicholas Brookes, Chief Executive, Bowthorpe Group.*

'If you have the right interface with people, they are really competing with you. They say: "There's no way I'm going to let him beat us."' *Barrie Stephens, Chairman, Siebe.*

'We are a very tough company in a soft way.' *Liisa Joronen, CEO, SOL.*

Although all of our high-performance companies put considerable effort into selecting and recruiting employees – particularly for key positions – in the end, they rely upon extracting extraordinary performance from ordinary people. They don't see a conflict between being hard and soft on their people; they are both at once. Hard, in the sense of pushing them to achievements they had not imagined they were capable of; soft, in the sense of supporting people with encouragement, praise and reward, and the resources they need to grow into the job. General Electric's Jack Welch talks about being 'hard-headed but soft-hearted' – in other words, being prepared to take tough decisions but being compassionate in dealing with the human implications of them. One of the characteristics we observed in talking to people at all levels in these companies was the sheer zest they had for the tasks they had control of. Although they are typically paid well above average, people in these companies come to work less for the money than because they enjoy it, as the following comments illustrate:

- 'People do enjoy working here. It goes back to being open and honest; that encourages an atmosphere where you can learn from your mistakes and afterwards laugh about them.' – David Spencer, Human Resources Director, Smiths Industries.

- 'We had a spoof video, in which the management team appeared in disguise. It brought some of the fun of television to everybody and cast all sorts of senior people in most unlikely guises. Everyone had a great time – it was very bonding for people to do it; it gave them a laugh and new insights into each other. One of the international hotel general managers came up to me and said, "Now I have it, in Granada you work very hard and you play very hard." I thought that was great. If on one day somebody gets the sense that not only is it important to work, but that there's real value in putting effort into having a good time, then you begin to get the balance. You have to work very hard to keep the fun quota up. Everyone is very busy. They put in long hours and perform to the limit. It keeps Granada feeling small. It's things like that that don't make it feel out of control.' – Stephanie Monk, Human Resources Director, Granada.

- Herb Kelleher of Southwest Airlines used to introduce himself to people in the field with: 'I'm from the general offices, and I'm here to help you. Ain't that a laugh?' As an ice-breaker it was remarkably effective.[1] Kelleher has 'turned up to work dressed variously as Elvis, Al Capone, Roy Orbison and Rhett Butler, depending on his mood'.[2] Kelleher, known to his staff as Uncle Herbie, appears in its commercials and even in a rap video for inducting new employees. He tells staff that flying with Southwest should be fun, and they take him at his word. On one much-reported flight at Christmas, all the crew dressed up as reindeer and elves and the pilot gently rocked the plane as he sang carols.

- Southwest Airlines encourages staff to play practical jokes, to dress up and make themselves look ridiculous – in short, to make coming to work a real pleasure. Staff at headquarters in Dallas wear casual clothes, and pictures of zany events featuring them and their colleagues are everywhere. The *Financial Times* quotes customer service supervisor Irene Schoenberg: 'I love coming to work every day. It's the lively atmosphere, the flexibility they allow us, and the fun we have. ... What we give the company, I think they definitely give us back.'[3]

- ASDA chairman Archie Norman maintains: 'The great battle is to create a workplace environment where people want to come to work, they believe that what the company is doing is a good thing, they enjoy being there and feel sufficiently secure that they behave with the same competence and confidence that they would behave with at home.' He explains: 'We're not doing it just because we think that it's a goody-goody idea; we're doing it because this is how we compete.'

- Wal-Mart's weekly business review meetings at Bentonville, USA, needed to be fun – why else should people give up their Saturdays? Sam Walton ensured that they were fun, indulging in what observers called 'cheerleading' and importing surprises, such as singing truck drivers.[4]

- 'Our starting point is to create an environment where people want to work. They want to be here because it's stimulating, they'll be extended and they'll enjoy it. ... You have to keep variety in the job, keep the stripes off as much as possible and do the unexpected.' – Bob Lawson, CEO, Electrocomponents.

- 'At Microsoft,' says Mike Murray, Vice President Human Resources and Administration, 'we've created a lot of wealth for a lot of employees. Many of them could stop working at age 33 or 34. It's only anecdotal evidence, but we think very few actually leave our company. What else would they do with their lives? Where else could they have such fun?'

- 'We all get on very well together. We all know each other extremely well and we all, if push comes to shove, support each other right down to the hilt. In terms of ambition, we are all ambitious for the organisation, but I think we would all put the organisation before ourselves. It's brilliant fun; it's great. It's got to remain fun.' – Rob Rowley, Director, Reuters.

- 'I've never had the same job satisfaction before. I wake up every morning with a buzz. That's something Berkeley has, a buzz all the time; all the staff feel that. I joined about ten years ago as a site manager and I've been through every discipline in the business to become MD. There has to be pressure, but pressure is what you make of it. The fun element is still there. It's not just a job at Berkeley; it's a life. Ask my wife.' – Colin Hutchinson, Managing Director of Berkeley Homes (Hampshire).

- At SOL, says Liisa Joronen: 'Work must be fun. The more I see happiness and hear laughter, the better results we get. Sometimes we have had 'a hat day', when people wear funny hats during an ordinary working day. When I travel, I buy all sorts of funny things for SOL. Speaking and walking toy animals, yellow teddy bears, funny yellow dresses, and all sorts of 'happy-face' things; watches, pens, bags, hats, pants, socks, earrings etc. Some I wear myself and some I give as presents for excellent performance. I am very childish and it is wonderful that I can be so in SOL.'

- 'I don't think we've discovered the Holy Grail. But we don't have too many people jumping ship. The environment is the key to happiness and a large part of the environment in Boots is the absence of too many constraints on people doing what they want to do.' – David Kissman, Personnel Director of Boots.

- 'For people deciding to work for us, the key differentiator between us and other firms is not pay. We do pay well, but not significantly more than other firms. What people do say when they join us is that they have a high degree of freedom, a lot of commitment, and a strong personal and social relationship with the company and other employees. On the social side, there are free lunches, parties, and sports activities.' – Claus Heinrich, member of the board of SAP AG.

• JCB's most famous promotional asset was the result of a bit of fun by demonstration drivers at the company's UK factory. The JCB circus – or Dancing Diggers as they are now called – have been performing exciting and memorable demonstrations for audiences around the world for some 30 years. The Dancing Diggers perform remarkable formation routines to music to show off the power and versatility of the JCB machines.

Working for these companies is so much fun, in fact, that it takes quite a lot to hire them away. At Vodafone, Sir Gerald Whent is proud that he has kept all but two of the key people brought on board when the company started. At Rentokil Initial, Sir Clive Thompson reports that: 'The people who leave Rentokil Initial are fired. Our managers are often headhunted, but they usually stay, even though they could make more money elsewhere.' Singapore Airlines, operating in a country with probably the most acute labour shortage in the world, where employees expect to be enticed elsewhere, nonetheless has one in five of its staff with more than 20 years' service.

N. Brown also has a low attrition rate among its valued managers. Says Chief Executive Jim Martin: 'If I had a manager come into my office and I wanted to keep him, I would take an involvement myself. Also, if head hunters call and boost the ego of the person, we put the question to them: "Where would you go where your level of authority is as great as it is now?" That is usually the issue that swings it. Money is only a motivator to certain levels.'

SAP also has a very low rate of turnover among its staff – less than three per cent a year. 'We did have some problems a few years ago, when SAP consultants in some subsidiaries were being lured away by other firms for much higher wages, but mostly they stayed,' says Henning Kagermann. Finding another job with the same level of challenge outside the company isn't easy.

The attitude surveys these companies run periodically reveal a remarkable degree of enthusiasm among employees. At Cadbury Schweppes' London headquarters, for example, says Human Resources Director Bob Stack: 'The Industrial Society, who analysed the results of our latest survey, said our headquarters had one of the highest motivations they had ever seen.'

In Boots The Chemist, three-quarters of store staff who had taken maternity leave returned to their old jobs – way above the national average. The company supports staff retention through a variety of family-friendly policies, including flexible working, term-time working, job shares and career breaks. What these policies do is more than provide an incentive – they say that the company cares enough to really want people to come back. So they do.

In part, this enthusiasm and positive feeling is a product of success. But, equally, it is an issue of culture. Says Granada's Charles Allen: 'Management is about taking people with you on a journey. I see business as a game and you have to create some goals and have some fun. Unless you have that fun and enthusiasm, you get nowhere. But, like football, you play to win.'[5] In essence, these companies are not only saying that it is alright to enjoy your work, but that enjoyment is a critical part of it. As we shall see in Chapter Eleven, the CEOs and chairmen of most of the high-performing companies provide role models for enjoying their work and being seen to do so.

That is not to say that work has to be fun all the time. It can't be. But the capacity to extract enjoyment from when things go well is important to buoying people up when things don't work out. Barrie Stephens, Chairman of Siebe, had something like this in mind when he asked John Major, the then British Prime Minister, if he enjoyed his job as Chairman of UK plc. The question was posed at a time when almost nothing seemed to have gone right for the government for some time, and its standing in opinion polls was near its all-time low. Recalls Stephens: 'He said: "I do!" I replied "You're lucky then, because most people enjoy their jobs at best 70 per cent of the time." You have to relish the sense of achievement, of beating the hell out of the competition.'

None of our interviewees or their companies had analysed why it was more enjoyable to work in their environment than in others that they had experienced. But certain phrases kept recurring within two overall themes: constant challenge and a feeling that more senior managers care both about the company and the people. For example: 'There's always something new to stretch you that little bit further'; 'Change is fun for us'; 'I've never had such freedom before – and I've never put so much into a job before'. And: 'The only thing more important to us than our customers is our colleagues' (ASDA); 'We expect people to put their families before the company' (Electrocomponents); 'I always tell new recruits to make sure they have interests outside the job.' (Atlas Copco).

The challenge culture
....

All of our case-study companies are very demanding of the people that work for them. They expect – and receive – results, as the following comments demonstrate:

• 'We set tough financial objectives. People are in a performance culture; they deliver results and they are rewarded. If they don't deliver, we have a fairly good track record of removing people. That's got tougher over the past five years.' – Bob Stack, Human Resources Director, Cadbury Schweppes.

• 'I give people a hard time,' says Microsoft's Bill Gates. 'When they come to meetings with me, they'd better be ready to respond to my questions in real time and at high bandwidth.' (In plain English, immediately and intelligently.)

• 'It's a culture that can be brutally honest about your performance but it leaves you in no doubt where you stand. There's no pussy-footing around issues, you get it with both barrels – either congratulations or the other side if things aren't going well. It means you know precisely what is expected of you.' – Martin Ellis, General Manager of UK Healthcare, Rentokil Initial.

• His boss, Sir Clive Thompson, puts it even more succinctly: 'We're a very mean company where failures are concerned. Part of our culture is to persecute failure and reward success.'

• At SOL, says Liisa Joronen: 'Our people set targets higher than anyone else's in Finland. My biggest job is to make them believe that they are as good as they want to be. There is no excuse. If they don't get the target, they don't get their bonus – we have no discussions. Every good company is tough in some way. It's very simple to be tough.'

• At IKEA, says Sven-Olof Kulldorff: 'People who don't like the competitiveness of producing results will not enjoy working at IKEA. This is not a philanthropic organisation. We want people who like to perform. We shouldn't have people who don't want to perform. We want results.'

• 'The good thing about this company is that people can get on with their work. It is not hierarchical, but the pressure is high. But pressure and achievement are related. If people come from other companies to us, they sometimes find the freedom and pressure difficult to adapt to,' says Henning Kagermann at SAP.

- 'Laggards won't be tolerated, because they betray everything their colleagues do', says Electrocomponents' Bob Lawson.

All of this sounds – and usually is – very hard-nosed. It smacks of fear as part of the motivation to perform. 'I'd be disappointed if I didn't generate a little fear when I visit branches,' says Rentokil Initial's Sir Clive Thompson. But the fear is fear of failure, not fear of the individual. And fear becomes confidence when people achieve beyond their expectations.

General Electric's Jack Welch generated a great deal of fear when he told managers: 'You are either the best at what you do or you don't do it for very long.' He then demonstrated that he meant it, by divesting non-performing businesses and people wholesale. It may have been traumatic, but it left the remaining managers in no doubt about what they had to do.[6]

PUSHING PEOPLE HARD

Granada's Charles Allen stunned his top team at Granada when he spelt out that annual profit increases of five or ten per cent were no longer acceptable; that he wanted to double profits every two or three years. What he was looking for, he explains, was 'a completely different thought process'.

He continues: 'I set very ambitious targets. I'm always looking to double the profits in three years. That's the starting point for setting targets. You have to challenge people dramatically to encourage them to go back and radically re-think what they are doing and how. If you go for a ten per cent improvement, then people just tinker; they get rid of a secretary here and there. That's not enough to stay ahead. It's really a freeing-up process. Doing it the way you've done it for the past ten years won't get you there. London Weekend Television is a good example. It was already a well-managed business when we acquired it, but we set even more stretching targets.'

'People who have delivered probably didn't believe they could do it three years ago. Sutcliffe Catering, for example, has almost doubled its profits with the same senior people as before. You give them real clarity of objectives . . . and back them.'

Adds his colleague Stephanie Monk: 'Within Granada, I've seen real added value from the headquarters, which has a management team that's very comfortable to talk about being unreasonable. That unreasonableness has prompted people to be creative and challenging in a way that they wouldn't have done had they had something that they felt was much more realistic by way of targets. I think people are more comfortable to look at incremental growth from where they are now, but the sort of challenge that's been thrown out from headquarters is such that people have had to think very radically and to re-appraise their businesses to think about doing things in very different ways. That's been really valuable and has been one of the reasons why, although we've had a change of leadership at the top and we've recruited some good new people in, we still employ lots of people who were here five to eight years ago. Yet the business is performing in a dramatically different way.

'We've had lots of conversations about it being unreasonable, but actually I have to admit that if I achieve my budget, I'm creating additional money for the business and I buy myself the room to make some radical changes in the future. Whilst everyone would love a quieter life, part of them acknowledges that success comes through this kind of very demanding focus from the centre.'

General Electric's Jack Welch declares: 'I've learned the value of stretching the organisation, by setting the bar higher than people think they can go.' Adds his colleague Steve Kerr, Vice-President for Corporate Leadership Development: 'GE is a challenge-driven, performance-driven company. It's very self-aware, even neurotic in a way, because of the very stretching goals we set. We have the ethic of an Olympian – of setting outrageous goals – but many people see themselves in this way. They moan and groan about the difficulties, like anyone else, but they resonate to the challenge. We take care of their inner needs by giving them stretch goals and the tools to achieve them. So there's a lot of self-selection of people. They know that, if you perform, you are looked after.'

For Boots, the concept of a challenge culture had to be grafted on to existing values. 'The first step was to stretch people, to make them believe that giant steps in performance were possible – that aiming for three to four per cent profit and cash growth wasn't good enough when you could be getting fourteen to fifteen per cent. It was a tremendous management challenge ... we had to get people focused on the right ratios, the right objectives.'

CLEAR TARGETS

The ability to achieve stretch targets, say our high-performing companies, lies in considerable part in the clarity with which people understand what they are meant to achieve. The more focused they can be, the more effort they will put into finding creative ways of achieving challenging objectives.

Clear, unambiguous targets make it easier for both top management and the subsidiary board CEOs to understand what needs to be done and to debate the best ways to make things happen. 'They may say all the right things in a meeting and impress the hell out of me, and be a good golfer too, but that's got nothing to do with it,' says Allen Yurko of Siebe. 'All I want is top line and bottom line results for the long term.' At SOL, in spite of the lack of central direction, there are targets set every month. Co-workers have to announce their own targets at a meeting of their peers.

'Successful teams are created by securing good leadership, providing clear-cut objectives and expecting them to achieve the extraordinary. When people understand precisely what is expected of them, they will usually deliver,' says Sir Colin Marshall of British Airways.

STIRRING THE POT

Many of our high-performing companies create a sense of challenge by not letting people stay too long in the same slot. One reason for doing so is to prevent people becoming too settled and complacent. But equally, it is to provide constant stimulation. Says Electrocomponents' Bob Lawson: 'We challenge people by moving them around: for example, accountants into the warehouse, or engineers into salesmen. We have very few specialists. We produce some very rounded people. The more you challenge the organisation, the better.'

At Smiths Industries too, says Human Resources Director David Spencer: 'We have lots of movement within the group, often taking people from one sector to another. It's about moving talented people around to give them continuous challenge. We find they are far more driven by challenge than by remuneration.'

Granada's Charles Allen explains: 'I learned a lot at GrandMet, when I worked in innovation. So, when I became involved in Granada, one of the first things I did was to change responsibilities for what people did. So, for example, if someone was responsible for programme making, then I made them responsible for broadcasting. That way you are presenting them with a fresh challenge. It helps them see the issues from another perspective. I suppose it puts them off balance, too.'

The bigger and more international the company, the more opportunity for this kind of challenge, says Michael Treschow: 'You can live a full life in Atlas Copco without feeling you get stuck, because you have the dimensions of the international life which means all the various countries. You have all the different businesses from big machines to small hand tools, with all different customers, different processes, and then you have all the different functions: sales, marketing, manufacturing. If I look at myself, even though I've been in one business area I've done all the functions. The interesting thing, I'd say, is doing lots of different things. If you have the idea that change is good for you and for the company, then you can live a long life in Atlas Copco without feeling you have reached some sort of limitation.'

It is also a priority issue for Marcus Beresford, managing director of Industrial Services at GKN: 'We have to get better at moving youngsters around the group. It's easy for a line manager to say, "If someone is so good, why should I pass him on to someone else?" We need to be a bit more mobile, otherwise we won't keep the bright people.'

Nonetheless, moving people around doesn't always work. Recalls Vodafone's Sir Gerald Whent: 'The biggest mistake I made was putting a superb technical man into a general management job, which was commercially biased. We always were a great believer that you can move people between skills and we have done that quite successfully, but I made a mistake there.' It goes to show that shifting people across functions needs to be done with careful attention to their strengths and weaknesses.

WHEN PEOPLE MISS THE TARGET

Of the subsidiary CEOs recruited by Siebe, one in four doesn't deliver. Those that don't are given counselling and support from the centre, but if they don't improve radically, they soon leave. 'It's not our style,' says Allen Yurko, 'to say "Joe didn't work out in this division, but we've got a smaller, less complex division over here where he might do better." ' The assumption is that the necessary entrepreneurial qualities are either there or not there.

Atlas Copco takes a more relaxed view. Says Michael Treschow: 'Our culture is more forgiving. Often managers who have failed have changed jobs and been given a chance to re-charge their batteries in another position. They later come back at the same level. I believe this is a good culture, because people see that you can afford to fail.

'For example, at divisional vice-president-level, a person just got stuck. We put him into another operational situation, which was more of a start-up. It involved moving outside Sweden to do a completely different job. He got involved in more project-based things and then three years later he came back as president of another division. No one felt that was strange. It gives a signal to the organisation that it's OK to fail, and as long as everyone is trying their best there's always room for another chance. It's so damn difficult to always be successful and it's not always in your own hands.'

The apparently toughest of our companies, Rentokil Initial, also takes a forgiving view. Says Martin Ellis, General Manager of UK Healthcare at Rentokil Initial: 'I'd call Rentokil Initial a meritocracy. No one is interested in my qualifications before I joined the company; what matters is what

I've done here. But if you have a failure or a difficult patch, the company is interested in not just what's going wrong but what you're going to do about it and how you plan to get back on track. As long as you've understood the reasons and show that you've learned from the problem, then that's OK.

'You have to justify performance in terms of the numbers and the trading account. The trading performance is the ultimate measure. At the end of the day, in the Rentokil Initial culture the only truth is the trading account – profit and loss. That's it. End of story. It produces a competitive atmosphere between managers, which most of us enjoy.

'Let me give you another example. I quickly realised that if I was to be a Rentokil Initial manager I'd have to be good on my feet, doing presentations. I was rubbish. But my manager allowed me to develop those skills. He allowed me to make mistakes and talked me through what I was doing wrong. That's an element of nurturing.'

'Reuters, too, tolerated failure among managers to an alarming degree,' says Patrick Mannix, Director of Personnel and Quality. 'I think it's probably on the whole been a strength in Europe, including the UK. I think it may have been a weakness in the States, where the expectation is that you are harder.'

At SOL, where targets are measured every month, some more often, it is accepted that not everyone meets their targets all the time. The centre's role is then to help them think the issues through, to help them plan how to get back on target. If they fail to improve, they usually choose to leave rather than let down their colleagues.

The lesson from all these examples is that high-performing companies take the achievement of targets very seriously. They don't accept excuses, but they do expect well thought-through plans for getting back on track and a proactive approach to bringing those plans to reality. At the same time, they are very constructive about temporary failure, where the will and the competence to do better next time are in evidence.

OPPORTUNITIES TO PROVE YOURSELF

For Vodafone, a critical resource is senior managers. It needs people who understand its business, yet have been exposed to demanding situations where they have had to demonstrate entrepreneurial skills and the ability to manage diverse operations. To cope with rapid expansion overseas (at time of writing, it is active in 15 countries) it has given relatively young managers responsibility for developing the business in another country – in effect, to duplicate the success of the parent company in the UK market. These managers are too valuable, says Sir Gerald Whent, to leave in the local company; and, moreover, it makes good business sense to allow the top slots in each country to be taken over by locals who have been coached into the role. Instead, they 'have gone out there, proved themselves and returned to bigger jobs.' A similar process takes place at Electrocomponents and ABB.

The nurturing culture

High-performing companies show they care in numerous ways. At Electrocomponents, for example, says CEO Bob Lawson: 'Our sales force are told not to open the mail first when they come home – that they should take time to say hello to their spouses. We try not to phone people at home, and our managers aren't allowed to say "tell him to phone me the moment he gets in."'

Southwest Airlines believes so strongly in the importance of looking after its employees that it publicly states 'customers come second'. Only by having exceptionally motivated employees, it reasons, can it deliver a genuine and consistent service differential.[7]

Microsoft retains very bright brains by keeping them loyal. It fosters an intellectual spirit – staff refer to the Seattle headquarters as the campus – and makes it easy for them to work long hours when they have an interesting and challenging problem to crack. The campus contains an all-night restaurant and pizza-delivery service and even a laundry to wash their jeans in![8]

SOL provides a wide range of benefits to its staff, not least of which is letting them manage their own time, as long as the job gets done. As *The European* describes it: 'Armed with portable computers and cellular phones, SOL staff can work where they want, at home or in the office, provided they meet democratically-voted annual targets involving the cleaning of the country's factories, offices, airliners, schools, and even zoos. SOL's open-plan head office in a former Helsinki film studio has virtually no hierarchy. Desks are communal and everyone answers the telephones and does his or her own paperwork in the absence of secretaries. The environment is one of paintings, comfortable sofas, fountains and birds. On Fridays staff going to the country for the weekend bring their children in for the day.'

When Liisa Joronen launched SOL in 1992, she set out to stand Finnish business culture on its head. Among the slogans she adopted were 'freedom from status symbols' and 'kill routine before it kills you'. She said she wanted a laughing office.[9] Corporate employee Jukka Suuniitty has absorbed the SOL values on working times: 'Normally I come in every day. Sometimes I take work home if there is an urgent deadline. Also I have days during the week that I might stay at home with the kids. It has taken many years to forget the old way of doing things and start to believe that you intuitively know how much you should work without checking the hours every day. I don't count the hours any more.'

Balancing challenge and nurturing

It's a theme echoed throughout our interviews, that there is a balance between the need to drive people to extraordinary achievements and the need to make them feel valued and supported. Geoff Hutchinson, Managing Director of Crosby Homes, describes a typical trade-off in his operating company: 'It's a fast-pace way of working. It's the same when we go out to sites; we use a Dictaphone to capture what's discussed. I don't mind talking about something once, but I don't expect to have to say it again. Once is enough – sort it out. The teams really enjoy it. They really want you to see the houses because they're proud of them. If I can't turn up on a site where I said I would, they're really disappointed.

'If you were a sub-contractor for me, say a carpenter, then I might come up to you after you've been working on something for two weeks and say I want to change it; it's not quite right or it could be in a better place. If you knew us, you'd be used to that, but you'd also know that when you called into the office on Friday afternoon your cheque would be ready. If you treat people with respect, then the next time you need them, they'll come and work for you again.'

How do high-performing companies develop this hard–soft, tough but fun environment? They share the following common approaches:

- recruiting the best people for the job;
- nurturing creativity and proactive behaviour;
- training and development to achieve great things;
- encouraging a genuine sense of ownership at all levels;
- recognising and rewarding achievement; and
- using communication as the driving engine of commitment.

RECRUITING THE BEST PEOPLE FOR THE JOB

'We aim to promote or recruit the best people we can find for every job, then unlock their potential and manage them correctly, so that we can ensure a greater return on our investment,' says David Spencer, Human Resources Director of Smiths Industries. While this might seem obvious, it is a fact that our high-performance companies appear to be more successful at recruiting and retaining winning employees. The reason seems to be that they pay more attention than most to the notion of 'fit'. By fit, we mean how well the person will slot into the organisation's values, rather than how well qualified they are to fill a particular post. Our case-study companies seek people who have the capacity to grow with the organisation, not just accepting the values but living them, being prepared to test their actions and other people's against the values, and to be vocal when they sense a divergence between action and values. All, without exception, do this for the top layers of the business; many for everyone in the business. This careful approach to selection by fit can also be seen in a handful of well known companies we did not study – for example, The Disney Corporation and The Body Shop.

'Fit' will clearly mean different things for these companies, because they have different cultures. For example, Southwest Airlines has far more applicants than it needs for every vacancy that occurs, so it can afford to be choosey. But hiring the right type of person is a critical part of retaining the culture and style of the organisation. It looks, of course, for people with a sense of humour and the kind of warmth necessary for good customer service. It also wants them to have a positive attitude and the interest and ability to work well with others.

Southwest places the right values much higher in its selection criteria than the right experience or expertise. Says Herb Kelleher: 'We'll take the guy with less experience if he has the values we are looking for, and someone else can take the expert. We look for attitudes. We'll train you on whatever you need to do, but the one thing we can't do is change inherent attitudes in people.'

People have to demonstrate compatibility with the culture, he explains. 'Part of the purpose of a probationary period is to determine that. You may be an excellent performer, but incompatible with our culture here. It doesn't mean there's anything wrong with you; there's just not a match. 'People write to me and complain, "Hey, I got terminated ... for purely subjective reasons." And I'll say, "Right! Those are the important reasons. We believe in taking subjective people!"'

Wal-Mart's Sam Walton saw the secret of being well managed as deceptively simple. 'It lay in attracting people well suited to their jobs. For Walton, this meant hiring individuals who exhibited the fundamental values of loyalty and, especially, hard work.'[10]

At IKEA too, recruitment interviews focus in considerable detail on culture fit. Will the candidate enjoy working in this kind of environment?

Does he or she share the same basic values about customers and colleagues?

SOL also looks for people with the right attitude. Says Suuniitty: 'We look for people's attitude towards service. How does he or she act when she meets people; their overall look; how do they speak to people? Do they look as if they take care of themselves?' Adds Joronen: 'In SOL the district manager hires his/her own supervisors and the supervisors hire their own cleaners. When you hire your own people you look very carefully at who you are hiring. You can't blame anyone else.'

Unusually for a retail environment, 90 per cent of Home Depot staff are full-time. The reasoning is that part-time staff can't have the same level of product knowledge. The company offers above-average salaries, but exercises considerable care in taking on only people who demonstrate the mix of enthusiasm, stamina and attitude.

A high proportion of the CEOs and chairmen in our sample of companies are personally involved in the selection of their top 150 or so people. For Sir Clive Thompson at Rentokil Initial, for example, this takes his involvement down three layers, to area manager. For Allen Yurko at Siebe, 'I interview every managing director we hire for our 160 companies. I want to know that they understand the culture. I try to scare them away by telling them how tough it is to be an executive here, that it's not comfortable, it's very intense. I tell them that they have the ball and they have to run with it. Three or four other people interview the person first. By the time I do, we'll know if they fit or not. It may sound simplistic, but it works.'

Jack Welch at General Electric calls the succession planning process 'Session C'. He personally takes responsibility for reviewing the development of the top 400 managers, monitoring their progress once a year in a process backed up by masses of information on each manager. The approach ensures that divisional executives also take seriously their own responsibilities for developing talent.[11]

Smith Industries looks first of all for managers with entrepreneurial ability. Then, says Human Resources Director David Spencer: 'We don't hire someone just on their track record; we look for potential, how they approach work and whether they will fit in. We need them to be flexible enough in their thinking to adapt to Smiths. You could almost say they needed to be chameleon-like, to blend in with the different environments they will have to work in.'

At GKN, Managing Director of Industrial Services, Marcus Beresford explains: 'Any senior appointment has to have my approval, and I do try to get a really first-class group of people in their early thirties who can progress quickly within the group.'

The question all these CEOs ask in recruitment of senior people is *'Does this person have the ability and motivation to flourish in our company's culture?'* The same principle applies further down the line, sometimes as far as the most junior positions. At Southwest Airlines, for example, says Herb Kelleher: 'When we hire new pilots, we bring our existing pilots into the decision. They participate voluntarily and on their own time, because of their dedication to Southwest Airlines.'[12]

At SAP, says Henning Kagermann: 'When we recruit people, in most cases we are looking at the potential rather than what they have achieved. We can train them up; what we need to see is whether they have the capability to absorb new learning.' Adds his board colleague Dr Claus Heinrich: 'At SAP the entry requirement is very high – in development, in research, everywhere. We have to think about the future of the company and we have to control and be very selective about the people we recruit. We only appoint someone if two development directors and one operations manager have seen the candidate and approved them.'

Having hired people with the right fit, high-performance companies seek to promote from within wherever possible. Whenever there is an important opening at Electrocomponents, says Bob Lawson: 'We always screen first the people we have. We recognise that we are always more critical of them, because we know their weaknesses. But that can be a positive thing.'

NURTURING CREATIVITY AND PROACTIVE BEHAVIOUR

High-performance companies nurture creativity and proactive behaviour in a wide variety of ways. In particular, they:

- encourage people to question and challenge;
- support individual initiative;
- welcome and value suggestions and ideas; and
- form teams instinctively.

Encouraging people to question and challenge
IKEA's founder, Ingvar Kamprad, tells employees: 'Encourage and enthuse, dare to question and have the energy to rejuvenate.'

Honda promoted the concept of *waigaya*, business improvement sessions, where argument and disagreement with the norm are encouraged. A *waigaya* session can be attended by people of all levels, from the shop floor to the president's office. One Honda president, Kiyoshi Kawashima, reportedly stepped down 'because the employees began agreeing with me 70 per cent of the time'![13]

Noel Tichy, in his study of General Electric, *Control Your Destiny or Someone Else Will*, begins by describing a training session where ten young managers were debating the alternative propositions that 'Jack Welch is the greatest CEO GE has ever had' and 'Jack Welch is an asshole'. The fact that such a debate could take place openly indicates the freedom people have in GE to address the controversial, to question openly what they are told from above.

GE tackled the issue of employee creativity through 'Work Out', a programme designed to stimulate discussion in an unthreatening atmosphere by employees at all levels. To emphasise that they could say what they genuinely thought, most of the discussions went on without managers present. Only when problems had been identified and solutions proposed were the managers invited in; and then they had to make decisions about each proposal on the spot, or at the latest within one month.

Welcoming and valuing suggestions and ideas

'One of the strengths of Smiths [Industries] is that we allow people to see where they add value. If you come up with good ideas, you get to see what the financial impact is. Because we are very open, people feel able to speak their minds,' says David Spencer, Human Resource Director.

There was a recent example of this at Smiths Industries' Vent-Axia fan company. A brainstorming session between technical and commercial staff led to the development of a unique, low-voltage light and extractor unit which could be installed in a shower cubicle. Sales people were initially difficult to motivate, so marketing demonstrated the unit to them by switching it on and then plunging it into a bucket of water. It continued to work. Seventy-five sales people were given a bucket each and told to repeat the demo to their customers. Within a year they had generated a new £1.5 million per annum business line.

On the wall of the office of John Rugman, GKN's corporate Head of Human Resources, is a quotation from a Japanese chief executive that says: 'You think the task of management is getting the ideas of the managers into the hands of the workers – we know that will never succeed.' GKN's Chairman Sir David Lees talks of 'a culture which makes it clear that good ideas and innovations are not the sole preserve of top management but can emanate from all levels in the company or group'.

Supporting individual initiative

Home Depot encourages employees to take the initiative on anything and everything. 'We give employees the tools to do the job, then let them do it. At every level, they are not afraid to make decisions,' Chairman Bernard Marcus told the *St Petersburg Times*.[14]

Daniel Bernard, CEO of Carrefour, says: 'This company has a long history of respect for people and a history of delegating responsibility. Managers do not have to call me before they decide on a plan of action, only when they make a mistake. We learn a great deal from mistakes.'

Microsoft carries out a regular empowerment survey of its employees, with some 50 questions. On a 0 to 10 scale, it consistently scores 7 or 8.

SOL's Liisa Joronen sees healthy internal competition as an important aspect of encouraging individual initiative. She explains: 'Our target-oriented and open information culture creates internal competition among individuals and groups. We also arrange all kinds of competitions. The most important competition last year was our internal quality competition. Because SOL could not apply for the Finnish Quality Award we launched a SOL Quality Award with the same rules and score-counting as the national one. The winner of the 16 areas won FIM 200,000 ($50,000). The amount was divided among everyone in the area. The competition was such a success that we have decided to renew it in 1997.'

Forming teams instinctively

'We allow plenty of room for the creative spirit to work here. To an outsider, we may not always appear to be entirely methodical,' says Smiths Industries' David Spencer. 'But on the other hand, we don't have prima donnas. Like Liverpool Football Club, we can weld the skills of the individual stars into a winning team.'

At Granada, says Stephanie Monk: 'I was fascinated when I first went to television, because it is a loose collaboration of people who are there because of the talent they had to offer and therefore they are very rule-averse. They also don't see themselves working in a conventional hierarchy or within the constraints of the job description. They therefore work together in a very collegial way and are very comfortable in a piecework situation. They come together and work on projects, they break up, they re-coalesce around another project. It's an approach towards working that is relevant much beyond that.'

TRAINING AND DEVELOPMENT TO ACHIEVE GREAT THINGS

Most of our high-performance companies spend way above average on training and development. Boots, for example, spends £50 million a year on training, and with 11,000 staff registered for National Vocational

Qualifications it is the largest user of NVQs in the UK. ABB spends more than $400 million a year on management education alone. It builds 'knowledge transfer' into its budgets as an important part of managers' time. At Singapore Airlines' airports subsidiary, the 8,000 employees each have at least five days' training each year. Newly recruited Singapore girls go through rigorous training that includes getting to know unfamiliar foods, such as cheese, that may be served to customers. For four months they practise serving each other, observed by instructors and videoed to show what they did well and badly. Only when they graduate are they allowed to serve real customers.

Home Depot believes it has to grow its own special people, who have the kind of creativity and customer attentiveness to fit its unusual culture. Chairman Bernard Marcus told *Fortune*: 'Where do we find these people? Nowhere. We make them. We tell them they'd better make it here because they won't be able to make it in another organisation. They'd be misfits.'[15]

Training at Home Depot usually starts at the lowest level and works its way up to the executive levels. The reasoning is that the people at the lowest level have more impact on the customer, and so it is far more urgent to train them first. New employees have to spend at least four weeks in training before they are allowed to serve customers on their own, and for some months after are expected to observe and learn from more experienced colleagues.

Training in high-performance companies is a core activity, one that deserves high-ability managers to run it and high attention by top management. At British Airways, for example, the human resources/training function has been a key posting for high flyers – including the current CEO, Robert Ayling. It doesn't have to be classroom training – far from it. For example, at Microsoft, Mike Murray, Vice President of Human Resources and Administration, says: 'On average, 70 per cent of a person's training and development comes from the job they are doing; 20 per cent comes from learning from managers and mentors; only 10 per cent comes from formalised learning.'

Among common attitudes we observed towards training in our high-performance companies were:

• *Active presence and involvement of top management.* At Smiths Industries, for example, says David Spencer: 'We run many development programmes corporately, bringing people together from around the world. The Chief Executive will almost always be there for dinner one day of the course. He meets and gets to know people at all levels.'

The presence of the CEO or chairman at training events emphasises that developing people's talent is a priority activity. Even more powerful is when the CEO takes on the role of trainer. Training is such a high priority at Home Depot that senior managers are all expected to take an active part. The Chairman and President both get involved in the training of every store manager. At Atlas Copco, leadership seminars are presented personally by CEO Michael Treschow.

- *Training is an essential part of promoting autonomy.* The more capable and confident people are, the more willing they are to take on greater responsibilities – and to let responsibilities go to other people. At SOL, for example: 'We try to train our supervisors to be so independent that they can organise their work and they get the support from here. The most independent ones discuss projects with their cleaners and they have better figures than the others,' says Joronen.

- *An investment mentality.* High-performing companies never see training as a cost; they always regard it as an investment. Says David Spencer of Smiths Industries: 'We invest in training the same way as we do in R&D; we want a return. By satisfying the businesses that there is a return, we get to invest more each year. We very rarely have to look externally for management recruitment. The CEOs of the businesses around the world have accepted the value of moving good people on, even though they may lose a talented young manager. One reason they have done so is that the CEOs preside at regular assessment centres, where these young managers are assessed and given guidance on their future development. The CEOs also act as coach or mentor to people from other divisions, who have been through the assessment centre.'

SOL insists that all cleaners receive training across the areas of the job and that they sign that they have had the necessary training. The training includes teaching them about the many measurements the company makes, from customer satisfaction to account profitability.

SOL also operates its own 'degree' – a five-module three-year programme covering training skills, public speaking, other communication skills, productivity and effective working, and an understanding of the SOL management philosophy.

Linking training to customer feedback is, in theory, easier, but few companies make the connection so overtly and directly as Singapore Airlines. So when customers reported that the cabin service was too mechanical, the training had to be adapted rapidly to suit. Says CEO Cheong: 'Our cabin crew, while pleasant and caring, tended to be robotic. As long as everything went well, fine. If something out of the ordinary happened that's not covered in the manual, they were in trouble. We took that very seriously and we changed our style of training. Previously, everything was set out in great detail – how to lay out the crockery and so on. We concentrated on the spirit of service and we were able to reduce the training time from around five months to three-and-a-half. We saved a lot of money in the process. What we got out of this was greater spontaneity.'

ENCOURAGING A GENUINE SENSE OF OWNERSHIP AT ALL LEVELS

When Southwest Airlines was faced with soaring jet fuel prices in 1990, the staff rallied round and bought $135,000 worth of fuel to help out. It wasn't much in terms of the overall additional costs of fuel to the company, but it was a gesture that showed they understood the problems.

High-performing companies develop a sense of ownership by:

• *Allowing and encouraging employees to take control of their areas of account-ability.* In retail, for example, Marks & Spencer encourages branch managers to feel personal ownership of their stores and, in turn, to spread that sense of ownership downwards to department supervisors. And Wal-Mart operates a 'store within a store' policy that makes people in a department responsible, in effect, for running their own business.

For a while, we were puzzled that our high-performing companies made so little of 'empowering' their employees. One or two, such as N. Brown, commented on changes they had made to put more authority to deal with customer queries and complaints into the hands of front-line staff, but for the most part this was an issue that they needed to be prompted about to discuss. When they were prompted, it became clear that, in most cases, it was so obvious and natural that they hadn't seen it as worthy of special comment. Few saw themselves as providing anything new or original in this respect. In getting the balance between control and autonomy as near right as possible, they automatically empowered the majority of people.

• *Involving employees in resolving business problems and opportunities.* Recalls Mike Killoran, Customer Services Manager at ASDA: 'A couple of years ago I was involved with re-designing the customer service desks in our stores. I organised a whole lot of listening groups in 15 regions around the country. These were broken down into three groups. The first group I asked to think about the physical aspects of the design; the second to look at the service we should be providing and the sort of training required to support it; the third group looked at the paperwork involved with doing a refund.

'A number of things came out of that. Group One came up with the idea that the height of the desk should be lowered by a few inches so that there was a good sight line for wheelchair users and children and so that it was easy for our people to make good eye-contact with customers. We also introduced a circular desk because it was easier to deal with more people and to put on an extra colleague if queues started to form. Then we went through every inch of cupboard space in detail to make the design more efficient. Those desks now go into every new store. Once introduced, too, we use listening groups to carry on tweaking the design.

'Group Two said the emphasis with training should be on interpersonal skills, so we've introduced training that focuses on that. Group Three managed to streamline the paperwork so that all that is required now is a single signature from the customer to do a refund. We posed the problem, and the solution was shaped by the people at the sharp end.

'Another example is our "VIP Scheme". Colleagues are invited to nominate a product line they think will sell really well. It can be people in the stores or even people in the back room who don't have much contact with customers. We then build a display in the stores with a photograph of that colleague. The person whose product wins gets the use of the company Jaguar for a week.

' "To listen naively" is another part of the ASDA Way of Working. It's integral to the role of the manager to listen to feedback without rationalising it. The danger otherwise (and we all do it) is that you rationalise ideas immediately and rule them out without thinking them through. The other thing is that listening is different to simply waiting for your turn to talk. So managers at listening groups listen naively and then go back later when they've really thought about an idea and say "yes, we can do that" or "no, we can't for the following reasons".'

• *Promoting share ownership and profit sharing.* At the time of writing, around 66 per cent of British Airways employees own shares in their own company. ASDA, too, has an employee scheme, and at Electrocomponents, says Lawson: 'We have a Save As You Earn scheme for everyone and a share scheme down to middle managers. We'd take it further down but we don't have enough issued shares. Currently about 57 per cent of the total worldwide workforce participates in the SAYE scheme.' ASDA campaigned vehemently against the Greenbury Committee's recommendations in the UK, which recommended limiting the proportion of shares available to directors and employees. ASDA's argument was that the more shares available to employees, the greater the incentive to perform and hence the greater the benefit to share-holders.

Southwest Airlines' profit-sharing scheme has created a fair number of dollar millionaires among long-serving employees. Money from the scheme is invested initially in the company's own stock, but after five years the employee can divert it to other funds. The problem with motiv-ating people through share-ownership schemes is that share values can fall as well as rise. Cautious rating of the US do-it-yourself industry as a whole has made Home Depot's stock stagnate recently. Given that Home Depot has rewarded performance not with sales commission but with stock and options, this is a potentially serious problem for one of the most admired US retailers.[16]

N. Brown has tried hard to involve everyone in sharing the firm's success. Explains Chief Executive Jim Martin: 'The senior executive group have received generous allocations of share options and have been rewarded very well. We've been anxious to spread the culture right down to the first line in our organisation. We've achieved that with the use of profit-related pay for all staff, given as an addition to their annual wage awards. A share Save As You Earn scheme was introduced, and we have more than 40 per cent of our employees saving on a regular basis from £10 to £250 per month. The first of the five-year schemes is maturing and there is clear excitement about the gains that they've all made, along with a recognition of how important profits are for long term success and security.'

RECOGNISING AND REWARDING ACHIEVEMENT

High-performing businesses tend to use the widest possible variety of methods to reward and recognise achievement. They recognise, firstly, that people are motivated by different things at different times and, secondly, that it is better to motivate people frequently and gently rather than in infrequent outpourings. One of the lessons learned by financial centres such as Wall Street, the City of London and Frankfurt is that massive year-end bonuses lose their motivating effect very quickly after the money is received. Indeed, that is the point at which many employees in that industry elect to move on.

The combination of medium-term reward and short-term recognition can be very powerful, however. Our case-study companies almost all focused managers' attention on achieving annual targets, but gave them plenty of encouragement and praise as they strove towards the target.

Medium-term reward

Managers at Wal-Mart are allowed to keep up to five per cent of the pre-tax profits from their store – giving them the potential, in extremes, to quadruple their annual pay.

To reward individual cabin crew for consistently demonstrating the service for which Singapore Airlines is renowned, the Winning Ways Award (Individual) was introduced in 1993. In August 1994 the scheme was extended to teams, with the ten teams earning the highest number of compliments winning cash vouchers of $2,000 each.

British Airways operates a profit-sharing scheme that has paid out 11 out of the past 13 years and usually amounts to several weeks' pay. Says Chairman Sir Colin Marshall: 'You get the best out of people by listening to them, keeping them informed and providing real incentives, such as a tangible share of profit for each individual. In short, to achieve success, you have got to teach people to succeed.'

'Microsoft, too, seeks and rewards tenacity, technical expertise, thinking, problem-solving and, often, willingness to trade high salaries for a longer-term stake in the company's profits.'[17]

Southwest Airlines manages absenteeism and good timekeeping by staff by providing incentives linked to travel. A perfect record on both counts for three months earns two free, space-available tickets anywhere in its network. The employee can use the tickets personally, or pass them on to friends.

At SOL, salaries are based on a mixture of basic salaries and a variable incentive based on a number of targets – for example, profitability, customer satisfaction, and customer retention. Each target they meet contributes to the bonus total. Supervisors' bonuses are based on how their cleaners perform.

With few exceptions, the compensation schemes perused by high-performing companies are tied both to the achievement of results and *demonstrating the values*. At GE, for example, the notion of boundarylessness is reinforced by the reward system. Says Jack Welch: 'Our behaviour is driven by a fundamental core belief: the desire and the ability of an organisation to continuously learn from any source and to rapidly convert this learning into action is its ultimate competitive advantage. We have made major changes in the compensation system to support this learning behaviour. Bonuses, as well as salaries, reward the *finding* and *sharing* of ideas even more than their origination. You can talk – you can preach – all you want about a "learning organisation", but, from our experience, reinforcing management appraisal and compensation schemes are the critical enablers that must be in place if rhetoric is to become reality.'

It isn't easy to get the balance right between rewarding for results and rewarding for values. Time and again we have encountered companies that espouse becoming a learning organisation as a core value yet struggle to make their managers behave in a developmental manner, even though everyone seems agreed that this is a generally 'good thing'. What happens in most cases is that, even if the bonus system contains some measures that reward developmental behaviours, these amount to only a small proportion of the total bonus. What counts most in bonus is still achieving the task, even though managers may be intellectually aware that the best way to do so is through growing the talent around them. Even where the influence on bonus from demonstrating the right values is large, the bonus is only one part of the reward package. Equally important are what managers are praised and respected for, by their peers and seniors; and what achievements are most likely to bring promotion or assignment to plum projects.

To get the balance right, an organisation's top management must create a climate where the *total* environment for reward and compensation is aligned with the core values. Then the system of financial reward can be managed so that people have to deliver both results and behaviours to earn their bonus – one without the other simply is not acceptable.

Short-term recognition

'Fun ... is recognition,' Southwest Airlines' Chief Financial Officer told the *Financial Times*.[18] Everyone in the company gets a birthday card from top management. Every promotion is recognised with a bottle of champagne and 'celebrations and awards break up the routine'. Rewards can be anything from 'formal employee-of-the-year awards to daily acts of recognition for good service. Informal rewards include gifts of [confectionery] or ice-cream, an hour off work, an impromptu party, or – very highly valued in the US – a parking space close to the office.'

Recognition doesn't have to be through high-profile activities or financial incentives. At one General Electric plant, one of the most successful motivational ideas was to give employees free coffee and doughnuts each month when they reached their quota.

'I have personally sent people's wives a couple of plane tickets for a weekend away, totally out of the blue,' says Electrocomponents CEO Bob Lawson: 'I never say why; they know. I like bringing people from deep down in the organisation to give presentations to the board. We might fly in a couple of Germans, who have won a safest factory award, on a Friday to make their presentation. They'll be joined by their spouses for the weekend.' Similarly, says Stephanie Monk at Granada: 'Charles [Allen] has been particularly good at celebrating success, whether it's somebody's birthday or a major corporate event. He will remember all sorts of peoples' birthdays and send flowers or a gift.'

By contrast, Reuters makes relatively little fuss of people. Says Director of Staff Development and Efficiency Programmes Martin Davids: 'It's not in the culture to applaud people. What we offer is a huge amount of buzz and excitement in product development, which comes from working with committed and loyal people.'

Says Sir Roger Hurn, Chairman of Smiths Industries: 'The way to get the best out of people is to make the managers truly responsible and pay people for success. Almost everyone in Smith Industries has some part of their pay based on the success of the business in which they work, right down to the shop floor. ... Whatever system they have – and they vary a lot across 60 businesses – the only central direction we give is "For God's sake, keep it simple!" If people don't understand why they're being paid or not paid a bonus, we've failed. They have to understand what the measure is and identify with it.'

Promotion and the opportunity to gain new experience can also be a strong motivator, particularly when they are seen to be fair and related to genuine achievement. Says Sir Clive Thompson at Rentokil Initial: 'This company is less political than most because everyone can be measured on their individual performance. Promotion is based on performance. It doesn't matter where you went to school or who you know. Promotion here is based on performance, not being a good chap. I have no favourites.' Allen Yurko at Siebe also places great store on promotion opportunities as a major motivator. He explains: 'The first incentive we give is they get the opportunity to perform. Our managing directors and senior managers like working here. We all like our families taken care of, but if you don't like what you do, money isn't going to help a lot. We survey them and they still say they like it here. We lose very few people by voluntary termination. Secondly, people get bigger opportunities. Less than half of the top 50 people here have the same job they were hired into.'

USING COMMUNICATION AS THE DRIVING ENGINE OF COMMITMENT

Communication is always best face to face

High-performance companies believe communication is too important to leave to passive media, as the following examples show:

- Says Southwest Airlines' Herb Kelleher: 'Communication is not getting up and giving speeches. It's saying, "Hey Dave, how are you doing? Heard the wife's sick – she OK?".'

- 'We keep communication very simple' says Dr Pepper/Seven Up President John Brock. 'We don't go in for reams of paper but a lot of face-to-face meetings, which involves a lot of travel. Once you start writing memos, a degree of bureaucracy always creeps in. By communicating in person we keep out the misunderstandings and irritations.'

- Face-to-face communication is also a priority at Siebe. Allen Yurko insists on between seven and ten personal meetings a year with each CEO: 'Occasionally, we use video conferencing, but we don't like it because we can't observe the mannerisms; you don't really feel like the person's in the room with you. When you meet face to face, you get a flavour of the business and the person behind it.'

- At Reuters 'no one writes memos' says Ros Wilton, Managing Director of the Transactions Products. 'A great deal of face-to-face and telephone communication takes place instead. CEO Peter Job picks up the phone to ask me or anyone else what's going on.'

- At ASDA, 'We're very much more open now than we were,' says Mike Killoran. 'I remember when the general manager of each store used to virtually keep the profit-and-loss account in a safe. Now we have colleague huddles where the manager explains what the sales figures are for the month and how they stack up with the business plan.'

- At SAP, 'People have a lot of opportunity to contribute. Not all decisions are made top-down. There is a great deal of open discussion. To be in a project team, which most people are, is very good – it engenders a great spirit and there is great egalitarianism,' says Henning Kagermann.

- Marks & Spencer stores have a weekly meeting between the three most senior managers and elected staff representatives, one from each area in the store. The meeting is chaired by one of the staff and the topics can cover almost anything in the business.

- Home Depot holds a quarterly video broadcast 'Breakfast with Bernie and Arthur' (the Chairman and CEO respectively). Every Sunday morning there is a broadcast by satellite television in which current topics are discussed, from company philosophy to new product ranges. Employees can telephone their own comments live to the show.

The one exception to the face-to-face rule is Microsoft, which places much greater emphasis on e-mail. 'It's a powerful tool, because it allows frequency of communication. You can be in contact with your manager three or four times a day. It develops continuity and familiarity in the relationship. It's been our primary means of communication for 15 years,' says Mike Murray, Vice President of Human Resources and Administration. The key to Microsoft's ability to make electronic communication work is that it uses e-mail not to replace human interaction, but to enhance it.

Openness

Openness is essentially about the climate of the organisation. It involves an absence of secrecy and of standing on dignity. At its extreme, anyone can talk to anyone else, regardless of rank. This is true of SOL, Microsoft, IKEA and several other of our cases. Some examples again:

- Southwest Airlines has avoided techniques such as '360-degree feedback' because, says CEO Kelleher, they aren't needed. People already feel free to tell each other about problems – and do, he says.

- Says Sir Roger Hurn of Smiths Industries: 'I believe in trusting people that work here ... we tell them far more than most companies.' Unusual for the UK, Smiths has had employee councils for 25 years, 'so people are used to having an influence on management thinking,' adds Human Resources Director David Spencer. 'We make sure people understand the business they are in. In most cases, they have almost as much information at their fingertips as their managers do. If there is bad news, we tell them as directly as we would good news.'

- Employees at Microsoft are encouraged to send e-mail messages to anyone else, no matter what their position.

- At Electrocomponents, says CEO Bob Lawson: 'The grapevine here is not run by bandits. It's a part of our natural organisation. If you try and suppress it you'll drive it underground. Just recognise it's part of life, don't feel threatened by it and don't abuse it. Being ordinary is part of the grapevine.'

- At SOL, says CEO Liisa Joronen: 'All our people have access to our figures. We try to be as open as possible. You cannot give too much information. How can they misuse it?' A monthly newsletter gives everyone in the organisation figures on all the financials and on a wide range of other topics, from absenteeism levels to customer satisfaction.

In summary...

High-performance companies do extract extraordinary performance out of ordinary people. They often do so by challenging those people to become extraordinary. The right people, with the right attitudes and behaviours in the right environment – it sounds too good to be true. And to some extent, it is, for there is at least one further key ingredient to the effective people balance – the style and quality of leadership, particularly at the top. Chapter Eleven shows how the right leadership can turn ordinary people into guided missiles on behalf of the company.

11 | VALUES-BASED LEADERSHIP
Leaders versus managers

'I don't think leadership is a complicated business.' *Sir Roger Hurn, Chairman, Smiths Industries*

'There's a huge difference between managing and leading. Every company has plenty of managers. Leaders motivate and inspire and dream dreams. Then they draw in others to help them achieve those dreams. Managers worry a lot about how they're doing things, rather than why they are doing them.' *John Brock, President and CEO of Dr Pepper/Seven Up*

There have probably been more books and academic papers on the nature of leadership than any other theme in management science. One estimate by a researcher in the mid-1980s identified more than 4,000 significant references. Leadership has pre-occupied generations of researchers because it is so difficult to define, so fundamentally important to the achievement of business goals, so alluring as a characteristic that every self-respecting executive needs to exhibit. Yet, for all the attempts to explain and analyse leadership, we are no nearer to packaging and wrapping it than we were 100 years ago.

Few people have had such an impact on the leadership debate as the American management writer Warren Bennis. Bennis simplified the debate about leadership by contrasting leaders against managers. He provides a distinctive list of differences, as follows.[1]

'To survive in the 21st century, we're going to need a new generation of leaders – leaders, not managers. The distinction is an important one. Leaders conquer the context – volatile, turbulent, ambiguous surroundings that sometimes seem to conspire against us and will surely suffocate us if we let them – while managers surrender to it. There are other crucial differences:

- The manager administers; the leader innovates.
- The manager is a copy; the leader is an original.
- The manager maintains; the leader develops.
- The manager focuses on systems and structure; the leader focuses on people.
- The manager relies on control; the leader inspires trust.

- The manager has a short-range view; the leader has a long-range perspective.
- The manager asks how and when; the leader asks what and why.
- The manager has his eye on the bottom line; the leader has his eye on the horizon.
- The manager imitates; the leader originates.
- The manager accepts the status quo; the leader challenges it.
- The manager is the good soldier; the leader is his own person.
- The manager does things right; the leader does the right thing.'

Well-intentioned as Bennis's analysis was, it may have done companies more of a disservice by depicting leadership and management as opposites. So generations of managers have striven to show that they are really leaders, because managers are really second-class citizens. We think – and our high-performance companies' experience bears it out – that management and leadership are not separable, although individuals may have a tendency to demonstrate one rather than the other. A leader without management skills is as useless as a manager without leadership skills. Says Electrocomponents' CEO, Bob Lawson: 'It's my personal view that most of our people are both – the good managers know when to lead and when to manage. Clear responsibility is the key. Then it's up to them.'

Much of the confusion between leadership and management can be dispelled, in our view, by defining the former as a role and the latter as a function. The function of management is about rationality, logic, systems and control; the role of leadership is about capturing hearts and minds, building consensus around goals larger than individuals, releasing energy. Our high-performing companies would argue that an important element of their success lies in selecting and developing people who can perform both the function and the role effectively.

Leaders only operate with the consent and goodwill of sufficient followers – by the authority of their personality and the respect they have earned; managers operate by virtue of the resources they control or can access – by authority of position. Our high-performing companies typically expect people to be managers when they deal with the routine, task-oriented aspects of their jobs, and leaders when they deal with the intuitive, visioning and people aspects. The balance will vary according to the individual's job and level in the organisation, but at the top, the emphasis is very much on leadership. Even at the top, however, the management function is an important element of their competence.

One of the simplest and most effective ways of distinguishing between the role of leadership and the function of management, is to take *authority* out of the equation. If the manager did not have the authority to tell people what to do, would they still do what he or she wants them to? Effective leaders get things done through influence rather than command. Indeed, they may often not have a view they wish to bring people round to; they may demonstrate leadership by helping the team come to its own conclusions about the best way forward. It is a myth that the leader has always to lead from the front.

At IKEA, they talk of three characteristics of a good manager, whatever level he or she operates at: leadership, the relevant technical skills and knowledge, and the ability to organise. In recruitment and promotion, these three characteristics are the first thing they look for.

Our case-study companies are not all sold on the virtues of leadership, however. Says SOL's CEO Liisa Joronen: 'I would have even less leaders in the traditional sense. That's the ideal model. More than two-thirds of business leaders are useless. I would like to go more to a mentor system with fewer leaders, but I don't think that will happen. If I had a factory here, I would not have one supervisor. Only when people are scattered do we need supervisors.' What she means is that every individual can be their own leader and manager.

Microsoft has given particular thought to what it expects of leader-managers. Explains Mike Murray, Vice President of Human Resources and Administration: 'Anyone who has people reporting to them has the word "manager" in their title. We expect the manager to get more out of his or her people. We have found that there are three key drivers of a successful manager at Microsoft:

- They make sure the group and every member in it have clear goals and objectives and performance measures.
- They must be very good at planning, the sometimes tedious process of figuring out the details of how to get there.
- They give continual feedback.

All our best-performing and most highly motivated teams have managers who meet these criteria. If one or more of these drivers is missing in the manager, then the team will not perform so well and people are likely to want to leave us.

'At higher levels some people have the natural ability to become a leader. These people are sensitive to critical issues, to the emotions those issues arouse and to the complexity within them. They also have the ability to seize the moment – they know precisely when to rally the troops.'

Our high-performance company CEOs share a number of characteristics in their own leader–manager style:

- *They are universally demanding of people who work with them.* For example,

Sir Gerald Whent at Vodafone admits: 'I ask a lot of people, but then I think people like to be asked to do a lot. Leadership is about keeping people going and giving them hope and inspiration when things get black; and about not letting people get too flamboyant when things go well.'

- *They communicate their excitement and enjoyment of the business wherever they go.* 'It's a super job', says Bob Lawson. A lot of them also seem to have a lot of fun and to spread it liberally. 'I use a lot of humour to release the pressure,' says Granada's Charles Allen. 'That way we can have an important management meeting to look at possible changes in the external environment that affect us, such as a change of government, with a very light touch.'

- *They have remarkable tenacity.* If they believe something is important and right, they will chip away at it continuously until they make it happen. Says Noel Tichy, a professor at the University of Michigan: 'The perseverance to repeat the same message day after day, year after year, with no end in sight, may be [GE's] Welch's greatest strength'.[2]

- *They are strong on developing the capabilities of people around them.* Says Barrie Stephens, Chairman of Siebe: 'You have to have inside you an innate sense of acute competitiveness and you have to be a natural leader. Those are the two attributes you need to build a world-beating company with a world-beating culture. Everything comes from that: the drive for quality, caring for people, and letting people make their own mistakes in a nursery environment.'

- *They encourage discussion and challenge to their ideas.* Rather than surround themselves with yes-men, they seek out people who will provide mutual challenge in thinking through strategic issues. For example, Tony Pidgley of The Berkeley Group maintains: 'I would rather work with rich people, who aren't worried about the next mortgage payment; if they don't agree with me, they'll tell me to **** off!'

- *They are highly visible.* Pidgley again: 'Further down in the business, our high-performance companies do expect leaders to be hands-on. The [local] managing director must open the post every day; he must see it. He must handle every complaint personally and see every house. ... If you aren't passionate about what you do, then you won't last long in this business.' And Barrie Stephens at Siebe: 'You can't do without visiting people regularly, eyeballing them, walking the plants and reviewing their performance. It must be done regularly and frequently, against a measured set of values set co-operatively between you and them.' Lord

Blyth at Boots 'dips in when he has to', says David Kissman, Personnel Director of Boots The Chemist. 'I'm always amazed by how much he knows about the business. He will often walk in to a store and say, "Why is the packaging like that?" or "Shouldn't we be displaying that product to better effect?" His knowledge is remarkable. But he does not sit on managers' shoulders. He is quite hands-off.'

Balancing leadership and management

The simplest way of describing how high-performing company CEOs manage this balance is that they make it an important part of their own accountabilities to promote both the role of leadership and the function of management. They encourage a holistic view of people's responsibilities, based upon the fact that you can't deliver challenging targets if you cannot both infect others with the challenge and support them with the infrastructure and resources to make things happen, to feel confident in taking sensible risks, and to pause, reflect and learn. They do so in several ways:

- they rely on values rather than systems to influence behaviour;
- they take seriously their own role as 'chief coach';
- they identify with the 'big idea';
- they emphasise inclusion rather than exclusion; and
- they set the example in their own behaviour.

RELIANCE ON VALUES RATHER THAN SYSTEMS TO INFLUENCE PEOPLE'S BEHAVIOUR

A major European subsidiary of a Japanese multinational recently had a new chief executive, whose brief was to ensure the company widened its marketing lead. The new CEO worked out a vision of the future, established a broad strategy and communicated it with gusto. No one indicated that they were in disagreement with either the vision or the strategy. Yet he met nothing but passive resistance. Puzzled and frustrated, the CEO brought in some communication consultants, with a view to pushing yet more communication into the organisation. The consultants took a different tack, however. They asked the employees about the values they held dear and the values they thought the CEO held. It rapidly became clear that the employees thought the CEO was aiming to ditch the company's 'commitment to product excellence' in favour of 'flavour of the month responses – poor quality products people would not feel proud to be involved with'. In fact, he was as committed to customer service as any of them; he just wanted to add a focus on 'speed of response to market demand'.

The lesson of this story is that alignment or misalignment of values exerts a very powerful influence on the way people behave and on their willingness to embrace new strategies. It's a lesson that our high-performance companies seem to be instinctively aware of. Their CEOs typically see their most important task as ensuring that the values are understood and lived by the top 100 or 200 managers; and that those managers in turn accept their responsibility for reinforcing the values in their operations.

Says Atlas Copco's Michael Treschow: 'Our structure provides a lot of autonomy. We have 16 different divisions. It's impossible to dominate them from the centre. I think it's very important to have that structure, but at the same time you cannot abdicate. You delegate the responsibility as far out as possible but it's your damned responsibility to keep it together as a group, with common values and common culture and common ideas and common systems, and the way we do things at Atlas Copco. That's my responsibility, to make sure it's not completely different here and there, because then we don't get the synergies.'

At Rentokil Initial, says Sir Clive Thompson: 'I see my job now as strategy leadership. By that I mean presence, not aura exactly, but the fact that you are there. The tension and apprehension that generates is very important – people caring because the person at the top cares. My role is also to protect the culture, and to give it bite, sharpness and aggression. But I don't think the business would change that much if I fell under a bus tomorrow.'

Says The Berkeley Group's Tony Pidgley: 'The culture is vital to the company. It's a culture that seems to breed here. I'm always here, for example. I'm not always doing much. Sometimes I might just be reading the newspaper, but it sets the culture – I'm here to do business if people want to talk to me.'

Cadbury Schweppes has a similar view, says Human Resources Director Bob Stack: 'We struggle with what leadership style and leadership model we should be reinforcing. The answer is, there isn't one in the kinds of terms that consultants think about. It is about the values. How you are able to deliver those values is down to you. We expect it to be different, based on cultural differences, market place differences, mature markets, developing markets and so on. Our expectation is that leadership is based on the situation you are managing, but that the common elements come back to the values.'

John Brock, President of Beverages Stream and CEO of Cadbury subsidiary Dr Pepper/Seven Up, bases his leadership style on three things, he declares: 'Firstly, a clear set of values so that everyone in the company knows what I think is OK and isn't. That's about integrity. Those core values never change. If you start to change them, you'll quickly lose your constituency. Secondly, a leader also has to be able to paint a picture of where he wants to go, for the whole organisation. That picture has to change when it needs to. The third part is hard work. I don't think there is any leader who can lead without being prepared to work hard and set an example.'

For Liisa Joronen at SOL, a hands-off style is difficult but essential. Her goal is for people to run the company themselves, with her simply there to set the tone and stimulate discussion. She recalls: 'I hope that they don't need me so much as people think. I was abroad for five weeks with my husband a year ago and when I came back it was just like a normal day almost. It was a good thing but sometimes you like to be more needed. I am happy if my people ask me to come to speak to them. It's a funny situation to be the company owner and let your people do what they think best. If we don't meet the month's target, I see all the time things that should be done in a different way. It's very hard not to tell people what they should do, but if I did then it would be my problem.'

THE CEO AS 'CHIEF COACH'

'Increasingly, I think leadership is about coaching and encouraging rather than dictating and being first over the wire,' says GKN's Sir David Lees. 'The best way of leading is to make sure you have got the best person you can raise to lead each of the individual businesses, and decentralise decision making to them, reserving the CEO for key issues and the strategy of the group.' At Bowthorpe, CEO Nicholas Brookes sees his role as coaching all 97 managing directors of the businesses, even though they do not all report directly to him.

Roger Mavity, managing director of Granada's Rental Division, gives an intriguing insight into the coaching manner of group CEO Charles Allen. 'I worked once with Terence Conran. You'd hear people who'd never even met him say, "Terence wouldn't like that." People seemed to have a very strong sense of what Conran would do in a certain situation. Strong personalities at the top sometimes radiate a vision like that, which is not even spoken. Charles is very clever at that. Occasionally, he'll drill down into an issue with question after question until he gets right down to the nitty-gritty. He knows that he doesn't have to do that all the time, because if he asks me a question, I'd better have thought it through. Very quickly, everyone in the organisation knows what Charles' priorities are, even people who have never met him.'

This personal attention from the top pays enormous dividends, says Siebe's Barrie Stephens: 'If you have a guy who's busting his balls for you, and you can spiritually put your arms around him and lift him up, then you have a guided missile.'

IDENTIFYING WITH THE 'BIG IDEA'

One of the fiercest debates about the nature of leadership is whether leaders need charisma. Some of the CEOs clearly do have a great deal of charisma. For example, when General Electric's Jack Welch talks to the troops, says Steven Kerr, GE's Vice President for Corporate Leadership Development, 'They get so energised. They don't know what part they are going to play, but they are damned well going to help him do whatever he asks.'[3]

At ASDA, says Mike Killoran, Head of Customer Services: 'Allen [Leighton] in particular is a tremendous motivator. I remember a meeting at Shipley [West Yorkshire] when I was in charge of the store there. It was the first time I'd met Allen and Archie. Allen came into the store with no jacket on and made straight for me. He shook my hand. He knew which stores I'd worked in and about me. I felt six inches taller. I think they did that for everyone in the company. It gave us back our sense or pride and restored morale.'

At least as many others, however, do not seem to be particularly charismatic. They are, however, *inspirational* in the sense that they communicate their own enthusiasm and belief in core values and core ideas – in particular, the 'big ideas' of Chapter Four. In effect, they become so associated with the idea that in the minds of the employees they *are* the idea. Says Granada's Stephanie Monk: 'Organisations have personalities like people. People need to have a sense of being able to identify with and commit to a situation. The role of the leader is to facilitate that and make it happen. They don't have to be autocratic and turn everything around, but people need to have the sense that there is one person taking the organisation forward. It's very good for people in the organisation when someone in a position of influence goes out to them and clearly is a bit out of the ordinary, [but] has something to offer and people can identify with them.'

It's also important, maintains Jack Welch, for the leader to exaggerate in order to make the point. He says: 'Everything I do has to look larger than life, or people can't see me. I have to jolt the enterprise, overstate and use hyperbole.' By asking for the moon, he may only get the strato-sphere, but that's a long way off the ground.

The more the CEO is talked about outside the organisation, in terms of his or her ideas, the greater the sense of identity between the leader and those people in the organisation who share and are also excited about the same values and ideas. Adds Monk: 'People read a bit about them in the paper and so they can identify with them. They've not got grey people heading up the organisation. They've got people with a bit of character and a few fairly outspoken things to say. I think more people like that than don't like that.'

Of course, it takes real leadership skill to merge one's own identity into the big idea. It also takes great communication skills and an ability and willingness to debate around the big idea with any audience. Above all, it takes self-belief and high personal integrity.

EMPHASISING INCLUSION RATHER THAN EXCLUSION

Keeping people informed is another important aspect of inclusion. As we saw in Chapter Ten, most of our high-performing companies go out of their way to ensure openness of information. For example, at Smiths Industries, says Sir Roger Hurn, 'I don't think leadership is a complicated business. People make it complicated because they overdo the secrecy bit. I believe in trusting people that work in this company. We tell them a great deal more than they would hear about in most companies, par-ticularly about the business they work in. We tell them everything and invite their comments. Leadership isn't complicated unless you make it so. ... You have to keep talking, keep being open, don't be secretive when you don't have to be, trust people who work with you with information in excess of that which can be found in the corporate accounts or that analysts know.'

Singapore Airlines also keeps people involved through extensive use of task forces and project teams, drawn from across functional boundaries. This gives rise to its own set of checks and balances. CEO Cheong explains: 'Quite often, when we want to look at a strategic issue, we set up task forces – sometimes of very senior people, sometimes of quite junior people – and we ask them to brainstorm and come up with rec-ommendations. Then we get comments that there are too many task forces and, "Why is decision-making so slow? Why can't we just get on with it?" Yet if you do decide something has to be done without consulting, then people say you are authoritarian. The pendulum swings from one side to the other and you constantly have to be fine-tuning the system. We don't think we should be an authoritarian organisation or a participatory one:

we need to have a mix that depends on circumstances and how far we have to move.'

A similar motivation inspires Southwest Airlines' CEO Herbert Kelleher. Loathing bureaucracy of any kind, he refuses to allow any form of permanent committee. Instead, he has created numerous temporary committees that often include people from all levels of the company, from senior management to ground and air crew.

The capacity to involve others and recognise their contribution, in terms of ideas as well as implementation, comes across in all our CEOs, even the toughest. They achieve in all cases, through including others in the thinking process. For example, of Bill Gates it has been said: 'Microsoft has been led by a man widely recognised as a genius in his own right, who has had the foresight to recognise the genius in others.'[4]

Another way Microsoft emphasises the level of partnership it desires with its employees is by matching dollar-for-dollar the amount of charitable donations it makes, up to $12,000 per head.

Few companies take such an inclusive approach as SOL, which has involved its employees – all of them – in all the major decisions it faced, with the exception of forming itself into a separate company. The top team, some of whom had worked with Joronen for 15 years, decided a name change was essential. So they went out to the employees and asked them for their suggestions on the new name. SOL was chosen because it means both sunshine and happiness. Says Joronen: 'The better people think, the better they are. If you think in a positive way, you really succeed.'

This level of involvement – well over half the employees made suggestions for the new name – helped gain ownership across the organisation. So did Joronen's efforts in visiting every branch to talk through the changes with the employees. Very often with a name change, it takes months, if not years, for people to stop using the old name as well. But 'SOL, formerly Lindstrom' became just SOL in only three weeks. Everyone, both customers and employees, was comfortable with the change.

LEADERS SET THE EXAMPLE

The notion of 'management by walking about' has taken a lot of stick in recent years, much of it unjustified. It's true that the leader who is wandering around the shop floor may be causing more disruption by his or her presence than can be compensated for in benefits to the business. But it's quite hard to set an example from an office desk. Senior managers who make genuinely useful visits to the shop floor have two basic purposes in mind:

- to listen and learn about what really happens, what employees really think and how the business really works; and
- to demonstrate and reinforce the business values.

The listening CEO

The older and more senior managers become, the more inclined they are to talk and the less inclined to listen. It is partly a sense of knowing so much; partly a matter of accepting the deference others give so readily to seniority and authority; partly a biological urge to pass on wisdom. (The latter is probably why so many retiring CEOs and chairmen have the instinct to write their autobiography!)

While there is, of course, a talking role for leader–managers in explaining ideas, sharing enthusiasm and building towards a common cause, really effective CEOs spend most of their time *listening and observing*. Significantly, this is also true of effective coaches and mentors. It's an issue Michael Treschow of Atlas Copco feels strongly about: 'The worst thing with top managers is when they are too creative. Organisations cannot stand creative management. I have to hold my tongue from time to time and remember not to think aloud. It always gives messages you did not intend.' Instead, the role of the CEO is to listen, ask questions and stimulate the businesses' own thinking.

Active listening can be an uncomfortable but rewarding experience, says Granada's Charles Allen: 'I spent a day with one of our rental engineers recently. I learned that we still came away from three customers out of the eight we visited without the kit working. That's something we now have to address. ... My main reason for going out isn't to see the sites, but to check what messages are getting through. I might ask a site manager about an initiative, to see if he knows much about it for example.'

Other exponents of the listening CEO include:

- Archie Norman, chairman of ASDA. One of his first moves on taking over at ASDA was to introduce a campaign called 'Tell Archie', which encouraged colleagues (ASDA's word for employees) to tell the new Chief Executive what was wrong within the company and where improvements could be made. Since then over 15,000 colleagues have done just that.

- Jack Welch of General Electric. Whenever he gives a presentation to groups of employees, at any level, he asks for personal feedback. Did they learn anything useful? Was there anything they didn't understand or caused them concern? The feedback helps him both to improve the presentation and to assess how well the message is getting through.

- Robert Ayling, CEO of British Airways. Ayling has an hour-long meeting every week with 15 or so managers from around the business, often including aircraft captains. A quarterly independent 'staff attitudes and trends' survey tells Ayling and his colleagues how well or otherwise they are doing in leadership and communication.

- Nicholas Brookes, Bowthorpe Chief Executive, writing in the 1995 annual report: 'I will continue to travel extensively and listen to ideas from those with the operational experience.'

- Charles Allen at Granada. Says Stephanie Monk, Human Resources Director: 'There's not a lot of formality. It's jackets off. When Charles comes to a hotel, he always goes and talks to everybody in the kitchen.'

- JCB's founder, Joe Bamford, apart from being a good engineer, was also a great listener. Says a colleague: 'No one, as far as I could see, had any great academic ability in the early days, but Mr Bamford could motivate people. He would listen to everyone and he was always challenging his senior people. He would listen, whether the ideas were good or not.'[5]

- Barrie Stephens, chairman of Siebe: 'Leaders have to be so unegotistical that, if you are stood on a platform communicating tactics and someone else suggests something better, you have to be able to say in public: "Your idea is better." '

Demonstrating and reinforcing the values

Because the CEO is the embodiment of the values, he or she has to be seen to live them. The CEO's behaviour will always be observed by others, who will use it as a role model. If the CEO doesn't really seem to mean what he or she says about a value, then the value itself becomes meaningless. Nowhere is this so true as when the CEO visits the front line. (And all of them do spend a lot of their time there – says Lord Blyth: 'We don't have absentee landlords. I'm in the stores continuously ... I pay quite a big price for that, because it takes so much time.') For example:

- Informality and lack of stuffiness are traits that the founders of Home Depot continue to role model to their employees. Executives visit the stores alone and without fuss.

- IKEA's founder, Ingvar Kamprad, who still plays an active role in the business although officially retired, established a reputation for deep-seated concern for his employees. He rarely enters stores by the front door; he prefers to come in via the loading bay where he can talk first to the warehousemen. Anders Moberg, Chief Executive of IKEA, flies economy class and never takes taxis when there is public transport available. He will often turn up to meetings on the bus.

- N. Brown's Chairman David Alliance 'has an almost evangelical zeal when it comes to serving customers well,' says Chief Executive Jim Martin.

- When the weather is good, SOL's Chief Executive Liisa Joronen sets the tone of equality by leaving her yellow car behind and riding to work on her bicycle. It reinforces her slogan, 'freedom from status symbols'.

- Granada's Chairman Gerry Robinson sets an example of working smarter not harder, while reinforcing the autonomy his managers have to get on and do what they think is right. He usually works only a 30-hour week, takes weekends and Fridays off and expects to be telephoned at home only in dire emergency. He told the *Irish Times*, only partially tongue-in-cheek: 'I think most work is pointless. There are only three or four things you do a day that have any effect on your business. The rest is a waste of time.'[6]

By demonstrating behaviours themselves, CEOs are better able to insist that managers down the line follow suit. At Marks & Spencer, managers have to have lived the work they expect others to do, by spending time in the jobs themselves, from stacking shelves to serving customers. It is all part of the apprenticeship.

At Siebe, says Chairman Barrie Stephens: 'When you are a small company and you have a problem in a factory 200 miles away, a leader visits it the next day. You listen and determine whether or how you can help. What counts is the fact that you are there, not at home with the family; that you care enough to be in the hot seat with them, even if there is little you can do. You could sit comfortably in your study at home and talk to the factory manager, but it's not the same. No one will tell you to do it, but natural leaders just *know*. When we look for leadership qualities, we seek people who have aggressiveness without arrogance.'

Another way in which the CEO sets an example is by what he or she is seen to focus on. Is their attention seen to be solely on the finances, or on the values? For example, Bowthorpe CEO Nicholas Brookes is adamant: 'I do not follow the share price by the minute or get too involved with minor movements. I believe in keeping my eye firmly on the business, and if that is going along strongly in the right direction, the analysts and the City will take care of the share price.'

It is equally important, however, says Atlas Copco's Michael Treschow, that the CEO be careful not to create clones of himself or herself. He explains: 'One of the things I'm deadly scared of is the opposite of diversity – homogeneity, or whatever the English word is – because the striving must be for diversity. Whatever we do has to be a mirror of the environment in which we live and act, and if we get too many people who think the same as I do, and too many people who would try to copy me, that would be dangerous to Atlas Copco.'

Management by example isn't only for people at the top, of course. Our high-performance companies expect managers at all levels to demonstrate the values of the business. At ASDA, for example, says Head of Customer Services Mike Killoran: 'Service with personality starts with how we treat colleagues. If we want our people to serve customers well, then managers must treat colleagues with courtesy and respect. The general manager of the store sets the tone. It's all about leading by example. For example, if we have a queue developing, we now have a "queue-buster" call that goes out in the store. Managers are expected to respond and lead from the front.' Similarly, at IKEA, says Sven-Olof Kulldorff: 'If you don't manage by example then you won't survive in this culture. You have to dem- onstrate basic things – for example, that you are open and that you're interested in people.'

GE expects all its senior managers to take and be active mentors and role models. Says Steven Kerr, Vice President for Corporate Leadership Development: 'We asked the head of our plastics business to lecture on a topic recently. He responded with "Why do you think I'm any good at this?" We pointed out that he was, but he wasn't necessarily aware how good he was. It was one of the best lectures we'd had.' The executive learned by teaching others – simply articulating good practice reinforced it in his own performance.

In summary . . .

High-performing companies do not share a particular style of leadership and management. On the contrary, they are diverse in their style and they encourage further diversity within their operations. They create 'natural' leaders by providing the example and the environment where leadership and management can thrive together.

Perhaps the last word on this topic belongs to Michael Treschow of Atlas Copco: 'We spent almost a year trying to figure out how can we train ourselves more in leadership, because I had a strong belief that better leadership would bring better results. To manage is to take care of things; managers are given their authority. Leadership is something that comes from below because people are willing to follow you. If you want to create great results you need to lead, you cannot just manage. So we tried for more than a year to figure out how we could train ourselves better in leadership. We went out and met many many consultants and read books, and we got rather frustrated because we couldn't find anything that fitted us. There's a lot of books out there. But all the books and all the consultants had one thing in common we didn't like, and that was the prototypes and the myth of leadership, the discussion of the super leader, the ideal leader, the born leader, the perfect leader. We didn't like any of this, because in reality we believe strongly that leadership is very much common sense. We have to de-mystify it and understand that many people are already good enough as leaders. Rather than dismantle people's confidence by telling them they are lousy leaders and they have to change themselves, we'd rather start at the other end and say, "Let's start with the basic assumption that all of us are here because we are acceptable leaders."'

Inevitably, however, the style of leadership within the organisation will be a reflection of the style at the top. So high-performing companies spend a lot of time and energy ensuring that the transition between one chief executive and the next will take place with minimum disruption to the business values and the consistency with which the other critical balances are managed. Chapter Twelve examines how they do so.

12 | SEAMLESS SUCCESSION
Gentle versus abrupt succession

'One of the great things of being a good business leader is knowing when to go!' *Sir Gerald Whent, Chief Executive, Vodafone.*

When high-performing companies seriously lose their way, it is more often than not associated with a change of leadership at the top. In some cases, the incumbent chief executive simply grows stale, hanging on too long before handing over; in others, a new, usually external appointee feels the need to introduce changes that, in hindsight, work against the company's core competencies.

Of course, there are situations where a new broom is undoubtedly needed: where a company is in crisis, where it needs to make a step change in order to keep growing (for example, from a family business to one that is professionally managed, or from nationally-focused to international, or from international to global), or where, as with Smiths Industries and GKN, it is clear to a far-sighted board that the company needs to emigrate into an entirely new sector or market.

However, for most of our high-performing companies, achieving a seamless succession at the top – and wherever possible lower down the organisation too – is a high priority, for number of reasons. Among them are the following:

- The pace of change within the company is to a considerable extent dependent on having clear anchors: a coherent vision or sense of purposeful direction, clear core values, and unambiguous targets. Interfering with any of these will almost certainly slow down the pace of change rather than speed it up. The time to consider a new broom is when the organisation is unable to deliver sufficient pace of change through these internal resources.

- The new broom almost always results in an exodus of talent, as cultures clash. In the tussle between old and new it takes time to sort out who will win out. People who perceive – rightly or wrongly – that the values are changing start looking for new pastures where the values they associate with still hold sway. Very often, it is the best, most talented people who find alternative jobs first. However, several of our case-study chairmen and CEOs suggest that an external appointment can take the sting out of being passed over, for the leading internal pretenders, so that they are less inclined to leave. The theory needs to be tested.

- The new CEO is not plugged into the networks of information and trust that are the real driving force of decision making in most organisations. Someone who comes in at the top *may never be* part of those networks – you earn your influence there by the quality and quantity of trade-offs you make with peers over a period of time. The outsider is almost bound to make counter-cultural moves – and so attract resentment and opposition – because he or she simply isn't part of the club and doesn't understand its unwritten rules.

External appointments at CEO level may be beneficial, however, when the company is in or heading for crisis. The company needs to act fast, bringing in new structures, removing costs and focusing on new objectives. In comes the classic turnaround manager, typically replaced a few years later, as he or she runs out of things to cut, by a more growth-oriented CEO. Thomas Ahrens, a Swedish consultant, has studied and written extensively on high-growth companies. He found that many of them overextend themselves, because they are not prepared for the maturing of their market. A turnaround manager is appointed and frequently restores the organisation to profit. But the soul of the organisation dies in this process. The entrepreneurial, free-wheel types leave of their own will or are fired. The organisation grows systems and procedures that constrain the remaining entrepreneurs from using initiative and intuition. These companies rarely if ever return to their high-growth habits, even if the market itself blossoms again.

What happens in such cases, in our view, is that banks and shareholders are concerned about getting the company 'back into shape', when they should be thinking about getting it 'back into values'. Positive change is always faster when it is aligned with deeply held values. So the turnaround manager needs to be someone who shares the core values of the business, and who has the skills to build the recovery on those values rather than try to impose new values. An external candidate may provide a new perspective, and a new set of objectives for the organisation – but so in high probability could a number of people inside the organisation. In our original study in *The Winning Streak*, we found that the most successful conglomerates often wiped out the existing top team of a new acquisition, if it had a poor performance record, and promoted the next layer. In most cases, these people knew exactly what needed to be done and had the energy and will to do it.

Because a high-performing company is, as we hope we have demonstrated, an orchestration of balances, it doesn't take much to put it out of balance. To pursue Peter Drucker's orchestral analogy, if the woodwind section starts to play an octave lower, or a fraction of a beat faster than the strings, what results is cacophony. The CEO is the conductor. Changing CEOs is like changing conductor mid-way through a symphony. It takes very delicate handling to make the transition without causing the orchestra to falter. Says Stephanie Monk, Human Resources Director of Granada: 'Succession, not necessarily immediately at the top but in the rest of the business, can be a huge opportunity for creating change, allowing creativity and innovation in a business by bringing in a new player who changes the dynamics. Change one ingredient in the recipe and the whole flavour changes, but recognising that requires some planning and attention.'

So most of the appointments of new CEOs to our high-performing companies are perforce insiders – people who understand the company and its culture, and recognise the value of its values.

Says Rentokil Initial's Sir Clive Thompson: 'I would expect the baton to be passed to someone inside the organisation.' And Anthony Pidgley is emphatic: 'We couldn't bring in outsiders to the executive board. People have to be part of the culture here. They need to be able to read the "Indian signs" – the trends and events in the housebuilding market that alert the company to dangers and opportunities.'

Singapore Airline's Cheong declares that it is 'unthinkable that the chief executive would be someone who is not familiar with the airline; somebody familiar to everyone, with whom everybody is comfortable.' SOL's Joronen is also doubtful about how an external candidate would fare. She explains: 'We have not recruited any outsiders as managers for a long time. We have excellent people waiting for new challenges, but if we needed to do so it would be very difficult for an outsider to come in. The culture is so strong and most of my people so excellent that it would really be difficult for any outsider to gain the trust, competence and confidence. Everyone in SOL must earn his or her status and respect, and it is tough.'

'It would be unthinkable for anyone to come in from outside to replace Bill Gates,' says Mike Murray, Vice President Human Resources and Administration at Microsoft.

At Southwest Airlines, says Herb Kelleher: 'Nobody is ever going to do things exactly like I do. That's a forlorn hope. ... What we'd be looking for is ... someone with the same spirit. ... If someone came into Southwest Airlines and said, "OK, Herb Kelleher is gone, and I don't subscribe to any of the things he did ...", I think that he'd last about a month. He'd be overthrown by the people, because the culture is stronger than the people.'

None of this is to say that the new CEOs are simply copies of their predecessors, nor that they come into the job without a hefty agenda of new things they want to achieve. Far from it. They tend to be independent-minded and questioning people, who see the potential to build on the strengths of the business. Says Electrocomponents' Bob Lawson: 'My successor should share the values of the business, but not be in my image. There should be no disruption to the organisation.' They may well introduce radical new visions of the future, but these are almost always *in addition to* rather than *instead of* what has gone before.

At British Airways, Robert Ayling, appointed as CEO in 1995, has built on the sound base left to him by the Chairman, Sir Colin Marshall, by finding new areas for improving the company within the values it already holds. So the notion of unleashing a 'war on the meetings culture' and encouraging greater decentralisation of decision making to people on the spot simply reinforced perceptions of good practice. Cutting the hierarchy (he more than halved the number of people reporting directly to him) was in the same mould.

The new CEOs are more than happy to make their mark by changing operating principles – within the values, of course – and therefore to influence the generation of new rules. All of this can usually be absorbed fairly readily within the company, because it does not require people to realign personal and organisational values.

Lord Blyth's superimposition of shareholder value onto Boots was likewise an addition to the values rather than a replacement. It was not an easy task, he admits. It took a lot of patient discussion, demonstrated example and commitment from the top to persuade people to take on a new value. Now, however, he says, 'The whole organisation is so imbued with it, I don't think we could ever turn back.'

Where the appointment of a new CEO has gone to an external candidate, it has provoked considerable debate and soul searching. At Smiths Industries, for example, Sir Roger Hurn's successor has had to be an outsider because 'the age profile of the obvious internal candidates was too close to mine. You could argue that we have failed to provide an internal successor, even though we have been very good at providing internal succession in the three layers below.' How this will work out remains to be seen, but there is clearly a strong meeting of minds between Sir Roger Hurn and Keith Butler-Wheelhouse, his successor. 'I share Sir Roger's obsession with cash and profit,' said Butler-Wheelhouse on appointment.

GKN went outside for its new CEO, C.K. Chow, because the obvious internal candidate preferred to continue running the automotive side of the business. Says Trevor Bonner, Managing Director of the Automotive and Agritechnical Products Division: 'The decision not to be considered for the position was mine. In effect, I pre-empted the board considering me. I've been involved in the automotive business now for 25 years, and that's something I enjoy and wanted to continue with.' The new CEO brings in experience of business in the growing markets of Asia–Pacific, but, admits Chairman Sir David Lees, there is always an additional risk in going outside. The Chairman's role in balancing that risk is crucial, he believes.

The selection process for succession

Few of the high-performing companies had detailed succession plans – indeed, some were strongly against them. Cadbury Schweppes' Human Resources Director Robert Stack points out that one of his first actions was to kill a bureaucratic succession-planning process at the centre, in favour of a more pragmatic approach that involves getting to know people better and letting the businesses themselves undertake most of the career planning for their people.

However, as we indicated in Chapters Ten and Eleven, almost all the CEOs take a strong personal interest in the development of the top two hundred or so people in the business. Says Granada's Charles Allen: 'I know the top hundred people in the business well, and the top three hundred quite well. That allows me to have a useful input into succession planning. I'm very logical, but I don't go in for formal succession plans.' Similarly, Lord Blyth takes direct responsibility for developing the top two hundred managers at Boots. This close interest enables them to identify and nurture possible successors long before those individuals are aware of it. Says Dominic Cadbury of Cadbury Schweppes: 'Succession is part of the management development process. If you have got an effective management development programme, you are going to present yourselves with successors.'

Few companies identify crown princes, however, as the following comments indicate:

- Electrocomponents' Bob Lawson: 'You want some options. The moment there is a guaranteed successor, why are you still around? Here, we have three people who are potential successors to me. Because the losers may walk, we have to have potential successors to each of them, too.'

- Atlas Copco's Michael Treschow: 'I have no idea who my successor will be. That's not my job. My job is to make sure there is a cadre of people who can do different things in the group, but whether one of those will be my successor I don't know, and I don't think that's important because that must be the privilege of the owners. The board makes the decision to hire and fire the CEO; if they feel that one of our people is the one, or someone from outside, I don't think I should have an opinion on that.'

- Dominic Cadbury: 'When we make a top-level appointment, it's abrupt in the sense that the decision has to be made on a single day. What we have not ever done is a gentle succession where somebody is groomed as a successor. In fact, if there's one truth about management succession at the very highest level, it's that it's almost always a surprise. It very frequently turns out to be someone who people did not anticipate. We try to provide ourselves with more than one alternative, so somewhere along the line you've got to make a decision. If you have only got one successor, I think that's not a very healthy sign of good management development.'

- Barrie Stephens of Siebe: 'I hired Yurko not as a successor but as a natural leader. His first assignment was Vice President of Finance at Robertshaw Controls. In 1990, I marked him out as having great potential. The City will tell you today that the handover was almost seamless. You have to pick the right people – competitive and natural leaders. If you have the right succession strategy, you will share in their successes because you are overjoyed. I had three in mind, but I never told anyone until I'd made my choice. So I didn't have the residual problem of creating one or two Cinderellas.'

- Sir Gerald Whent of Vodafone: 'I think one of the great things of being a good business leader is to know when to go! Your body gives you an early warning of when to go. I don't believe in nomination of successor, I think its demotivating for everyone else. If you start saying "this is my successor" five years before you go, first of all they can't wait to get rid of you and, second, in five years people change. I don't believe in nomination. People believe that when the time comes, the hat goes into the ring. We have got to give the nomination committee time to look outside as you don't always have the next Chief Executive in your company. While there are people within the company that could do the job, you have got to give the nomination committee time to look. The way it will work is if there is anyone better than an outside candidate internally, then they will get it.'

Building a high degree of strategic consensus among the top team

Our high-performing companies spend a lot of time discussing issues among senior managers to gain a consensus about the right way to tackle issues. Although they may be led by strong, sometimes charismatic, personalities (as many of them are) the emphasis of discussion and decision making is on the team rather than on individuals. Singapore Airlines CEO Cheong took issue with one of our questions, concerning what he had achieved. He explained: 'We don't look at it that way. I know in a lot of companies the chief executive represents the company and he makes or breaks it; but over here we talk about we rather than I.'

At Reuters, says Patrick Mannix, Director of Personnel and Quality: 'Peter [Job] has brought a far more open consensus style. He's certainly enabled the senior management group to work much better as a team. If the company is very dependent on the chief executive, then you have got a hell of a problem when it comes to succession.' Adds the Chief Executive himself: 'We have a collegiate style at the top, which helps a lot. People here are used to that style of give and take. There is a series of safe and steady hands, which is exceedingly important. I think that's overlooked sometimes.'

It helps if there truly *is* a team at the top. Most of our high-performing companies have a very cohesive top team, although the CEO or chairman attracts most of the publicity. Too much of a personality cult can, of course, make smooth succession difficult. Archie Norman at ASDA is genuinely concerned that that shouldn't happen. 'It comes with the ticket. It's regrettable because it tends to create an over-simplification, both in the public eye and internally. It's obvious that I haven't turned round this company single-handedly – I've done it with a team of people, particularly with Allan Leighton, who is now Chief Executive, and Tony Campbell, Trading Director, with Phil Cox. We have been a team throughout.

'The personality cult tends to belittle the effort of others who don't get the same profile. It's a hard thing to manage. In our case, Allan Leighton is my closest business partner and we've worked extremely well together for five years. I brought him into the business and the succession was a completely natural process. I will stay as chairman because I am devoted to the company but I won't be doing it full-time. Allan will want to make changes and develop the company more, but so would I have done if I'd been Chief Executive.'

Peter Job of Reuters refers to the problem of an over-dominant figure at the top as the Banyan tree. He explains: 'Nothing can grow in the shade of the Banyan tree. I think everyone has their own formula for running a business, but part of that should be the subordination of the ego. You can walk around any country graveyard to remind yourself that you will be under grass eventually. It's sensible therefore to say, "How long do I want my company to go on after me?" This one has been going since 1851.'

Ensuring that potential CEOs spend long enough in the company to understand how it works

It takes time to become steeped in the values and competencies that have underpinned a company's success up to that point.

Canadian-born Allen Yurko (now an American citizen) was with Siebe for five years before he became CEO. In that time, he was groomed progressively for the top job. He recalls: 'The Chairman, Barrie Stephens, didn't want to fall off the deep end and have someone else start from scratch. So, long before I knew it, he had set up a strategy for a seamless transition. By the time he told me about it, he had been grooming me and probably several others for the better part of 18 months. He gave me bigger assignments, introduced me around the City as one of his board members and so on. He started in 1991 with a transition that wasn't going to happen till 1994.'

When Sam Walton, founder of Wal-Mart, retired in 1984, his ultimate successor David Glass was asked about the transition the company would have to go through. He replied: 'There's no transition to make, because the principles and the basic values he [Walton] used in founding this company were so sound and so universally accepted.' Glass had been in the business for eight years, sufficient to both absorb the business philosophy and influence it before his appointment as President and CEO.

'One of the reasons we've had a seamless transition is that he chose a person who agreed with his culture ... I don't remember much conflict or areas we disagreed on ... though we did have occasional differences of opinion when we were talking strategy. We both remained flexible enough to home in on what we both agreed with.'

Robert Ayling had a varied apprenticeship for the chief executive's job. Having joined British Airways from the Department of Trade team that set up the privatisation of the airline back in 1983, he eventually became Personnel Director, then Marketing Director (at a very tricky time, when the airline was involved in a dispute with Virgin over alleged dirty tricks), and Managing Director in 1993. He thus had more than two years to prepare for taking over as CEO and to be groomed by both Sir Colin Marshall and the previous Chairman Lord King.

Marks & Spencer, too, likes to grow its own top management – to the extent that external appointments at any level are relatively uncommon. Marks & Spencer views the creation of promotion opportunities at all levels as a critical part of employee motivation.

However, that does not mean that you always have to be a career lifer in a high-performing company if you want to get to the top. On the contrary, the most typical pattern is for people to join the company at middle management and work up. Says Cadbury Schweppes' Human Resources Manager, Bob Stack: 'There clearly is a premium on promotion from within, particularly at the senior levels. For example, I was for a time the only one of the top 150 executives hired directly from outside and, even today, that figure would be less than ten. However, we don't have a lot of 25-year service people here – in fact the average length of service of the top 150 is ten years, including prior service in companies we have acquired. ... John Sunderland, who we have recently announced as the new CEO, does have 28 years service, essentially back to his graduate days, but he's a rare commodity these days.'

What the new CEO does seem to need, however, is breadth of experience within the company. Sunderland has extensive experience around the world in different roles within Cadbury. Says Stack: 'John Sunderland has been groomed very well, actually, in the sense that he worked on both sides of the business, confectionery and beverages. He's worked in at least four different countries and, in his earlier days, in a number of different functional areas.... The kinds of assignments he's had include the start up of Coca-Cola Schweppes beverages and the integration of Trebor Bassett. He's been in difficult management situations: South Africa, Ireland, the US.'

For many, if not most, of our case-study companies, it is an operating principle that managers move around continuously to broaden their experience – of the company as much as of different operating environments.

Using the retiring CEO as chairman–mentor

In relinquishing the role of CEO to an outsider, Sir David Lees at GKN has effectively defined his own new role as Chairman. 'What we hope we are going to achieve,' he explains, 'is the new chief executive bringing thoughts from outside, while I ensure continuity.'

Reported the *Financial Times* of Smiths Industries: 'The chairman and his new chief executive have agreed to adopt a partnership approach to running the group. Sir Roger [Hurn], who shuns the non-executive sobriquet, is expected to remain close to the centre of things. But it will be Mr Butler-Wheelhouse calling the shots.'[1]

A chairman–mentor is particularly valuable when there has been a strong CEO who has been very closely identified with the company for a long time. At Bowthorpe, for example, says CEO Nicholas Brookes, his predecessor John Westhead 'was the first person to realise that we were at the stage that no one single person could lead if we wanted to continue to grow. It was getting too large. John gave the orders and we did have very successful execution of those orders. So John was the first person to admit we needed to go outside, and that we needed a change of management. There is always a temptation not to let go of the reins ... but he has been so professional. He is still on the board, as Deputy Non-executive Chairman, but supporting me whenever I need it. The succession has been handled extremely well.'

At IKEA, founder Ingvar Kamprad appointed Anders Moberg as President in the mid-1980s, but remained as Chairman. Kamprad selected a young man in his mid-thirties precisely so that he would have time to grow into the job. The handing over of the reins has been almost imperceptible, but it is clear that Moberg now operates with a high degree of independence. He shares the same values as his mentor and, when Kamprad eventually departs, IKEA executives expect to see little change in culture or style. It would, in any case, be very difficult to change the values, says Vice President Sven-Olof Kulldorf: 'The values are so strong throughout the organisation that if somebody tried to go against those values, there would be a revolution which, either would remove that person or would result in lots of people leaving.'

Says Stephanie Monk, Human Resources Director at Granada: 'A mentoring relationship means you have to care, be willing to put in time, have a relationship of confidence and trust; but where it's been successful, the chairman is really very much acting in the role of coach, wanting to bring on the chief executive and sharing the limelight and grow someone to the point where they step back.'

In summary...

Gentle versus abrupt succession is the last of our ten critical balances, which high-performing companies insist on managing well. But how do they make sure these balances receive the attention they deserve? Read on.

13 | KEEPING ALL THE PLATES SPINNING

Achieving all the balances

'You can't watch every plate all the time. But GE is better than average at knowing when to give each plate a spin. Constant experiments, surveys and focus groups with customers all help to tell us when a new spin is needed.' *Steven Kerr, Vice President for Corporate Leadership Development, GE.*

In the foregoing chapters, we have outlined ten critical tensions that high-performance companies manage effectively. These are not the *only* tensions these companies have to manage – far from it – but they represent the common issues where they take pains to ensure that conflict is minimised or removed altogether. As we have seen, the way in which each achieves the balance that is right for its specific circumstances and values varies considerably. What works for, say, Reuters, will not necessarily work for Granada or Singapore Airlines.

That led us inevitably during our research to consider whether there were any underlying competencies that enabled high-performing companies to both establish the right balance for their business in the first place and adjust it to circumstances as they evolved. So about half-way through the research, we began to search back through our interview notes for underlying competencies, and then actively to seek comment from executives and other employees about them.

The result was that three core competencies – in addition to being able to manage the balances – emerged time and time again, across all sectors and all types of high-performance company. Those three were:

- a challenge-driven culture;
- a sense of rightness – most obviously demonstrated in an unswerving commitment to integrity in all the company's activities and relationships, but also in the way people knew instinctively how to balance difficult trade-offs; and
- 'simplexity', a remarkable ability to simplify the complex without being simplistic.

A challenge-driven culture

A challenge-driven culture is one where the organisation is constantly providing people with new opportunities to learn, to stretch their capabilities and to prove themselves. It is also normally strong on reward, although the rewards may be as much to do with a sense of achievement as finance.

Says David Spencer, Human Resources Director at Smiths Industries: 'People who are really good won't work in an environment that's not challenging. The challenge doesn't have to be the bottom line, but that's a large part of it for our people. The wider challenge is to be at the top of the pile in our chosen niches. We don't have mission statements or written corporate objectives that spell it out; but it's tangible – a constant awareness of the desire to be at the top in most of the things we do.'

A similar environment permeates Microsoft. Says Mike Murray, Vice President of Human Resources and Administration: 'As an intellectual asset company, our assets are not products or buildings, but our people. We strive to hire people who have a compelling need to achieve in their lives. So it's never been a problem to provide an environment of challenge.

'We carry out research into why people leave Microsoft (our actual attrition rate is very low for the industry, at 7–8 per cent). The primary reason is that they no longer have a great job. When they lose their enthusiasm, when they feel they can't contribute, they walk away. It puts a lot of pressure on managers to assess whether each employee is in a great job assignment.'

Being challenge-driven helps high-performance companies manage difficult balances in a number of ways:

- Because they attract bright people, allow those people to put forward ideas, and give them space to experiment and learn, there is a constant flow of new perspectives on old problems. So difficult trade-offs are re-examined time and time again through new eyes. Occasionally, this results in radical change, but on a day-to-day basis it becomes a steady process of erosion, rubbing away at the hard edges of a problem until they become smooth.

- In order to achieve challenging goals, people have to think in different, more radical ways. The question, 'Is there a better way?' becomes the rule, rather than the exception. When a better way is found, it will almost always have a knock-on effect on other aspects of the operation, leading once again to discussion around critical balances.

- A challenge culture allows people to question the business values, or at least the way they are applied. If the values are strong enough, this process reinforces them and increases people's understanding of them. Strong values also usually make it relatively easy to get the balances right.

- Challenge-driven cultures tend to be associated with clarity of objectives and clear priorities. The greater the clarity, the easier it is to recognise where the emphasis on any of our balances should be.

A sense of rightness

An intuitive feel for what is right, across a wide range of circumstances, is something that grows within a company. It is built up in an organisation by a combination of empathetic recruitment, self-selection in the people who work there (and who bring compatible values), experience, anecdotal reinforcement and the style of top management – plus a lot of even less tangible influencing factors.

Most of our high-performance company CEOs have spent a lot of effort trying to transfer that intuitive feel for what is right. They share their vision of the kind of company they want it to be and gain people's commitment to the broad idea. But they are constantly drawing attention to yet another detail of the picture, shining the light of the vision and values into yet another corner and helping people think through the implications. Sometimes they are so far ahead of the masses that they have to actively sell the new ideas. For example, Liisa Joronen at SOL needed to spend a lot of time discussing with people before they were willing to give up the status symbols of management.

Two themes recur frequently in this context: openness and integrity. The concepts permeate almost every speech these CEOs make to internal (and often external) audiences. For example, on integrity:

- For David Wellings, Chief Executive of Cadbury Schweppes, integrity is a critical part of the relationship with the consumer. 'If Cadbury's was regarded as an unethical company by the consumer, then I would be devastated, because I think it would weaken the brands. . . . I am totally concerned that people who work in this organisation see us as an ethical company – if they don't, they leave it,' he told *Management Today*.[1]

- 'Increasingly, in an ambiguous business environment, people like the confidence of knowing we are all concerned about integrity. It's very difficult for people to be working in a situation where integrity is not important,' says Stephanie Monk, Human Resources Director of Granada.

- General Electric's Jack Welch is accustomed to asking staff: 'Can you look in the mirror every day and feel proud of what you are doing?' He was driven to make ethical behaviour a higher business priority by a lapse of integrity that caused GE to be struck off US Government procurement lists for a short period. Jealous of the company's reputation as much as concerned at the loss of business, Welch made it his personal mission to ensure that every employee got the message.

- At Microsoft, the top team has identified six key success factors for the business. Integrity is not on the list – but for Bill Gates and his colleagues, it is implied in all the other factors. They simply aren't achievable without absolute integrity, he maintains.

- 'Integrity? Ignore it at your peril. If you've got it, protect it. If you haven't, go get it. It's deep down in the organisation. It's not dependent on one individual. It's implicit,' says Electrocomponents CEO Bob Lawson.

- Siebe Chairman Barrie Stephens tells managers around the world that he expects to hear business rivals describe the company in these terms: 'They are wicked competition, but boy, are they straight!'

 And on openness:

- Commercially right and ethically right are two sides of the same coin, says David Spencer, Human Resources Director of Smiths Industries. 'Sir Roger [Hurn] set the tone, by always laying bare the facts to people, whether they were City investors or employees.'

- 'The thing that I noted about Gerry [Robinson, Chairman] early on,' says Stephanie Monk at Granada, 'was his absolute honesty to the point of brutality. There is no subject that Gerry is unprepared to be honest about. He doesn't dissemble, so he will talk very honestly about all sorts of things, including difficult things. When we first went into Forte, he answered every question and was very comfortable to say when he did not know the answer or to tackle difficult questions about redundancy. A great lesson I have learnt from him is [that] there is nothing like the truth for seeing you through the most difficult situation. It pays to be more frank rather than less.'

However it happens, that intuitive feel is there in our high-performing companies and it is widespread. Even though they are highly decentralised, there is a remarkable commonality of approach among their subsidiaries around the world about making judgments. This is more than sharing values; rather, it can be seen as a *collective wisdom*. Collective wisdom can be seen as the ability to combine strong shared values with the ability to extrapolate from shared knowledge and experience.

Collective wisdom aids managing the balances in several ways:

- it enables people to link back to the values and put them into context with their own and others' experience;
- it helps ensure that both sides of complex issues receive adequate attention; and
- when time is of the essence, it allows people to make instinctive decisions about where balances should lie, in the knowledge that these will normally be not far wrong.

'Simplexity'

Simplexity aids managing the balances by reducing complex issues to manageable proportions. For example:

- Southwest Airlines bases its entire business on keeping every aspect of service at the simplest level. There are no complicated problems with menus, because it serves only snacks and drinks. Its frequent-flyer programme is very easy to calculate, because it simply tots up the number of flights rather than air miles. It only has one type of plane, so maintenance is relatively simple and inexpensive.

- Rentokil Initial keeps costs low and customer satisfaction high by limiting product choice. For example, says Martin Ellis, General Manager of UK Healthcare: 'Healthcare offers a small number of services. For example, a competitor might offer 12 different soap dispensers, but we offer just one. Offering more products like that actually dilutes the service as you have more things to manage. We offer one soap dispenser, which we have developed and are confident will work. That way we can optimise our service routing and scheduling because we know we won't be called to the site to fix the soap dispenser. It's a similar approach to the other core divisions. The objective is to simplify and to make the service unique so that a competitor would find it impossible to copy. That's how we justify higher margins. The key word is "unique".'

- IKEA maintains its low prices in large part by offering basic product ranges in a uniform manner.

Most of our high-performing company CEOs are passionate believers in opting for the simple solution wherever possible.

- Said Southwest's CEO Herb Kelleher in a 1994 interview: 'Our annual report emphasises getting back to basics. Business has gotten so complex that we've forgotten the basics: do what your customer wants, be happy in your work ... all these little things. The way I dignify it is to say, "Remember Einstein's criterion: if you've got a choice between two theories, neither of which is overtly provable, pick the simplest one. It's always right!" Later, when the means are available to prove it, the simpler one will inevitably prevail.'[2]

- At Smiths Industries, 'We make simple, efficient products to fit a niche. We also have simple processes. In particular, we manage our people in simple ways – we don't have complex remuneration systems, for example. If we do become complex occasionally, it is because we haven't spent the time to make our objectives clear. A term we often use is "commercially sensible" – it involves finding simple, easily understood solutions and applying common sense,' says Human Resources Director David Spencer.

- Electrocomponents' CEO Bob Lawson comments: 'We say that we operate a simple business in a complex market. We try to make it as simple as possible for our shareholders, our customers and the people who join us. The key is clarity: if you can't express the issue in terms a non-expert can understand, you don't understand the subject and/or you haven't got a solution.'

- The Berkeley Group's Tony Pidgley: 'Accountants want to systematise us, but we're actually very simple. We buy the land; we develop the land; we sell the houses. The real skill is getting the right product on the right land. That's what it's all about in our business.'

- At Granada, says Stephanie Monk: 'Gerry [Robinson, Chairman] is very keen on simplicity. He tries to strip things back to very simple principles and ask a few important questions. He doesn't get bogged down in masses of analysis, doesn't look to make something difficult. If it can be done easily, why make it difficult? Or if it's hugely difficult, are you sure you are doing the right things? That's very good in terms of pace and resource and freeing up time and also adding value to other people's work. If you are immediately responsible or you have got a functional responsibility, you can see huge complexity and infinite shades of grey. It can be very helpful from the top if you have a focus which is "Let's cut through all this. What are the three important questions, the big issue, or the five really crucial things we need to achieve in the businesses here?" It has an effect on the way our operating reviews work. People come to a meeting with well thought-through proposals, because volume isn't important. It's a few good ideas or the right answers that are important, rather than volumes of research or masses of possibilities.'

- Says JCB's Joe Bamford: 'I always count the number of parts first. Generally, I find that other people use more parts than I would. Better to keep it simple.'[3]

- Siebe chairman Barrie Stephens used to keep his 'magic six' key measurements for the group and each of its businesses in a sixpenny notebook with a biro. He still has them today, as a constant reminder not to let the business get too complicated. 'If you start a business off in the right direction, with lots of velocity and keep things simple, you will go a long way,' he says. His colleague Roger Mann, Finance Director, introduced a lot of 'simple financial systems that still deliver today. If systems are forceful, simple and practical, they'll survive!'

- Says GE's Vice President for Corporate Leadership Development, Steve Kerr: 'Jack Welch is always looking for an analogy to make complex topics simple. He points out that all businesses are basically a system of input, throughput and output, and so there is always a lot to learn from how other businesses do things.'

- At IKEA, founder Ingvar Kamprad wrote in his testament: 'The key concepts behind simplicity are words like efficiency, common sense and doing what comes naturally. If we do what feels natural, we will avoid complicated solutions. The fewer the rules and the shorter the instructions, the easier and more natural it is to stick to them. The simpler the explanation, the easier it is to understand it and carry it out.'[4]

Stories akin to cutting the Gordian knot abound in these companies. Managers may talk about 'cutting the crap' or 'getting to the heart of the issue'; whatever language they use, they recognise that anything that increases the complexity of the business increases the chances of things going wrong. So they wield the sword of simplicity wherever they see an opportunity – in production systems, in organisation structure, in management processes, in job descriptions and in anything else that takes up time, resources or energy.

Simplexity is in itself a balance – between reductionism (reducing complex data or phenomena to simple terms) and holism (regarding complex systems as irreducible wholes). Sometimes it is necessary to take a complex problem apart, to understand what each part does, and build practical solutions from the components up. Yet at other times, the problem requires the leaders of the organisation to step back and metaphorically walk around the issue until they understand the *meaning* of the complexity they see. Almost invariably, such understanding reduces the problem to bigger but simpler issues, which lend themselves to bigger but simpler solutions.

What differentiates high-performing leaders from others who wander about slashing at problems with the weapon of management machismo (from the axes of plain old cost-cutting to the epées of Business Process Re-engineering or Value Based Management) is that they seek first to *understand* the big issue, not just at an intellectual level but also at an emotional, intuitive level. When they cut the Gordian knot, they do so because they know deep within them that this is the right thing to do. That inner conviction is what gives the determination to make things happen and the ability to carry others with them. It is the complexity of their understanding that enables them to achieve a simplicity that is elegant, credible and readily communicable.

A basic tenet of simplicity is to keep the rules to the minimum and allow people the maximum flexibility to use their common sense. This is particularly true in those businesses, such as the airlines, that have multiple opportunities for success or failure directly with the customer. For example, the 'moments of truth' for an airline passenger are frequent and many. British Airways and Singapore Airlines devote a great deal of resources to simplifying each predictable interaction and training staff to respond flexibly to the unexpected.

Home Depot's co-founder Pat Farrah tells employees: 'This is a basic and simple business. People create problems by not trusting their own judgment. By creating a committee. By constantly needing validation. You guys are empowered. You can find 99 per cent of the answers in the aisles, where the customers are.'[5]

At Microsoft, says Mike Murray, Vice President of Human Resources and Administration: 'Simplicity is a result not a strategy. Our industry is very complex because of the rate of change in markets and technology. You end up with complexity squared. We try to get round it by hiring very, very smart technical and business people – people who are able to understand complex issues and narrow them down to actionable items, who can gain commitment from others to move forward. If a manager in our business doesn't perform, it's often because he or she can't cope with making complex issues simple.'

Complexity can creep into an organisation very easily, so CEOs such as Archie Norman at ASDA spend a lot of attention rooting it out. ASDA has deliberately not followed fashion among its competitors in managing promotions to customers. Says Norman: 'Our promotional programme is biased against complexity: that you have to buy certain products to gain bonus points, for example. The risk is that this approach can be manipulative and customers find it complex. That's not to say it can't work, but we prefer to keep it simple, to concentrate on giving customers reassurance, trust and confidence that our prices are permanently low.'

A problem for many companies in approaching simplexity is 'simplicity for whom?'. What appears to a customer to be a very simple operation – for example, buying fresh strawberries in mid-winter – may require a great deal of organisation behind the scenes. However, our high-performing companies seem to have learned the lesson that reliability in delivering simplicity to the customer usually requires a vigorous approach to simplifying what goes on behind the scenes. IKEA simplifies the customer interaction in large part by making the customer do much of the work – a trade-off the customer readily accepts as part of the value-for-money deal – but to cope with international expansion, it has also had in recent years to simplify its logistics significantly. Nowadays, an increasing proportion of its product is delivered direct from the manufacturer to the stores.

The robustness of M&S's behind-the-scenes systems is what supports the quality of service at the customer interface. In recent years, the company has concentrated on simplifying systems so that staff spend less time out back looking for items not on show and more time dealing direct with the customer.

Reducing complexity often benefits both the customer and the company. For example, at N. Brown the practice of listening to customers identified that having one order delivered as separate items could be very annoying, especially if the deliveries were spread out over several days. Packing orders for the same customer together in the warehouse, rather than letting the delivery organisation put them together, not only reduced hassle for the customer, but saved N. Brown the cost of multiple delivery.

And now...

In the original version of *The Winning Streak*, we included a control group of companies that were not high performers, to test whether the characteristics of excellence were genuine distinguishing factors. For this study, we have had the benefit of being able to look back at those high performers in the original study who had fallen from grace. Chapter Fourteen includes an analysis of a selection of those companies, compared against the ten characteristics of balance from the current study. It also looks at some companies outside the original study, whose experience illustrates what happens when companies don't keep all the plates spinning together.

14 | THE LOPSIDED COIN
Where poor performers fail: a comparison

Throughout this book the emphasis has been on *sustaining* success, the processes and practices whereby companies ensure that they evolve, adapt to new circumstances and foster managerial learning. The achievement of success, however, is often said to carry the seeds of failure. Past strong performance can introduce organisational arrogance; the entrenchment of top management, bringing complacency in decision making; a strong resistance to change, in the belief that past policies will always ensure success; and a reduction in the responsiveness to new information, with inevitable consequences for organisational learning.[1]

We have argued that avoiding such pitfalls is a difficult process, and to achieve it firms must constantly make judgments concerning the ten balances we have described. But are these attributes peculiar only to successful companies? Of course they are not.

The position, we argue, is that successful firms *manage the balances better.* In order to demonstrate this, we have selected seven less successful companies to examine. Four of these companies come from the original 1980s study of *The Winning Streak*, which will allow us to identify the reasons why firms initially characterised as successful have suffered over the last 12 or so years. A further three firms were identified from a number of sources to be less than successful in their particular sectors.

In this book we have concentrated largely on processes and practices that are internal to the firm, and we have devoted less attention to the contextual factors that surround individual firms and that may have an important effect on performance. This does not mean we are promoting a universalistic approach to the management of companies, in which the application of various attributes can be used across company type and sector to achieve success. Rather, we argue that firms must manage the balances we have identified in light of the changing environmental circumstances, and in light of other contextual factors that are associated with their organisation. Firms are not dominated solely by their contextual situation; managers have strategic choice, whereby they can shape the direction and structure of their organisations in ways that can give them important advantages over competitors. Our considerations in this book deal predominantly with this area of managerial discretion.

The companies we have chosen for comparison here are (from *The Winning Streak*): Trafalgar House, United Biscuits, Saatchi & Saatchi and Allied Domecq. The remaining three are Wang Computers, AEG, and Fisons.

The comparison companies

TRAFALGAR HOUSE

Trafalgar House, the construction and engineering conglomerate that also has the Ritz Hotel and the QE2 as assets, has had a turbulent time since the company featured in the first version of *The Winning Streak*, where it was described as 'one of the most consistently profitable stars of the stock market'.

The two key concerns for the group have been focus and controls. The company's success from the 1970s to the early 1990s was primarily driven by acquisitions. The pursuance of the acquisition strategy proved to be disastrous when, in 1991, at the height of the recession and the Gulf War, the group bought the Davy Corporation, an engineering firm that had been brought to its knees by an oil rig contract 'taken on at a ridiculously low cost because the company was so desperate for business, and which turned out to incur huge additional costs'.[2]

Some of the costs filtered through to Trafalgar House, diluting shareholder wealth. The purchase of 40 per cent of the British Rail engineering arm BREL two years earlier had also proved to be ill-judged and, by 1991, with the failure of the group to divest its hotels business, there was strong downward pressure on the balance sheet.

In addition, the problematic 'accounting practices' of the company attracted the scrutiny of the Financial Reporting Review Panel, which forced the group to readjust its 1991 profits to show a large loss,[3] when the Ritz hotel and other properties were overvalued by £350 million.[4] The scale of the losses (£437.2 million) would have broken the company's banking covenants had it not been for the injection of facilities from HongKong Land, which provided £300 million of lending facilities through its 25 per cent shareholding.

Sir Nigel Broackes left the board in December 1993 (he was given the title of Honorary President) and was replaced by Simon Keswick, Chairman of HongKong Land. The new board instigated a business review, and independent valuations were made of the group's properties,[5] but there remains concern that the group's core businesses – construction and engineering – show few signs of coming out of the doldrums. In March 1996, Kvaerner, one of Norway's largest engineering groups, took over Trafalgar House for £904 million.

UNITED BISCUITS

United Biscuits, formed from the amalgamation of a number of leading UK food companies, manages such well known brands as McVities, Crawfords and KP. Other major brands, such as the Wimpy and Pizzaland chains (to GrandMet in 1989) and Terry's chocolates (to Kraft Jacobs Suchard in 1993) were sold as the firm attempted to focus on the core businesses of biscuits and snacks.

Since *The Winning Streak*, the group has continued to pursue a global expansion strategy, with North America, Europe and Asia–Pacific the markets where UB wants to have a significant presence. But commentators have argued that expansion into Europe has 'come too late', while the US market entry through the Keebler business failed when, after years of making losses, the business was put up for sale in 1995.

Problems came from stiff competition in both markets: Unilever and Nestlé in Europe and Nabisco in the US. The group, too, has been hit by the rise of own-label products, which have pushed down prices on branded biscuits. Since 1990, there has been a series of acquisitions in Europe and Australasia, which have widened the firm's geographic spread. The UK remains profitable, but price competition and a rise in raw materials pricing has led to sharp decreases in margins.

A major problem for the company was that, in the words of Chairman Sir Robert Clarke, 'we diversified too far.' In effect, United Biscuits lost focus. The selling of the restaurant and chocolates businesses has been followed by the disposal of Ross Young's, the UK frozen food division, again marked as peripheral to the group strategy of building an international biscuits and snacks empire. Though the UK base remains strong, overseas expansion has been patchy.

SAATCHI & SAATCHI (RENAMED CORDIANT)

Saatchi and Saatchi was the world's most famous advertising agency throughout the 1970s and 1980s. Started by brothers Charles and Maurice Saatchi in August 1970, it relentlessly pursued the strategic aim of creating a large agency, making numerous acquisitions and persuading the City that advertising was a sound investment. The agency became the world's largest in 1986 following the acquisition of the US firms Ted Bates and Backer & Spielvogel, and it had many high profile accounts including, famously, the UK Conservative Party, which it helped to two election victories in 1983 and 1987.

The rise of the group was assisted by the boom in the mid-1980s that saw advertising spend increase dramatically in all sectors of the economy, and between 1981 and 1987 the firm's earnings grew at a compound rate of 38 per cent per annum.[6] But from 1988 onwards, profits started to dip as the economy took a downturn. To compound the danger, the firm indulged in some unlikely ventures, such as the acquisition of the Hay Group in 1984 (sold later in 1990) and making a bid for the Midland Bank in 1987.

Negative cash flows in 1988 were compounded by concerns over financial management. As one commentator stated, the group allowed 'working capital and capital expenditure to continue careering out of control long after the good times had ended'.[7]

Maurice Saatchi handed the reins over to Robert Louis-Dreyfus, who promptly sold the management consultancies and cut costs, particularly in staff numbers. Though this intervention prevented the collapse of the group, the prognosis remained cloudy and profits failed to impress.

Matters came to a head in 1994 when Maurice Saatchi was ousted from the board of the agency by US fund manager David Herro amid accusations of poor accounting practices. The culture of the organisation, it was argued, had lost touch and had become arrogant and complacent (the bid for Midland bank being a prime piece of evidence). Maurice and Charles promptly set up a rival agency, called M&C Saatchi, leaving Charles Scott to chair the former Saatchi & Saatchi, now renamed Cordiant.

The brothers' standing and charisma ensured that a number of big clients followed them to their new agency, among them British Airways, Dixons Group, Mirror Group and Qantas, and M&C Saatchi has already set up a worldwide network to service its multinational clients. It has focused on what the old Saatchi & Saatchi was good at.

ALLIED DOMECQ

Allied Domecq, the alcoholic drinks and retailing group, has been called the 'aunt sally' of the sector and, because of doubts about its performance, has long been rumoured to be a likely bid target.[8] The group changed its name from Allied Lyons in 1994 with the acquisition of Spanish drinks company Domecq for £995 million.

Under the Allied Lyons name, the group had operated in a variety of markets – food, drink, retailing and a number of unconnected ventures.

In 1985, Australian company Elders made an unsuccessful bid for Allied, since when the group has tried to become more focused, with the aim of transforming itself into an international spirits and retailing company. Lyons bakeries, Tetley tea, 900 pubs and a Dutch brewery were sold (for £763 million) in order to achieve focus and raise funds for the purchase of Domecq. But the acquisition trail has been fraught with difficulties.

The Domecq acquisition took place just before the recession and followed the devaluation of the peso in Mexico (one of Domecq's big markets), both of which slowed the growth in the spirits market. The merging of Tetley beer and Carlsberg UK has been beset by problems, affected by falling demand in the industry (the market is shifting towards take-home sales of premium beers) and severe price competition. The merged firm is one of the worst performers of all the big UK brewers. Allied Domecq has said it now wants to get out of brewing.

Issues concerning control have also been to the fore, particularly in 1988 when the group lost £150 million speculating on the foreign exchange markets. The bureaucracy of the firm has been said to stifle innovation and reduce flexibility, and the group remains subject to strong takeover rumours.

WANG LABORATORIES

The demise of Wang Laboratories, the US computer products and services firm, highlights many of the concerns raised in this book, in particular the issues around succession and controls.

Founded by Dr An Wang in 1951, the company grew rapidly, initially through the manufacture of specialised electronic systems. Then, in the 1960s, it emerged as the market leader in programmable calculators. The firm's impressive record of research and development continued with the development of the first word processing system in the early 1970s. Continued growth was maintained by the development of systems that integrated data, word, voice and image processing, and the introduction of the VS series of minicomputers. Dr Wang's own standing as a front-rank scientist fostered a strong sense of personal loyalty from his employees, and the firm's revenues in the period from 1965 to 1985 grew from $1.8 million to $2.33 billion.[9]

However, the company was late on a number of key trends in the industry – most importantly, the move from closed (or proprietary) systems to open systems. This left Wang with products that were not to the then industry standard and so were vulnerable to low-cost producers offering greater compatibility. There was also late entry into the personal computer (PC) market, which was highly damaging to its competitive position.

Wang's practice of pricing products high when first introduced to the market and then savagely cutting the price 12 months later did little to enhance its ability to capture market share.[10] Problems with late deliveries, under-resourcing of the advertising department and announcing new products before the company had the capability to deliver them also caused customer frustration and often defections to the products of competitors.

A central problem with the company was the absence of any sophisticated controls: 'Under Dr Wang, the company did not have good financial controls. Wang Labs had no reliable product-line earnings statements and often did not know what return its various offerings brought.'[11]

The decision of Dr Wang to announce his son Frederick as successor to the top job provoked a major crisis in the firm. Senior managerial and technical staff departed and the resultant talent debit undermined to a considerable extent the company's core capabilities. The appointment of Fred Wang as President and Chief Executive Officer in 1986 coincided with two years of huge losses. He resigned in 1989.

He was succeeded by Richard Miller, who instigated a turnaround strategy. Through rationalising the operations of the firm, savings of $400 million were made in 1990, and $600 million of assets were sold. Two-way communication and devolution of responsibility replaced the old autocratic culture, and the control systems were tightened considerably. However, though the patient is out of intensive care, it is fair to say that it is not a healthy subject even now.

AEG

AEG was one of Germany's oldest and largest industrial groups until 1996. Its demise is a story of poor financial management, lack of focus, backing the wrong core businesses and the failure to act quickly in the face of poor performance.

The group has a strong history of innovation – inventing the first high performance railway locomotive, the tape recorder and the Pal colour TV system, now the industry standard in the West.[12] From its beginnings in 1883, exploiting the invention of the light-bulb, the company 'began its long expansion into almost everything electrical and – later – electronic'.[13]

At its height, the group was a vast conglomerate selling everything from nuclear energy to typewriters and refrigerators. This lack of focus was to prove disastrous, as resources were allocated to businesses that turned out to have slim growth prospects – white goods and energy equipment – while good long-term opportunities, such as electronic components and transport systems, were pushed down the priority list. Large-scale investment in nuclear energy and mainframe computers, stemming from the 1950s, saw little return, and the group's financial performance was hit hard.

The oil crisis in 1973 ushered in a decade of survival management. Despite restructuring and the selling of assets, the group did not fare significantly well and in 1985 Daimler-Benz took the group over in pursuance of its strategic goal of becoming an 'integrated technology company'.

But AEG's fortunes did not change. Daimler's strategy backfired badly and it returned to the concept of being a 'transportation group', which left AEG high and dry. The individual businesses are now being sold off or closed, and estimates are that 10,000 employees will lose their jobs.

FISONS

The case of Fisons illustrates the crucial issues of succession, the dangers of an inward-looking insular culture, and problems over both managerial and technical controls, all of which caused the company difficulties in the early 1990s.

The company had grown from its historic roots as an agricultural fertiliser business to encompass pharmaceuticals and scientific instruments. The company operates on every continent and in over ten countries worldwide. The fertiliser business was sold to Norsk Hydro for £59 million in 1982 as part of a corporate restructuring aimed at increasing competitiveness on a global level and reducing company debt.

The company focused on three core 'growth' businesses – pharmaceuticals, scientific equipment and horticulture. Strong organic growth, driven in particular by the performance of the respiratory drug Intal, saw impressive profit growth during the 1980s, and this was augmented by acquisition activity, with the 1989 purchase of VG instruments for £270 million making Fisons the fourth-largest scientific instruments producer in the world.[14]

The strategy and the vision of the company did not appear compelling to analysts and investors, who argued that the three businesses had little synergy and the company's presence in them was merely opportunistic rather than strategic. Chairman and Chief Executive John Kerridge's announcement that Fisons was to 'go it alone' in the pharmaceuticals business also caused concern, with the trend for partnerships in the industry to offset the enormous R&D and marketing costs.

Kerridge resigned as Chairman and Chief Executive in January 1992, to be replaced by Patrick Egan as Chairman, who announced a more participative style and a new openness to external constituencies, and Cedric Scroggs as CEO. Problems with gaining US approval of the drug Tilade, stemming from the company not meeting US regulations in relation to manufacturing and testing (a scenario that was repeated with the drugs Opticrom and Imferon), showed the firm had problems in quality control. This concern was exacerbated by the lack of strategic urgency in trying to gain the rapid reintroduction of withdrawn products into the US market.

Improper sales practices amongst the pharmaceuticals sales staff in 1993[15] also showed managerial controls to be in poor shape. Many blamed the excessive bureaucracy of the company (its lack of simplicity) with 'up to six layers of management between the chief executive and individual members of the salesforce'.[16] The resignation of the Finance Director following controversy over Fisons' accounting practices in the pharmaceutical division on 11 December 1993 also sparked the sacking of Scroggs as Chief Executive at a board meeting two days later.

The appointment of Stuart Wallis in September 1994 as Chief Executive ushered in a new rationalisation programme. He found six separate headquarters sites in the UK, poor balance-sheet controls and a large number of underperforming assets.[17] The scientific instruments business was disposed of in March 1995, a large proportion of the research and development arm was sold to Astra for £202 million, and headquarters was moved from Ipswich to London. The strategy of selling divisions worked in terms of turning its debt pile into profit, but there were concerns that it would not bring sustainable growth. Before Fisons had the chance to find out, it was bought out in a hostile takeover by Rhone-Poulenc-Rorer for £1.7 billion in late 1995.

A discussion of the issues

Having examined these brief case histories, what do they show in terms of the findings of this book? As a first step, let us map some of the problems of the companies against the 10 balances identified as important to sustained performance (Table 2).

Table 2: *Winning Streak II* balances and the 'poor' performers

	TH	UB	SS	AD	WL	F	AEG
Control and autonomy		x		x	x		x	
Long-term strategy and short-term urgency	x	x	x	x			
Evolutionary and revolutionary change		x	x	x	x	x	x

Table 2 (contd)

	TH	UB	SS	AD	WL	F	AEG
Pride and humility	x		x		x	x	x
Focus and breadth of vision		x	x	x		x	x
Values and rules			x			x	x
Customer care and customer count				x	x	x	x
Challenging and nurturing people					x		
Leaders and managers	x		x			x	x
Gentle and abrupt succession			x		x	x	

Key: a cross marks a prominent problem of the particular company.

CONTROL VERSUS AUTONOMY

The issue of controls was a major one for the companies identified as less successful. For Trafalgar House, Fisons and Saatchi & Saatchi, control of the balance sheet was not as tight as investors would have liked, which led in some cases to overvalued assets and a reduction in credibility in the eyes of the market, followed by the disposal of businesses. Poor controls on foreign exchange business caused crisis at Allied Domecq, while the degree of autonomy given to businesses and managers at Fisons had dramatic consequences in terms of the instances of improper behaviour of some sales staff in 1993. The unwritten rule that there be 'no surprises' clearly was violated in these companies. Bureaucracy was prominent at Allied Domecq and particularly at Fisons, which at one time had six headquarters sites in the UK.

LONG-TERM STRATEGY VERSUS SHORT-TERM URGENCY

Pursuance of long-term strategy while neglecting short-term urgency is a recipe for disaster. Trafalgar House's acquisition policy led them to buy the Davy Corporation at the height of the recession and in the middle of the Gulf War. The resultant costs almost drove the company over the edge. Allied Lyons' purchase of Domecq again could not have been worse-timed. For Saatchi & Saatchi too, the acquisition trail has led to serious problems in terms of company health, as the need for cash flow was overlooked in the quest for greater scale. At United Biscuits, the continuance of the US strategy as Keebler was consistently losing money showed too much commitment to the wrong long-term policy.

EVOLUTIONARY VERSUS REVOLUTIONARY CHANGE

Most of the companies in this sample have attempted to refocus and restructure in a bid to improve performance. But the emphasis has been on enforced revolutionary change. For Saatchi & Saatchi, it led to the break-up of the agency, for Fisons a near-death experience brought three chief executives in three years and a divestment programme that saw the firm eventually swallowed up by Rhone-Poulenc-Rorer. Wang fell into 'Chapter 11' difficulties in the US, as the effort to claw back market share and reputation proved immensely difficult. In these firms, evolutionary change had not been an option; only drastic surgery could save the patient, and now the patient is barely recognisable.

PRIDE VERSUS HUMILITY

Saatchi & Saatchi's bid for the Midland bank is one of the clearest examples of hubris. Fisons' John Kerridge, who boasted that the firm should adopt the strategy of 'go it alone' in the pharmaceutical business, when all indicators pointed to the value of mergers and partnerships, also shows the danger of overweening pride. Wang's promotion of products before it was capable of delivering them to customers showed that pride in the technology led the firm to underestimate the importance of marketing and distribution.

FOCUS VERSUS BREADTH OF VISION

All the firms in the sample have attempted to redefine their core businesses, but with varying success. For United Biscuits, the decision to expand into Europe came, according to some commentators, ten years too late, by which time Nestlé and Unilever had developed dominant positions. AEG sold everything from nuclear energy to typewriters and white goods, and problems with resource allocation between the businesses led to the group often backing the wrong horses. Saatchi & Saatchi lost focus through expansion into management consultancy and almost into banking – too great a breadth of vision was harmful to the health of the company.

Timing is important in determining the success of refocusing or expansion. Trafalgar House spent too long in divesting its hotels business, and United Biscuits waited a long time before selling its frozen foods concern.

These decisions, though strategically sound, were hampered by the lack of speed in implementation.

VALUES VERSUS RULES

Because the companies were undergoing, in the main, revolutionary change, there was a divergence between the old values of the firm and the new, with consequent dissonance from the perspective of the employee. The disruption to old ways of working meant that new values took time to be internalised. Further, underperformance in the companies led to rationalisation and redundancies, which drove down morale. The turn-around at Fisons, the shake-out at Saatchi & Saatchi, the large-scale job losses at AEG, as three examples, have all altered the culture and changed the psychological contract between employer and employee. The gap between organisational rhetoric and reality is wide, and there is little basis for the sharing of value systems.

CUSTOMER CARE VERSUS CUSTOMER COUNT

Examples of companies ignoring the demands of customers are rare, but certainly Wang Laboratories' service quality – slow delivery times, and marketing that led to expectations the company could not fulfil – was seen to be a major cause of the group's problems. Fisons' problems with manufacturing controls in the development of drugs can also be viewed as an example of a lack of focus on delivering to customer expectations and specifications. Allied Domecq's (along with other brewers') practice of maintaining high prices for beer sales in pubs was against customer wishes and influenced the large switch to take-home beer sales from retail outlets.

CHALLENGING VERSUS NURTURING PEOPLE

The threat of collapse and fear of redundancy do not provide a climate for nurturing people – and certainly do not bring a sense of 'fun' to work. Though there is definitely a challenge to working in such conditions, the possibility that the firm does not have a long-term future tends to sour the sense of opportunity. At Wang, senior executives thought that their path to the very top would be blocked as Dr An Wang installed members of his family in the highest positions. So strong a presence of a chief executive may also inhibit the degree of power and opportunity to build a track record that ambitious employees desire.

LEADERS VERSUS MANAGERS

The companies described in this chapter have had some very powerful leaders: Sir Nigel Broackes, at Trafalgar House, John Kerridge at Fisons, Dr An Wang at Wang Labs, Sir Robert Clarke at United Biscuits, Maurice Saatchi. They all have different styles of leadership and all faced different problems in the running of their companies. The attribution of blame for problems in company performance has landed, to a large extent, at their doors, though this of course paints too simplistic a picture. It is interesting, however, that in terms of their successors, there has been a strong bias towards appointing outsiders, which may suggest a lack of depth in their firms' management.

GENTLE VERSUS ABRUPT SUCCESSION

In the majority of cases, the succession process in these companies has been problematic. At Fisons, John Kerridge resigned 'due to ill health', while his successor Cedric Scroggs was sacked. The Saatchi brothers were removed from the board due to shareholder pressure. At Wang, the appointment of Dr An Wang's son as successor to the top job caused concern in the company and the departure of senior-level executives as a result led to poor performance and Fred Wang's eventual resignation just two years later.

In summary...

The discussion has provided some evidence that companies that have been less than successful in recent years have seriously misjudged several of the balances identified by the findings of this book, and this has had important consequences for company performance. This is not to say that, of the companies portrayed as successful, we could not find similar instances where difficulties have arisen because of similar lapses in judgment. However, the findings seem to suggest that successful firms get it right more often, and if they get it wrong the imbalance does not persist long enough for it to become critical.

15 | SAINSBURY – AN ACTION CASE STUDY

When the plates begin to wobble

'We haven't always been as good as we should have been at the big change.' *David Sainsbury, Chairman*

'When a company ceases to be nimble, it's not that they are not working hard. It's because they are getting drowned in the business of staying alive.' *David Sainsbury*

Five years ago, Sainsbury overtook Marks & Spencer as the UK's most profitable retailer and over the previous 20 years the group had grown profits at a compound rate of 23 per cent per annum.[1] In that same year, 1992, David Sainsbury took over as Chairman and Chief Executive from his cousin Lord John Sainsbury. By 1995, Sainsbury made £800 million in pre-tax profits and was still the country's largest and most profitable grocer. The company, which opened the first supermarket in the UK in 1950, was featured in the original *The Winning Streak* book and despite a number of problems for it (notably the purchase of Texas Homecare from Ladbroke in 1995), we had every intention of including the supermarket group in *this* book as an example of a firm that exhibited solid business performance in a highly competitive sector. After all, profits in 1996 were £854 million and Sainsbury was still earning more money than Tesco, its main rival. Furthermore, the group still achieved higher sales and profits per square foot than any other supermarket group.

The events up to and including January 1997, however, forced us to rethink. A profits warning depressed the shares by 13 per cent, wiping £1 billion off the group's stock market valuation and eroding the family's personal stake by £375 million. What's more, for the first time ever Tesco overtook Sainsbury as the UK's leading grocer and has since overtaken it in profit.

What had happened? Rather than drop Sainsbury from our case list, we decided to treat it as a living case study of how an excellent company copes when some of the plates begin to wobble. Does it focus on regaining the spin in the plates that have slowed, perhaps to the detriment of the rest? Does it focus on what is going well and allow one or two plates to fall? Does it react with calm planning or barely concealed panic?

Measurement against the ten balances
....

We commissioned one of the research team to compare the observations of external commentators (including, by proxy of the press, some of Sainsbury's competitors) and what had emerged from our interviews with David Sainsbury and a cross-section of people within the company in the context of recent events. We wanted to assess, in particular, which plates had begun to wobble, and how deftly the company was acting to restore their spin. Taking the ten balances in turn:

CONTROL VERSUS AUTONOMY

Sainsbury's culture under Lord John Sainsbury was one of tight reporting lines and 'power concentrated in the hands of an inner sanctum at the top of the company'.[2] The capacity for autonomy at store level was and is constrained by the need to maintain consistency across the group as a whole.

Says David Sainsbury: 'It's about discipline and constant standards. If you have very sophisticated systems, it's really quite easy to make them go wrong. For example, if people start playing around with the space given to products in the stores, you very quickly get inconsistency in quality and product ranges. So, for example, if a manager wants to carpet his store, we would have a clear view that he hasn't got the authority to do that. We would want him to put the ideas to people in the business who are concerned with that area. They would look at it and say "right, let's try it" or not.'

This approach to control is typical of large retailers – Carrefour, for instance, provides a similar story. With Sainsbury's having 380 supermarkets serving 10 million customers a week (and over 140,000 full and part-time employees), the issue of consistency is crucial. Nevertheless, the supermarket manager does have some freedom to innovate, particularly in the area of customer service. For example, Durham Store Manager David Milburn spends a large part of his time gathering ideas for improvements from his staff and experimenting with them. He gives an example: 'One idea from the staff was that we should have someone going round the shop acting as a customer helper. Normally we are very reactive – a customer asks someone filling shelves where something is and they'll stop what they are doing and show them. The idea was that we would be more proactive by actively asking customers if they have found everything they need. The customers seem to really love it.'

Under David Sainsbury, the balance has shifted several steps towards the autonomy end of the spectrum, with greater opportunity for debate around business issues, but it has not been easy for traditional Sainsbury managers to adapt. Nonetheless, there is no evidence that this particular plate is out of balance. The move towards greater local initiative, based on more accurate information about local customers, is inevitable. If anything, Sainsbury could be said to be ahead in its attempts to shift this balance.

LONG-TERM STRATEGY VERSUS SHORT-TERM URGENCY

The market strategy of Sainsbury's supermarkets is to be the customer's first choice for food shopping in the UK. This strategy has relied on a clear focus on quality and choice underpinned by strong locations, insisting on high-quality suppliers, and majoring in own-label brands. Innovations such as cashback, promotion of health-conscious foods and the provision of a wide range of quality wines have also been part of Sainsbury's success story.[3] The group has also invested heavily in information technology and made improvements in the supply chain. But innovations by competitors, in particular the loyalty card at Tesco, saw the gap between Sainsbury and the rest disappear. Six months ago, as performance dipped, Sainsbury reviewed every area of the business. David Sainsbury said: 'There is still a long way to go, but we will turn this company around.'

It would be hard to criticise Sainsbury in terms of its attention to the long term. The group has consistently taken a far-horizon view, both with regard to its supermarket businesses and to its diversifications into other areas of retail. But did it lose its sense of urgency? Having overtaken Marks & Spencer, did key managers pause for breath? An external observer would find it hard to conclude otherwise, and David Sainsbury has been open in his admissions of *mea culpa*.

A company spokesman points out that there is a strong cyclical effect in the food retailing market, with the major players alternately experiencing rapid growth and increased competitive edge. But high performance companies generally have the capacity to rise above competitive cycles, ensuring that the competitive gap is never allowed to close.

Sainsbury *has* reacted with urgency, especially since the appointment of a new CEO. However, with the possible exception of its U-turn on loyalty cards, it has avoided panic measures. The emphasis of this business remains in the long term and it is relearning how simultaneously to maintain short-term urgency.

EVOLUTIONARY VERSUS REVOLUTIONARY CHANGE

David Sainsbury is refreshingly candid: 'We have always been good at incremental innovation. If you look at our product ranges, we are constantly introducing new products and new ways of merchandising. We haven't always been as good as we should have been at the big changes.' To stay ahead, the company needed to have locked into revolutionary change as its rivals began to catch up. Opening up the gap now will require more effort, although at least it will be easier to convince people of the urgency.

Gaining control over the focus of change is a key part of Sainsbury's recovery strategy. Says David Sainsbury: 'In recent years, there has been a real danger we would be overtaken by initiative fatigue. So I take pains to prevent it. There's a real danger of endlessly having initiatives instead of sitting down and saying: "Which ones are really important? Which are the ones that we have to get right and how do we do them?" We were in danger of drowning in initiatives a year ago, so we reviewed them all to identify those that really matter in the supermarket business. Now we have a much stronger sense of what the priorities are.'

Curiously enough, Sainsbury's emphasis on long-term thinking may hold the key to regaining the balance between evolutionary and revolutionary change. Defining the big, captivating vision is easier for the far-sighted company than for the company whose primary focus is on overtaking its rivals. And its ability to launch numerous initiatives shows that the group is capable of rapid change when needed. What remains to be seen is how well Sainsbury can marry revolutionary change with a sufficient sense of urgency to regain both its differentiation in the marketplace and its superior profit performance – and to sustain them.

One thing is for sure – Sainsbury has not lost its capacity to innovate. Analysts and press commentators were surprised, for example, at the speed with which it added financial services to its product range in 1996.

PRIDE VERSUS HUMILITY

If one accusation has been levelled at Sainsbury's by its rivals more than any other, it is that the company is arrogant and self-satisfied. For example, *The Sunday Times* declared that the culture 'of deep conservatism and an unwillingness for self-examination, which bordered on arrogance, proved disastrous',[4] while a senior executive in a rival supermarket chain was quoted as saying that 'Sainsbury has always been very arrogant and that arrogance has allowed them to take their eye off the ball. This whole experience has been very sobering for them.'[5]

However, David Sainsbury told us: 'This has always been a culture of endlessly wanting to improve things. It's down to the psychological make-up of the people who run the business – people who continually strive to do things better. We've always been very proud of what we do, but that is always balanced by a deep sense that no one is secure. We know that our market changes rapidly and that, if you don't get it right, you can very quickly be out of the top league.'

Where does the truth lie? The experience of our other high-performance companies suggests that rampant success always stimulates similar criticism. Equally, the hubris trap is clearly one of the easiest to fall into. In the end, however, whether the cause was excessive pride or 'adrenalin drain' – the energy loss athletes so commonly feel a while after a great and successful exertion – the net result was a dangerous complacency. The shift of management style, to greater involvement and debate, has the potential to restore the balance between pride and humility at Sainsbury by allowing competitive concerns to surface more quickly from the branches. Indeed, the tenor of our interviews with Sainsbury managers suggests that this is already the case.

FOCUS VERSUS BREADTH OF VISION

As the company that introduced the supermarket into the UK, Sainsbury remains determined to maintain its focus on being a leading retailer. The supermarket business remains the largest part of the group, accounting for three-quarters of group sales. The other retailing interests include the hypermarket company Savacentre and the DIY chain Homebase, which has successfully integrated Texas Homecare (bought from Ladbroke in 1995 for £290 million). Sainsbury claims to be the only UK food retailer with a properly thought through divestment strategy. The pattern of Sainsbury's acquisitions reflects the company's long-term perspective. It has a track record of turning round less successful businesses through considered investment rather than relying on rapid cost-cutting. Sainsbury seems to have kept this particular plate spinning consistently and has rightly ignored criticism from outsiders expecting more rapid results.

VALUES VERSUS RULES

When top management appears to falter in its commitment to a value, it is a dangerous time. At Sainsbury, 'customer value' has long been and still is a core value. A deep part of the mythology and culture of Sainsbury is the company's stand against trading stamps, on the grounds that they meant worse value for the customer, who ended up paying not only for the prizes, but for the costs and profits of the company administering the stamps. Steadfastly refusing to follow the fad, in spite of pressure on its sales, Sainsbury emerged as the consumer champion, with a greatly enhanced reputation.

On the face of it, the recent trend for retailers to introduce customer loyalty cards is a re-run of the same battle. Sainsbury's immediate reaction was to reject them out of hand as another gimmick that did not add value to the customer in the long run. The phrase 'electronic green shield stamps' is one David Sainsbury now regrets using, but it set a tone of expectation within the company. Internal debate and observation of how other retailers were using loyalty cards gradually made top management realise that loyalty cards could in fact be an important vehicle for adding customer value – more customised offers could help strengthen the relationship between Sainsbury and its customers.

Says Robin Whitbread, main board Director: 'What we've done now is to realise that the card is more of a means to an end, a way to establish more information about your customers, and communicate much more effectively with them. That is actually quite hard to do when you have a high number of customers passing through your stores each day. I remember when I started in the company in the 1960s. I worked behind the counter in our store in Weybridge, Surrey. Back then you could talk to regular customers. Now the card will help us to know who shops regularly with us so we can communicate more effectively.

'We originally felt it would add a significant cost to the business, which means you either lose profits in the short term or you have to recover the cost from customers. Given the fact that we wanted to retain our "good value" offer, it is not a decision we took lightly.'

The problem this turnabout caused for the company was internal as well as external. Were the old values being abandoned? Did top management have the same degree of commitment to value for money? Just how much employee confidence in the values was damaged isn't clear. However, top management was undoubtedly faced with the need for rebuilding confidence.

It no doubt helped that the debate was relatively open, so people could feel involved in the decision. However, it would be a mistake to assume that such debates were not already built into the company culture.

An illuminating example of how deeply values issues have traditionally been debated in the company comes from David Sainsbury: 'When I joined the business, this building was our warehouse with a little bit of office on top. You came up in a lift and it was a real grocery headquarters – you smelt the cheese. As the company grew, it was no longer efficient to have a central London warehouse. The modernists wanted to decentralise warehousing to depots around the outskirts of London. The traditionalists said it is fundamental to what this business stands for in terms of quality that buyers can go downstairs and check the quality of goods going through. The simple answer was to have samples brought in, but at the time people debated it hotly, because there was a real issue of whether we would lose something integral to the business. You have constantly to ask yourself, "What are the fundamental values, and what is just a manifestation that has to change as you go along?" '

Has the balance between values and rules been lost? Almost certainly not. Sainsbury is still a company managed primarily by values and one where the values are an important factor in attracting and keeping key staff. Maintaining consistency in the values messages – walking the talk – will remain a challenge, however, as the group evolves.

CUSTOMER CARE VERSUS CUSTOMER COUNT

Sainsbury positions itself to balance high quality and choice with price competitiveness, and it relies on service innovation to keep it there. It carries 22,500 lines and claims to provide lower costs than its main rival Tesco – although it has a hard time establishing that perception in customers' minds. Like the high-performance airlines, it is concerned to ensure that the entire service experience is differentiated from the competition. Explains David Milburn, the Store Manager of its branch in Durham, England: 'Our challenge now is to make sure that we are always first-choice with consumers in range, availability and price. So our whole team of 420 people are targeted at promoting an atmosphere of pleasing the customer. That means having a greeter on the front door, for example. It's very important to get first impressions right. The last impression is also vital, as it determines whether they come back next time. This is a very difficult position to recruit for. You don't want them just handing out baskets. They should really be greeting customers, especially the high-spending ones who need a trolley, not a basket. We want them to get away from the "have a nice day" approach – our customers don't like that. The same principles apply in our cafeteria and petrol station, as those are often the last point of contact with the customer.

'Another change we have made is to have teams of five cashiers and one supervisor. So rather than ringing a bell and having someone come out of the back office to deal with a query, the supervisor is right there and can deal with 90 per cent of the issues.'

Sainsbury is also good at managing customer recovery. For example, says Milburn, 'A lot of complaints are to do with the fragile products we handle. Sometimes people say, "Maybe I left it in the car too long". Then we say, "No, we want to replace it." Those situations often turn out to our advantage.'

The issue for Sainsbury here is not that it has lost its customer focus – far from it – but that the pace of innovation in service has gradually been matched by its rivals. Again, this plate shows no signs of wobbling.

CHALLENGING PEOPLE VERSUS NURTURING PEOPLE

'Engaging the customer comes more naturally to some people than others,' says Sainsbury's Nigel Broome, Director of Retail Human Resources: 'We now have a four-stage process, which is designed to filter out of customer-facing roles people we don't think will be good with customers. There are a number of companies we have learned from in this area. TGI Friday actually auditions staff. We've also talked to Virgin Our Price about how they get enthusiastic sales staff. In their case, it's easier to recruit young people who are enthusiastic about the product. PC World is the same – it has good customer service because it recruits young techy enthusiasts. It's much more difficult with food – vital as it is, it's not going to be someone's hobby. So we have to find other ways of instilling enthusiasm.' Hiring people with the right kind of manner and interest in other people is a good starting point.

Sainsbury has recently introduced a new recognition scheme for managers and employees. Explains Nigel Broome: 'The JS Guild allows them to aspire towards a gold, silver or bronze level in their field. Bronze is the basic stuff; silver is to do with product knowledge, gold is about the wider environment. It's a chance for staff to gain recognition for their knowledge and skills in the food sector.'

Like Marks & Spencer, Sainsbury has always tried hard to live up to its values of employee welfare. This is another area of strength, on which recovery can be reliably built.

LEADERS VERSUS MANAGERS/GENTLE VERSUS ABRUPT SUCCESSION

We have drawn these two balances together because the issues are so closely entwined for Sainsbury. The culture embodied by Lord Sainsbury was one of autocracy and decision management vested in the hands of an inner circle of directors. This approach, it has been claimed, is unsuited to the fiercely competitive pressures in the retail sector of the 1990s. New managers have been brought in, particularly a new Chief Executive, Dino Adriano, and Kevin McCarten as Marketing Director, as David Sainsbury attempts to free up managerial initiative and move away from the former culture. However, some commentators have claimed that it is precisely the shift from the old culture that is at the root of the problems. A senior executive at a rival super-market said: 'Lord Sainsbury ran an incredibly tight ship. The staff were used to being barked at, and then the extremely nice David Sainsbury took over with this loose management style and everything ground to a halt.'[6]

The successor to a charismatic leader always has a hard time. The *Financial Times* reported the succession at the top of Sainsbury with: 'They are moving from a benevolent dictatorship to a democracy. That tends not to go too smoothly ... no-one knows how to make decisions.' While it sorted out the new style of leadership, Sainsbury seemed to lose some of its sense of direction, said the newspaper, referring to a 'series of U-turns in the past three years'.[7]

In some ways, Sainsbury is the exception to the rule in respect of seamless succession. On the one hand, David Sainsbury knew the company inside out. He has been a main board Director since 1966 and was made Finance Director seven years later. He has been effectively groomed for the role almost from birth! So his succession in 1992 should have created few waves. What made it an abrupt – and therefore potentially disruptive transition – was that his style was so radically different, that it required an equally radical shift in mindset for managers in the business. In the end, that shift only came about by replacing some of the top team.

Could it have been handled differently? Perhaps a more progressive transition would have given people time to adjust, but that can be hard to achieve while a long-term charismatic predecessor is still around.

What counts for the future is that there has – in spite of confusion over loyalty cards – been no change in the values of the company. David Sainsbury is as committed to the core values as was Lord Sainsbury. The lesson, therefore, for other companies, is one of communication. It would have been wrong for David Sainsbury to attempt to be a clone of the charismatic Lord John. After all, it was the personality of the company, rather than of the individual, that needed to be preserved. But clarity and continuity of direction and values both needed to be reinforced strenuously throughout the transition and beyond. Had this happened to the level that was needed, perhaps none of the other plates that wobbled would have done so.

In summary ...

Despite a profits warning, the loss of shareholder value and the relegation to number two retailer behind Tesco, Sainsbury 'remains a force to be reckoned with'.[8]

Looking at the group's recent problems in terms of our ten balances is instructive:

Control versus autonomy	Still spinning well
Long-term strategy versus short-term urgency	Needed more emphasis on urgency
Evolutionary versus revolutionary	Seeking a new balance
Pride versus humility	Complacency has been an issue
Focus versus breadth of vision	Still spinning well
Values versus rules	Minor wobble quickly corrected
Customer care versus customer count	Still spinning well
Challenging people versus nurturing people	Still spinning well
Leaders versus managers/Gentle versus abrupt succession	Arguably the source of the company's problems – but also the way out of them

In short, Sainsbury's problems can be traced to two major wobbles: a leadership transition that had a much more disruptive effect than expected; and a gradual slide into complacency. Other losses in balance followed as the organisation attempted to restore stability.

The good news, in Sainsbury's case, is that none of the plates has dropped or appear likely to do so.

Moreover, the company is already on the recovery trail, financially. To a considerable extent, this can be said to be due to the strength of the underlying characteristics that made it into a long-term high-performance company in the first place. Our interviews with Sainsbury managers demonstrated that they do understand and value simplexity – although the logistics of maintaining 22,500 lines in so many stores are difficult, they are achieved by and large by avoiding unnecessary complication. They do perceive and respond to the challenge of their jobs and are keen to incorporate new challenges within the constraints of consistency of the customer promise. Though it has been tested in the past three years or so, there is a clear 'sense of rightness' about what the business stands for, and this may become stronger as the new leadership style becomes more established.

Maintaining the balances, however, is a top management task. The top management team did fail to keep a consistent eye on all the critical balances for the business; as some plates lost their impetus so did the business as a whole. How soon Sainsbury returns to the ranks of high-performing companies will rest in large part on how well top management can regain the ability to keep all the plates spinning together.

APPENDIX: CASE-STUDY COMPANY PROFILES

ASDA
....

When Archie Norman joined ASDA in December 1991, the company was in dire trouble. A misguided strategy to take the supermarket chain upmarket, combined with unsuccessful diversifications had taken the Leeds-based group to the brink of bankruptcy.

One of Norman's first moves was to introduce a campaign called 'Tell Archie', which encouraged colleagues (ASDA's word for employees) to tell the new chief executive what was wrong within the company and where improvements could be made. Since then, over 20,000 colleagues have done just that.

At the same time, he re-focused the group's strategy, taking it back to its roots as a champion of low prices for ordinary people. Value for money became the company's credo once more, and he sold off non-core businesses including Allied Carpets and some food manufacturing operations.

The company that emerged was highly focused. Morale soared (despite an unavoidable programme of redundancies) and the company began a spectacular comeback. Most telling of all, perhaps, Norman worked with the company's strengths and recognised its limitations – a principle he calls 'trading where you are'. As he explains: 'Everything was wrong except that the company still had a heart; the spirit was still there, the idea of what it should have been was still there, and we still had our stores. What we couldn't change, which is very long-term, is the fixed capital base – the store base. That has been built up over 25 years. It will take at least another 25 years to alter.'

What the company did have was over 200 large stores, many of them 50 per cent larger than its competitors' equivalent – it pioneered the Superstore concept in the UK. Norman made that work for the company, creating a vision based around volume and value. 'Our basic beliefs are all interlocked,' he says. 'They're all built around a single idea of the type of store we run for customers. It's all about volume, value for ordinary working people and their families, large stores, wide range, and service with personality.'

ASDA also moved into clothing, launching the 'George' brand with designer George Davies. With its sights set on becoming Britain's second family clothing brand behind Marks & Spencer, it has now brought the business into the ASDA group.

By 1995, customers were flocking to the rejuvenated ASDA at a record level of 5.5 million a week. Profits jumped 27 per cent to £251 million (and rose again in 1996 by 26 per cent to £316 million).

In the process, Asda's confidence in itself has been restored. It has re-introduced traditional craft skills – training in-store butchers and bakers – and by recognising the contribution of its people it has brought excitement to its stores so as to make shopping fun for its customers.

In 1997 Norman, still just 42, became Chairman, passing the Chief Executive's baton to his deputy, Allen Leighton.

Atlas Copco
....

Atlas Copco, the Swedish engineering group, was founded in 1873. Today, its activities include the manufacture and maintenance of air and gas compressors, power tools and assembly systems, motion-control products, and mining and construction equipment and related activities.

It operates through 16 divisions split amongst three business areas: compressors, construction and mining, and industrial. In 1995, 96 per cent of its sales of more than £2 billion came from outside Sweden.

Despite its apparent complexity, the company's President (Chief Executive) Michael Treschow insists: 'You should always be able to explain to your grandmother what Atlas Copco is in three minutes. If you can't do that, then there is something you have missed.' To make that task easier, the company has recently produced a simple picture book that spells out the basic values, the mission, the strategy and the structure of the group. The mission, for example, is to be the world's leading company in its businesses.

Treschow, who has led the company for the past five years, is a firm believer in allowing managers the freedom to manage, a belief that was tested in the early 1990s when the recession hit. Throughout the downturn, however, no edicts were issued from the centre and decisions about redundancies or other cost-cutting measures were left with the managers running the businesses.

Treschow's confidence was vindicated by the company's strong recovery. In 1995, it had its best year ever, recording a 45 per cent increase in profits. When it comes to the latest management techniques, he is equally unwilling to impose initiatives from the centre. 'It's no fun as a manager to have initiatives imposed on you from head office, or to be told this is the year of customer focus or quality circles,' he says. 'I'm very allergic to that sort of concept. Rather, this is the year of even tougher targets than last year and, in order to make those targets, you'll need something extra and here is a toolbox. Make your own Mona Lisa.'

Much of the company's success, he believes, comes from the enormous diversity of its people and the career opportunities it offers. 'We are also very, very persistent,' he says. 'People know that once we have decided something we are like a bulldozer; even if the bulldozer moves slow, it means we're getting there.'

The Berkeley Group

Tony Pidgley, Chief Executive, has led Berkeley Homes (The Berkeley Group) for 20 years. He is a man with no formal training, who has sustained just about every ingredient of business success by a combination of instinct and common sense enhanced by experience. He has a legendary sixth sense for market trends in the cyclical housing sector epitomised by his famous perfectly timed decision to 'go liquid' in 1988.

'We're in the business of adding value to land to make profits,' he says. 'Equally, we're in the business of being market led – otherwise we don't have customers and we don't have a business.'

What is it that makes Berkeley Homes Britain's most successful house-builder? Pre-tax profits have grown consistently to over £40 million despite recession in the housing market. The group's market capitalisation is now over £500 million; earnings per share have almost trebled in the last five years. This has been achieved by attention to quality, detailed design features, effective land buying, a passion for quality and a degree of customer focus rarely seen in the industry.

The group wants customers to be proud of their homes and make money in the resale, and it also wants employees to feel a sense of pride and also be involved, such as in photographing an interesting chimney stack, roof design or window shape they come across on their travels. Innovation to Berkeley Homes is often how to go backwards – for instance to deliver to the customer a Queen Anne-style home with traditional features but modern comforts and space.

'We give all our customers a moving-in pack – all the documentation they need about their house in a leather binder. They cost us £80 each. The thing is you buy a new car or fridge and you expect that, but you buy a house – probably your biggest expenditure – and you don't. Most people have a dream; we try to sell them that dream.'

The company has focused on 1 per cent of the total UK housing market, but has been brilliantly creative in land buying, pleasing the environmentalists by cost-effective buying of 'brown' land in cities rather than just new greenfield sites, converting it to attractive and profitable projects through skilful reclamation.

CEO Tony Pidgley practises the art of delegation as a key factor in success, creating an extraordinary degree of job satisfaction. 'They love to run their own business. They learn about success and failure.' Indeed, 'I've never had the same job satisfaction before,' says a senior executive. 'I wake up every morning with a buzz. That's something Berkeley has, a buzz all the time. All the staff feel that.'

As Tony Pidgley said to us: 'Twenty years ago when we started out, housing was not product-led. We decided that it should be. That was the niche we decided to enter. In that respect, we could lay claim to changing the housing market.'

Boots

Founded in 1877, Boots, with its strong tradition of enlightened customer service and a presence in the UK high street, has one of the strongest consumer brand names among UK businesses. Boots the Chemist is the largest retail chemist chain in the UK, with strong performance in healthcare and beauty products, and the division accounts for three-quarters of group turnover.[1] The division has 53,000 employees in more than 1,200 stores, mostly in prominent high street locations, and it is this core business of managing chemist shops that has been the engine for success.

Supporting the Boots the Chemist business is Boots Healthcare International, which undertakes the research, development and marketing of over-the-counter drugs. Strong brands include Strepsils, Optrex and the pain relief drug Neurofen. Boots Contract Manufacturing also acts in support, and 'supplies private-label and contract manufactured cosmetics, toiletries and healthcare products'.[2] In addition, the group has Boots the Optician – the second-largest chain of opticians in the country.

With the arrival of Sir James (now Lord) Blyth as Chief Executive in 1989, Boots diversified further, buying Ward White Group, which included the bicycle and car parts chain Halfords, the home decorating business Fads, and the Payless DIY stores, for £900 million in total. A year later, Boots formed a joint venture with W.H. Smith, putting the Payless stores and W.H. Smith's Do It All business into one entity, jointly owned by Boots and W.H. Smith. Boots were thought to have overpaid for the group and concerns remain – the DIY business in particular is facing large problems with the end of the property boom having caused overcapacity in the market, and both Fads and Do It All are making losses. These elements are thought to be candidates for disposal.

Despite these problems, Boots has maintained a strong reputation for reliable, trusted products and services, and performance of the group as a whole remains solid, with £443 million in operating profit on £4,125 million turnover in 1996. The key to the company's enduring stability has been its focus on value-based management (VBM), which guides its strategic decision making. In practice, business managers have a good deal of autonomy to be innovative and entrepreneurial, provided they can demonstrate the value-adding potential of their proposals. This decentralisation is a relatively recent phenomenon – ten years or so – and represents a major break from the culture of paternalism which infused the company before. Sir James Blyth became a life peer in 1995, and took over as Chief Executive of Boots in 1994. As he said to us, 'We have decreased control systems and continue to do so. If you don't need a policy in the centre you shouldn't have it. You can't dismantle 100 years of control if you don't trust the managers on the ground.'

The clear strategic focus of value-based management has turned around the Halfords business (contributing £22 million profit in 1996), and given clear management accountabilities. In addition to the VBM approach, Boots is fanatical about customer service. Lord Blyth says: 'We are obsessed by our customers. We do a lot of research . . . we regard it as a major source of competitive advantage.' Competitors are rigorously scrutinised, too, so that Boots can undertake retail engineering – allowing the group to maximise margins by pricing products differently in different areas according to social mix. Boots was also at the forefront of innovation in information technology, ensuring the effective stocking of stores through electronic point-of-sale (EPOS) technology and gaining better understanding of customer purchase decisions.

Bowthorpe

Bowthorpe, the electronics and electrical components group, has grown organically and through acquisition to encompass over 80 businesses throughout the world, and it has earned a reputation for strong performance in the very tough components market.

The company's core strategy has been to manage niche businesses, defined as £1 million turnover or less, and to be in the top three players in each niche. There has been strong decentralisation in the group, with no emphasis on seeking significant synergies across businesses. 'Not until recently had all the managers met together,' says CEO Nicholas Brookes, who took over in January 1996. Changes have now been implemented to take greater advantage of the synergies that exist between businesses, but the basic principles of autonomy and the avoidance of unnecessary bureaucracy remain key.

The major reason for this high level of autonomy is to ensure that the innovative and entrepreneurial drive of the businesses is maintained. A centrally-imposed culture or set of systems 'would smother the creativity and entrepreneurship. What I do encourage ... is a culture based on such principles, and we want to be an entrepreneurial company, we want to encourage teamwork. These elements of culture we do want – they are very general to all the businesses,' says Brookes.

A test of the success of the company is given by Brookes: 'If you look at the acquisitions most companies make of entrepreneurial companies, very often the entrepreneur takes his money and goes off to do something else. That's their nature. For us, in many cases, the entrepreneurs are still with us and are still thriving.'

A major incentive to enhance the retention of key technical staff is the introduction, by Brookes, of a technical career ladder, to sit beside the managerial ladder, 'so that an innovator who is not interested in managing people should be recognised and be able to progress away from line management. This has been very well received.'

The spread of business and geography has provided some defence against economic slowdown and, as the *Financial Times* claimed: 'Most competitors in the components business would give their eye teeth to be in Bowthorpe's position.'[3]

The strategy of the group originated with John Westhead, Managing Director from 1980, and the group was very much dominated by Westhead's vision for the firm. Westhead retired in January 1996 and became Non-executive Deputy Chairman. His successor, Nicholas Brookes, was recruited from Texas Instruments, and for six months shadowed Westhead in preparation for the role. Brookes said: 'A key factor in the success of the group is its pipeline of innovative products, some of which are developed through joint projects between operating units and universities in the UK and overseas, thus utilising the latest research in specific technical fields.'

The group is in the process of focusing the number of core businesses down from 12, and is encouraging greater information sharing across the businesses. More acquisitions will certainly be part of the strategy but the R&D capability means organic growth is also likely to be impressive.

British Airways

When Sir Colin Marshall took over as Chief Executive of British Airways in 1983, he found himself in charge of an organisation whose morale was in tatters. His impact on the company has been little short of miraculous. He preached the theme 'Putting People First' – reminiscent of his experience with Avis under the catchphrase 'We Try Harder'. He has a first-class brain under very careful, rational control, with enormous powers of continuous concentration. He is a superb motivator, not least by his own example of hard work, continuous questioning and constant pursuit of improvement.

Many of the business leaders interviewed for this book regard British Airways as one of their most admired companies. It is one of the most profitable airlines in the world at a time when a number of national flag carriers are subsidised or protected. Annual pre-tax profits are well in excess of £500 million and the market capitalisation has trebled in the last five years to over £5 billion.

From the outset 15 years ago, the task was clearly set out – 'to be the best and most successful airline in the world'. 'This can only be achieved if we deliver a consistently high quality of service to our customers,' said the Chief Executive. All BA's staff are put through a programme on how to make customers feel wanted. 'In an industry like ours, where there are no production lines, people are our most important asset. Everything depends on how they work as a team,' said Sir Colin.

In the process of change, massive job cuts were made to increase efficiency; new younger managers were put in place after being identified as having real potential. Delegation down the line, to allow responsiveness to customers, also enriched jobs. Sir Colin's style has been a combination of giving autonomy but remaining close to activity, constantly questioning.

Inevitably in the politicised and highly competitive world of airlines, tough and tense battles have been fought over new destinations, landing slots, fares, new terminals and sloping playing fields. British Airways has held its own through intensive bargaining and has maintained its revered performance.

The strategy is now globalisation, to recognise the realities of the 'shrinking world'. The challenge, to acquire complementary airlines against national resistance and then to inject the BA culture, will test the current and future management.

Sir Colin, now Chairman, has passed the CEO baton to Robert Ayling, promoted from within. Robert Ayling has not rested on his predecessor's success. Complacency is impossible as he aggressively challenges the appropriateness of current management structures and approaches in the new environment. British Airways' fundamental 'people first' culture will remain as global ambitions are driven ever higher.

N. Brown

N. Brown, the Manchester-based home shopping group, has a sparkling record of 20 per cent compound growth over the last 25 years. The N. Brown name is not immediately recognisable, and deliberately so, the firm preferring to push the brands of its catalogues – J.D. Williams, Oxendales, Heather Valley, Fifty Plus and Ambrose Wilson – to give consumers the impression they are dealing with a small and personal firm. The strength of the brands, plus a marketing operation based on a highly detailed customer database, provide the keys to the success of the company.

Sir David Alliance acquired a number of small home-shopping companies in the late 1960s and early 1970s, reversing them into N. Brown in 1972. The firm has prospered by focusing on home shopping aimed at distinct markets of middle- to older-aged consumers. Sir David, who is Chairman, is still the major shareholder with 41 per cent of the equity, and 'has an almost evangelical zeal when it comes to serving customers well' says CEO Jim Martin. N. Brown's success has been through organic growth supplemented with a few small judicious deals.

The core strategy of selling to older women has been supplemented by expansion into children's wear, menswear, the younger female market (over 30s), footwear, and now, home and garden. The focus is consistent: 'We are retailing to people who prefer to shop from home,' says Jim Martin.

Central to the effort is a sophisticated database marketing process that makes N. Brown 'perhaps the most complex mail-order operation in the world' according to its Marketing Director. The company endeavours to know its customers fully, 'their tastes, their expectations of quality and their size specifications'.[4] This information, gathered from purchases and from 'focused selling propositions in national newspapers and magazines' is used to segment customers and tailor products and offerings accordingly, with the underlying philosophy that 'there is no such thing as an average customer'.

The company has developed a customer-service index, which has identified '40 to 50 critical issues in the business relationship between the company and the customer' against which the company scores itself so as to measure progress and success. This process is aided by the fact that

N. Brown is a direct-order company, rather than an agency mail-order company – they deal directly with the end-user.

The company places a great emphasis on research to gain a better understanding of customers' needs. Amongst a number of initiatives, it carried out a size survey involving 700 women to improve its clothing specifications, and in turn launched a successful new catalogue, Classic Combination. In a similar style the company has created a new footwear fitting service, Shoe Tailor.

N. Brown's commitment to the customer is also shown by the fact that the company keeps the highest levels of 'in-stock' in the industry (90–92 per cent), which ensures high availability and speed of delivery, and the company recently decided to pay for postage on customers' returns (at a cost of £2.5 million a year).

The combination of Chairman Sir David Alliance and CEO Jim Martin is highly respected in the City and internally: 'They are open-minded enough to be always looking for the next thing, the next opportunity or innovation,' says Nigel Green, Marketing Director. A bid for Littlewoods in 1995 failed and while the firm is still looking for other targets, prospects for organic growth remain highly impressive.

Cadbury schweppes

Cadbury Schweppes has a proud history dating back to the nineteenth century. From its early Quaker roots, confectionery manufacturer Cadbury brought to its business a keen awareness of social and ethical concerns, which remains to this day.

In the 1970s, the company diversified into soft drinks through the merger with beverages company Schweppes, achieving a powerful point-of-sale presence. From that base, it has continued to grow its portfolio of global brands, adding the US soft-drinks company Dr Pepper/Seven Up in 1995.

In recent years, the company has built on its position as market leader in many Commonwealth countries, to become a truly global company. In many of its markets it faces fierce competition. Often, it has succeeded against bigger rivals by 'playing larger than its size', and relying on speed and flexibility for competitive advantage. As current Chairman Dominic Cadbury explains: 'When you are competing with Coca-Cola, Pepsi[Co], Mars and Nestlé, there isn't a lot of room for arrogance because you can frequently be looking at levels of performance which keep you right on your toes. We are not humbled in any way by comparison with them, but we certainly have a realistic sense of the intensity of the competition.'

The 1990s have seen profits jump from £360 million in 1991 to almost £650 million in 1995, and Cadbury Schweppes was among the first Western companies to establish manufacturing operations in Poland and China.

Throughout all the changes, too, the company has remained true to its guiding philosophy. In 1976, its values were distilled into a document entitled *The Character of the Company*, written by the then Chairman Sir Adrian Cadbury. They involve a commitment to: competitive ability, quality, clear objectives, simplicity, openness and responsibility to employees, customers, suppliers and shareholders.

For its thousands of employees working in 190 countries around the world, those values provide a powerful cultural glue and a clear understanding of what the company stands for. So, for example, when Eastern and Central European markets opened up after the fall of the Berlin Wall, Cadbury Schweppes managers knew – without reference to London – that unethical practices of any kind were not an option.

The company continues to see its reputation as a major source of competitive advantage. Dominic Cadbury puts the company's ongoing success down to the pride of its people in their performance: 'You've got to be fundamentally a competitive person. If you are competitive by nature, by instinct, the buzz comes from the company succeeding and all the satisfaction that gives to everyone involved.'

Carrefour

Carrefour is France's biggest hypermarket operator, with a market value of FF 54.9 billion. With 115 hypermarkets in France and strong domestic growth potential, the group has performed consistently well, but it is its overseas expansion where real growth opportunities have been identified. With a presence throughout Europe and America, there has been a big push into the Far East, including China.

The company's success has stemmed from its pioneering of the concept of the hypermarket. This simple guiding structure – everything under one roof, self-service, discount prices, free parking, segmented product offering[5] – has provided the foundation for domestic success as well as proving a readily adaptable template for expansion overseas. This concept, allied to a mission that states that 'all of our efforts are geared towards customer satisfaction', has brought continual adaptation as the company seeks to fulfil and anticipate customer demands.

Chief Executive Daniel Bernard says: 'Our focus is to continue our growth by moving into different places. In France, we live with very mature customers. If you compare our consumption curve with 20 years ago, we are at the top. We have introduced many new ideas. In particular, we were among the first to develop shopping by car, moving out of the town centre. Now this is all done and we have to develop more qualitative techniques in order to continue to grow. We face a new period – a new game, new paths. We have to buy in new technology – this will be very important.'

Carrefour faces a number of key tensions: maintaining customer loyalty in the face of increasing competition; and becoming fully global and decentralised while ensuring high standards and quality. In terms of customer loyalty, Bernard says: 'Customers have the behaviour of investors. They are very clever and are always comparing what you have to offer. So we have to ensure quality. We have developed supply chains which reach from the farm to the store and we chart the quality at each link. We have an association with farmers, which means we can offer a better ratio between quality and price than others.'

The emphasis on quality is reflected in the store design: 'The store must be a place where people can be happy and go and get everything they need. There has to be some spectacle. For example, our fish counters are like theatrical experiences, beautifully arranged and dramatic. We have got to permanently improve to keep customers. And we must present the best price. Combining these ambitions is a constant challenge,' says Bernard.

Innovations in merchandising, products, store layout, as well as offering financial services, have given Carrefour a competitive edge. The exploitation of global synergies in such areas as logistics, purchasing and data processing have served to give the company a highly competitive offering.[6]

The management of the global business demonstrates the decentralised style of Carrefour and its inherent nimbleness. The key to ensuring control and consistency across countries has been to foster the values of the company. Daniel Bernard says: 'In Carrefour, you have to rely not on recipes and policies but on values. This ensures that you can have entrepreneurs who can go anywhere with a suitcase. So rules no, entrepreneurialism yes. It demands a new characteristic – you have to be able to control flows of organisational information in order to transfer knowhow.'

The company tries to adapt to the environment of the countries in which it operates – after start-up, the company aims to have on average 95 per cent of local nationals as employees. Nearly all responsibilities are delegated, and central HQ is extremely small: 'We have 110,000 people worldwide but only 35 people in central HQ. The centre is for finance, control and organising for synergies, and to shape overall strategy. Management by charter is not for us.'

The company has a long history of enlightened treatment of staff and of delegated responsibility. 'In this company, managers do not have to call me [the Chief Executive] before they decide on a plan or action. With global expansion, opportunities for career advancement are strong,' Bernard declares.

Electrocomponents

Chief Executive Bob Lawson has had two periods at Electrocomponents – the first, in the 1980s, resulting in his abrupt departure as an executive; the second, from 1991 to the present, when he was asked to return as Managing Director.

Electrocomponents sells electrical components to engineers and technical people, through locally produced catalogues. Says the company's 1996 Annual Report: 'Electrocomponents supports a rapidly developing international group of operating companies. Each company is dedicated to the distribution of electronic, electrical and supporting products within their respective countries. Each offers a high level of service to its customers. It is this service offering, combined with a broad product range, that provides the group with its market lead.'[7]

It aims to be its customers' principal secondary supplier, depending on rapid delivery (a couple of hours in some circumstances) rather than volume orders. But the volume orders can mount up. For example, every dealer's desk in the City of London is worth on average £20 in annual sales of spare parts!

Lawson's philosophy is simple but powerful. He believes in making Electrocomponents a company people want to work in and want to perform well in. And he believes passionately that the company should never give a customer a reason for trading elsewhere on products that Electrocomponents should supply.

The results have been dramatic and largely organic growth in an apparently very mature industry. Profits before tax have nearly quadrupled in the four years 1992–6, while sales at RS Components, the main company within the group, have nearly doubled over the same period.

General Electric

More has probably been written in the past ten years about General Electric and its charismatic leader, Jack Welch, than any other company save perhaps Microsoft. Since Welch took over GE in 1981, the company's annual revenue has grown from $27 billion to $29 billion, while profit has risen from $1.65 billion to $7.28 billion. The average annual return to shareholders has been 23 per cent.

Welch took over a successful giant of a company that was in his own words 'arrogant and internally focused'. He rapidly gained the nickname 'Neutron Jack', dark humour for a perception that his visits to plants usually left the buildings standing but wiped out the people.

However, Welch had a clear vision of the future and a deep recognition that GE was living on the past – and the pension was due to run out. He reshaped the group, selling off anything that did not meet his exacting performance standards, including some companies, which observers inside and outside saw as the family silver. Those standards included an insistence that a GE company had to be first or second in its market.

Welch also set out to change the attitudes of everyone in the company – a task he recognises requires constant encouragement from him. He introduced the notion of stretch targets – constantly raising his demands of managers to encourage them to contribute more. He promoted the concept of boundarylessness – an enhanced form of employee involvement that required people at all levels to contribute their thoughts and ideas, saying, 'The only way to be more competitive was to engage every mind in the organisation. You couldn't have anybody on the sidelines.' Boundarylessness even extended to encouraging people attending management courses to discuss whether Jack Welch was the saviour of the business or an asshole.

Welch takes a hands-on approach to employee development, personally reviewing development plans for hundreds of executives and playing an active role as a course tutor.

GE is currently the world's largest company by stock value ($170 billion), with 239,000 employees in 100 countries. Yet for all its size, GE is remarkably nimble. Says Welch: 'We have to walk, talk, act and think like a small firm.' One of the sources of this nimbleness is the company's abandonment of the detailed, bureaucratic strategic planning processes it pioneered. Instead, it has moved to much more locally focused, flexible strategies that help individual businesses stay number one or two. Welch himself is regarded within and without the company as a master strategist, 'one of the best game players ever to run a business ... always thinking three or four moves ahead of the competition'.

He spends a large part of his time promoting the core values of the group, maintaining: 'Everything I do has to look larger than life, or people can't see me. I have to jolt the enterprise, overstate and use hyperbole.' The result is that the organisation often appears to be in constant turmoil. However, Welch declares that 'if you plan small changes, you get none.'

GKN

GKN is one of the UK's largest and most profitable engineering groups. Once heavily dependent on the highly cyclical automotive components market, the firm has expanded into the helicopter business with the purchase of Westland and has rapidly developed its Chep pallet hire business, in line with the broad strategic aim of 'smoothing out the business cycles through a balance of products and geography', says Chairman Sir David Lees.

In addition to the core businesses, there are also 'performance businesses' (for example, pressings, tractor cabs), which the company 'couldn't afford to invest in heavily but are useful profit makers', says Lees. The portfolio of businesses gives the group strong cash generation and, in the three core businesses, there is considerable growth potential.

The group stresses the goal of 'absolute excellence' in its product areas, in particular in the major automotive driveline business: 'In the automotive industry, every level is cost-sensitive, so what the component manufacturer has to do is differentiate itself,' says Sir David. Research and development (a £60 million spend per year) are strongly emphasised and this is closely tied to the group's whole approach to the customer, which is 'not to sit on our butts and wait for the customer to issue drawings to half-a-dozen manufacturers, but actually to get in to where the vehicle is being designed and say "if you give us the specification we will tailor the solution which will give you optimum cost and drive characteristics."'

A key element in the success of GKN has been the company's capability in business partnerships, which are present in its three core businesses. These have been crucial to the group's drive to become a global operation. The group has around 20 major joint ventures throughout the world, which have brought expert local knowledge to the group's technical expertise. Lees says 'partnerships have dominated my period as Chief Executive. Partnerships for us have always been positive and they are an important part of growing the business.'

The strategy of three core businesses, and the firm's success, are relatively recent phenomena – perhaps only three or four years' duration, although the gestation period has been considerably longer. Sir David Lees, who has held the role of Chief Executive from 1988 until recently, has stepped down to be replaced by C.K. Chow, a Hong Kong citizen, formerly a divisional director of BOC. The appointment of Chow is intended to reflect the group's international ambition, but Sir David will be a hard act to follow.

Granada

Granada's Charles Allen took over as Chief Executive of one of Britain's most successful companies in early 1996 as his predecessor and 'other half', Gerry Robinson, moved up to become Chairman.

In discussing Granada's success, Allen often points to the 'tough but fun', unstuffy, youthful culture that he and Gerry have built up throughout the company. The insistence on openness and 'no surprises', combined with a determination to set and achieve challenging targets, have made the company one of the City's favourites over the last few years.

Since joining Granada in 1991, Robinson and Allen have increased operating profit from £88 million to £388 million. The huge respect that they command from City analysts was demonstrated by their success in acquiring the Forte Group in January 1996, principally on the back of their promises that they could turn the business around and deliver true growth in shareholder value. Allen says: 'A strong relationship with the City is one of the key factors in our success. They have to believe in our strategy, and our ability to turn that strategy into real profit growth.'

According to Allen, when he and Robinson joined Granada it had lost its direction, and over 80 per cent of profits came from the rentals business. Their main drive has been to refocus the group, putting growth business areas such as media, hotels and restaurants in the centre stage. Allen believes it is the Granada culture that has driven this success, as he strives to strike a balance between autonomy and control. He says: 'We give people tremendous autonomy when things are going well, but as soon as they are not, everything is pulled in very tightly.'

He describes Robinson as the man whose vision creates a clear image of where he wants the company to go. Allen sees himself as the man whose skill lies in jointly creating the strategy and knowing how that vision can be realised – who not only understands the destination but understands how to reach it.

IKEA

The story of Swedish furniture company IKEA began with the vision of one extraordinary man, Ingvar Kamprad, its founder and first Chairman. That vision remains the guiding principle for the business today. It is 'to contribute to a better everyday working life for the majority of people, by offering a wide range of home furnishing items of good design and function, at prices so low that the majority of people can afford to buy them'.

Born in the barren country of Small-land, Kamprad grew up during the Great Depression of the 1930s. He took the qualities of resourcefulness he saw around him to heart and built them into a winning business philosophy. Now in his seventies, he refers to the values he instilled in IKEA as his 'testament'. Those values are set out in a document written in 1976 (revised in 1992), and remain unchanged even though the company now operates in 28 countries and has a turnover in excess of £865 million.[8]

It's a home-spun philosophy that combines the virtues of simplicity and making do (the company led the way in using recycled materials in furniture, for example) with determination and a deep-seated commitment to equality and innovation.

IKEA permits no status symbols among managers and refers to all employees as co-workers. The principle is reinforced by the example of Anders Moberg, the company's current President (ie Chief Executive). When travelling on business, for example, Moberg flies economy-class and refuses to take taxis when public transport is available.

Building on its early experience in Sweden – when a visit to an IKEA store could involve a day's travel – the company also tries to make shopping an enjoyable experience rather than a chore. Outlets include an IKEA restaurant with reasonably priced meals, and they also provide crèche facilities and activities to cater for children. (On special occasions, it even employs clowns and conjurers.)

IKEA has also succeeded where many European retailers have failed, successfully taking its formula to North America. The experience, however, was not without lessons. Puzzled at first by poor sales of beds and other lines, it quickly learned that although Americans liked the simplicity of its designs they wanted furniture to match their larger homes. The answer? Bigger furniture. It hasn't looked back since.

Microsoft

Microsoft's recent history has been of remarkable growth in one of the most competitive industries in the world. Under the leadership of Bill Gates, it has grown from a two-man operation in 1974 to a company with over 20,500 employees, and more than $8.8 billion a year in sales.

Microsoft attributes its success to concentration on six key factors:

- a long term approach;
- results orientation;
- teamwork and individual drive;
- a passion for its products and customers; and
- continuous customer feedback.

The company hires very bright, creative people and retains them through a combination of excitement, constant stretching and good workplace conditions. (At less than 8 per cent per annum, labour turnover is low for the IT industry.) A relaxed attitude to dress code and a broad indifference towards hierarchy is balanced by demanding attitudes towards performance.

When people leave, Microsoft research has shown they do so because the challenge has run out. So a major responsibility for Microsoft managers is to keep injecting challenge into people's work.

In keeping with its product emphasis, Microsoft's lifeblood is its e-mail and intranet systems, which are the main methods of communication. Anyone can and does contact anyone else, regardless of job title, with ideas, suggestions and requests for help.

Perhaps the most significant test of the Microsoft culture is that so many of the original employees are still there. A lot of people in their early thirties have become millionaires with their stock options. They could comfortably afford to retire for life, but as Mike Murray, Vice President of Human Resources and Administration, expresses it: 'What else would they do with their lives? Where else could they have such fun?'

Rentokil Initial

When Sir Clive Thompson took the helm at Rentokil in 1982, he set the company an extraordinary goal: 20 per cent growth in profits and earnings per share per annum, for ever. To achieve that goal, he re-focused the business, moving away from the provision of residential services and other less-profitable activities, to concentrate on contract-based industrial services where customers were prepared to pay for quality.

Fifteen years on and the strategy is unchanged. ('Only a lousy strategy needs constant revision,' he says. 'A good strategy lasts.') The figures speak for themselves. Over the past decade, profits have grown, on average, by 23.5 per cent a year and earnings per share by 24.4 per cent per annum – a remarkable performance for a 70-year-old business operating in highly competitive markets.

Best known for its pest control operation, today the company provides a variety of other industrial services, including office and retail cleaning, medical services, hygiene services and the supply and maintenance of plants to business premises.

Rentokil Initial (the name was changed in 1996) now operates in more than 40 countries, including most of the major economies in Europe, North America, Asia–Pacific and Africa. In each market, the brand offering and philosophy is the same, something for which Sir Clive makes no apologies. 'We maintain central control. Marketing, for example, in all our services is in exactly the same style in every country – like McDonalds. We say this is what we provide, this is what we are good at.'

Within this clearly defined framework, the 600 Rentokil branches operate as profit centres in their own right. The UK headquarters acts as banker and co-ordinates group activities – such as strategy and marketing – and has total control over acquisitions. As Sir Clive explains: 'Six hundred different branches means that it's hard to make large mistakes.' He applies the same principle to the company's recent £2 billion acquisition of BET: 'It looks big, but in practice it is probably 50 trading businesses which we will sub-divide into more than 100 opportunities to get it right or wrong.'

It's also a company that believes in results. As one Rentokil Initial manager put it: 'It's a culture that can be brutally honest about your performance, but it leaves you in no doubt where you stand. There's no pussy-footing around issues. You get it with double barrels – either congratulations or the other side if things aren't going well.'

So why is the company so successful? 'Our competitive advantage is that we provide services on our customers' premises,' says Sir Clive. 'It's not easy. They see what we do and we do it better than anyone else.'

Reuters

In the words of its Chief Executive: 'People find it difficult to understand what Reuters actually does.' People commonly associate the company with the international news wire that bears its name, but in reality media products only account for some seven per cent of the company's revenue. The core business of Reuters is the supply of information products to the financial community.

Reuters Chief Executive Peter Job joined the business as a journalist over 30 years ago. For him the core values of the company are the same now as they were back in 1851 when the company was founded: speed and accuracy. 'Given that these are two mutually exclusive propositions, it's not surprising it has taken us 150-odd years to try and bring them together!' he adds, explaining that the photograph of President Chirac of France on the cover of the 1995 Reuters annual report is there to bring home the point that on the occasion of the French resumption on nuclear weapons testing, Reuters had news of the explosion five minutes before its competitors.

For a company of its size, Reuters' financial performance is almost legendary. In the 11 years to 1996 its turnover increased by a factor of six to £2.9 billion, and profits increased from £54 million to £701 million. Job explains this performance lucidly: 'We are simply saying that if we have something good, we should carpet the world with it. Over the last ten years our main challenge has been to occupy the empty hills.'

Now that there are perhaps fewer empty hills, Reuters is focusing on the development of newer business areas, in particular that of transaction products that allow traders to buy and sell instruments from their keyboards. Such developments are allowing Reuters to use its core technological competencies to construct and mine a whole new seam of products that will over the coming years undoubtedly challenge the power base of many of the world's physical financial exchanges.

Keeping the feel of a small organisation whilst ensuring the benefits of scale and global reach is one of the secrets that Job alludes to in explaining Reuters' sustained success: 'We're not one huge company. We're actually a large number of small- to medium-sized business units that are all made to feel part of a global nexus. While on the one hand we encourage people to be Russian in Russia, on the other they are plugged into a strong global network.'

And Job's final piece of advice to the committed Reuters-watcher? 'Don't be deceived by the grey suits! While it may pay us to appear conservative given the markets we're in, underneath our minds are constantly whirring. Ours is a special form of conservatism: radical conservatism!'

SAP

SAP is the world's fifth-largest software company, and was formed in 1972 when five IBM software engineers left to set up their own company. In 1995, turnover was at DM 1.15 billion (£523 million) and pre-tax profits at DM 223 million, up 67 per cent and 80 per cent respectively on the previous year.[9]

The basis of SAP's success was the product R/2, which provided standard business software for mainframe computers. But in 1992, the launch of R/3 saw the company grow at an amazing rate. R/3 is standard business software for client–server applications – the technology that breaks down computer systems into front end 'client' workstations and back-end 'server' processors so that data is handled by networks rather than stand-alone PCs. This product 'provides a range of financial, logistics, personnel, and other applications which companies can buy off the peg and have altered to their needs instead of spending heavily on "made to measure" solutions ...' where 'internal product flows and financial trends become much easier to monitor.'[10]

The company is now the market leader in client–server applications, outpacing US giants such as Oracle and PeopleSoft and the Dutch-based Baan company. The company appears to be well-placed because the world market for such products 'is in its infancy' and because 'companies buying similar packages will have a tendency to choose the programs their main customers and suppliers have already adopted.'[11]

As the company grows, it is looking to penetrate the markets of the US, Europe and Asia–Pacific. But the focus remains firmly fixed on the development and marketing of standard business software. As executive board member Professor Kagermann says: 'The focus is not to transfer skills outside this area – we need to maintain the focus to continue our success.'

In common with many software companies, SAP experiences constant change as the demands of this highly volatile market change. But two things keep the firm ahead of increasing competition: the quality of the products, and the strength of the partnerships the firm has forged with suppliers and customers. Says Kagermann: 'We still have the best product. We have many blue-chip customers – they have chosen SAP and we have developed very strong relationships with them, servicing their needs and keeping close contacts with them. Second, we started very early with partnerships. We had that debate early on and it has really worked for us. We would rather work through partnerships than progress through acquisitions and mergers. This is particularly so when we partner with very large firms and we would never have the money to buy them. With smaller firms, it takes too long to buy and you can lose flexibility when you buy firms. Making a partnership can be done in a week and you retain the flexibility that such a relationship can bring.'

The company's culture has remained consistent throughout its history: informal, team-based, non-hierarchical, with innovation and entre-preneurialism encouraged. The rapid growth of the company ensures there are considerable opportunities to build a career within the company.

As a German company, the emphasis is less on the short-term financial results and more on the long-term development of relationships with key clients as a major strategic aim. The expansion of the firm has brought concerns about control: 'It is different when you have to control a firm of 40 people and then to control a firm of 9,000 people,' says Kagermann, but the key has been to 'ensure that the company values are maintained. These values are reliability and trust – these are our major strengths, apart from the technology. We have trust and belief in each other.'

Siebe

Barrie Stephens, Chairman of Siebe, talks about luck whenever he describes Siebe's success. He took over a small company in 1963 that was virtually bankrupt and turned it into a thriving international group. Says Stephens: 'I had to pledge my house to pay the wages. On my birthday, I had to let 100 people go. Now we have sales of £3 billion and market capitalisation of almost £5 billion.'

Then he and Finance Director Roger Mann had the good fortune *not* to be able to sell two very small, apparently dull and poorly performing businesses making control equipment. He explains: 'Roger and I bought a company called Tecalemit in a hostile bid. We looked inside the cookie bag and there were a couple of control companies, with combined sales of less than £1 million. I said: "What do we know about controls? We'll fix them up and sell them." But no one wanted them. Then we made other acquisitions and they had a few little control companies too. We started to look around at the big control companies, such as Honeywell, that we were competing with and decided there had to be something in this for us too.' He told *Management Today*: 'I decided this was for us. It was sophisticated, clever, all the people in it were global players and we were able to operate under their guns.'[12]

Siebe is now one of the world's leading control instrumentation companies in its own right, and one of the most consistently profitable engineering companies in Europe. Growth has been a mixture of organic and acquisition, with a heavy stress on new ventures in North America. Siebe owns, among others, Compair, Robertshaw Controls and Foxboro. It has a reputation for achieving remarkable turnarounds – the ailing Foxboro, for example, almost doubled its market share in the six years after Siebe acquired it.

Stephens set out six simple financial measures in an exercise book within his first few weeks at the helm and these remain the bedrock of Siebe's management system. He and his successor as CEO, Allen Yurko, maintain a hands-on style of management, carrying out regular reviews of each business with the team responsible. The financial measures form part of that review, but of more interest and concern is how the business is geared for the future. Each business is expected to launch at least five new products each year. They do not have to develop all of those products, but they do have to get them into the market. Each business is also expected annually to have five critical strategic objectives, which it will partially or wholly achieve within the following 12 months and on which the unit's top management focuses.

Singapore Airlines

From a domestic market of only four million people, Singapore Airlines has become one of the world's great air carriers – the world's second largest airline in terms of market capitalisation. It has established a strong and well-deserved reputation for quality of service that has fuelled rapid growth and sustained profitability through the global airline recession. It consistently appears as the Asian airline offering the best quality of service, a reputation it maintains through a very heavy investment in training and a continuous flow of service innovation.

Managing Director Cheong Choong Kong operates out of a sprawling office complex alongside Singapore Airport. He is reluctant to accept personal acclaim for the airline's success, pointing out the company's culture emphasises teamwork rather than individual achievement.

The company's reputation for service quality comes from a long-term commitment to differentiate itself in this way. All passenger-facing staff, and especially cabin crew, undergo months of intensive training before they are considered ready to work with customers. Customer opinions are tracked continuously and used to develop further innovations that help the airline stay ahead on service reputation. From hot towels to in-flight communications, Singapore Airlines has consistently been the innovation leader.

Singapore Airlines' six core values – customer awareness; safety; pursuit of excellence; caring for staff; integrity; and teamwork – were only written down in recent years, but have driven the business since its beginnings. It now has around a hundred subsidiaries, including engineering and airport management. It has weathered the ups and downs of the airline industry with remarkable consistency – due at least in part to a policy of steady investment in growth.

Smiths Industries

Sir Roger Hurn, who oversaw the transition of Smiths Industries from an instrument supplier to the motor industry, with a residual clock and watch business, into an engineering group in aerospace, medical systems and general industrial products (ranging from hosing to ventilation fans) recently handed over the reins as Chief Executive to Keith Butler-Wheelhouse. Sir Roger remains as Chairman.

The transition was remarkable in that, even though the company shifted the entire focus of its business, it did so without once allowing steady improvement in profit to falter. In 1981, the year Sir Roger became Chief Executive, the company reported pre-tax profit of £16 million on sales of £368 million. In 1996, the year he relinquished that role, it reported pre-tax profit of £170 million on sales of just over £1 billion. Dividends also increased every year throughout this period.

Sir Roger Hurn started out as an apprentice at Rolls-Royce and worked his way up. It taught him a lot about managing change, he says – not least, the importance of changing only one thing at a time, so you can measure the impact. 'I don't think leadership of a company is a complicated business,' he says. 'It's about being open and trusting, and keeping it simple.'

Sir Roger describes the company's strategy as 'pursuing high-value niches with technology and marketing pluses. ... We are not chasing market share any more. I don't think it is relevant to our business.' He lives, eats and breathes the company he shaped, and places a high premium on developing the kind of relationships with customers, 'where they want to do business with *us*' rather than with anyone else.

Smiths Industries also has a reputation for taking big risks where the circumstances warrant and the potential returns are sufficient. Its development of computerised decision-making software for commercial aircraft, for example, was a $60 million act of faith based on customer relationships and technological intuition.

SOL

Liisa Joronen runs the Finnish company SOL, a nationwide cleaning and waste management operation whose clients include Finnair, Ericsson and Nokia. The company's distinctive bright yellow jackets and even more dazzling growth figures have raised eyebrows in the conservative world of Finnish corporate affairs.

When Joronen founded SOL in 1992, she set out to turn Finnish business culture upside down. A member of a powerful family-owned Finnish industrial group, her experience as Chief Executive of her father's national laundry chain Lindstrom had convinced her that radically different management techniques and styles of working were required in the future. By the early 1990s, her far-sighted father could see that his headstrong daughter would not take no for an answer, so he sold her the cleaning business and let her get on with it.

The first task was to choose a name for the business. She asked her workers for suggestions and SOL – meaning sunshine – was selected. She also asked them to help design the first SOL head office (SOL Studio) in a converted film studio, and again later when the company moved to its current larger premises (SOL City).

SOL's slogans include 'freedom from the office', 'freedom from status symbols' and 'kill routine before it kills you'. The open-plan office in Helsinki has virtually no hierarchy. Desks are communal and no one has a secretary. The environment is one of paintings, comfortable sofas, fountains and brightly coloured walls. Armed with portable computers and mobile phones, staff can work wherever they like, at home or in the office, provided they meet democratically-voted annual targets for cleaning the country's factories, offices, airliners, and even zoos.

'If you trust your people 100 per cent, they will do almost anything for you,' says Joronen – or Liisa as she is known to everyone in the company. 'Happy and satisfied people do better work. Left to their own devices they also set higher targets.'

The fact that she launched SOL in the depths of the worst economic downturn in Finnish history is testament to the strength of her beliefs. Not only did the business survive – and it actually made a profit even during the worst years of the recession – it has also achieved a turnover of $50 million and is currently growing at 20 to 25 per cent annually, posing a serious challenge in Finland to Danish-owned ISS, the world's largest cleaning company.

For all its emphasis on the soft aspects of management, however, the success of the company is grounded in its grip on Total Quality Management. Joseph Juran, the American management expert and one of the founding fathers of the Quality movement, was so impressed that he described SOL as 'the future of quality'.

Southwest Airlines

Southwest Airlines, based in Texas, is the most consistently profitable US airline. Its strategy for success is simple: to specialise in short-to-medium-range flights to convenient airports on high-density routes within the US, keeping costs to a minimum. Indeed, simplicity is the basic philosophy at Southwest – fares are extremely low, a single class service only is offered (no first or business class), and there are no assigned seats and no meals. The company only operates one aircraft type – the Boeing 737 – to simplify scheduling, maintenance, flight operations and training; and the 'ticketless travel' concept provides fast and simple boarding for passengers.

Quick turnaround of aircraft and frequent flights have added to Southwest's popularity and seen the company grow from its Texas base to become the biggest operator of flights within California, flying to 46 airports today. Turnover in 1995 was $2.87 billion, with profits of $18.3 million, and the airline employs 20,000 people.

Keeping fares lower than competitors has meant that the firm has to keep costs low. Operating costs at Southwest are among the lowest in the industry – costs per seat mile are 19 per cent below the industry average.[13] The key to maintaining this low cost structure is through high productivity. John G. Denison, Executive Vice President of Corporate Services, said: 'Southwest continually achieves the highest asset utilisation and employee productivity of any US airline ... thanks to our culture at Southwest Airlines, we do not have to motivate our employees with programs to reduce costs; rather, it is their goal each and every day.'[14]

The culture at Southwest Airlines is indeed unique. The company is big on recognition for employees – formal and informal awards presentations, birthday cards for all employees – and a reluctance to set down explicit rules for employees to follow has engendered a high commitment culture. Add to this a heavy dose of fun encouraged when dealing with customers and it adds up to a strongly individual climate which passengers seem to love. Leading this spirit is the now legendary figure of President Herb Kelleher, renowned for his jokes and pranks. He defines his approach to the management of people as follows: 'People are very, very gifted. They can do a whole lot of things. And if you give them the opportunity to expand beyond the horizons that the organisation tries to define for them, you will be amazed at what they can produce.'[15]

Southwest focuses a great deal on recruitment. In 1995, 124,000 people applied for 5,473 jobs: 'We hire people with attitudes that are outrageously positive. Our employees enjoy working together as a team and take pleasure in team results, rather than emphasising individual accomplishments.'[16]

Vodafone

Vodafone is a spectacular success, building a £8.5 billion business in under ten years and being instrumental in the rapid growth of the mobile phone industry. The strong focus of the business – 'we are in mobile telecommunications ... this is a single business; it has a lot of small companies but it's all the same orchestra,' says CEO Sir Gerald Whent – has produced a clear strategy. Its global expansion has been successful in developing cellular networks worldwide. He draws the analogy between global telecommunications and a theatrical production. Vodafone's role in that production is that of a top-class actor; he sees no reason why Vodafone should try to run the whole production.

The firm is highly decentralised, with Vodafone empowering managers at all levels to take decisions quickly to ensure a highly entrepreneurial culture. Businesses are kept small to engender a flexibility and fast response to customers. In this highly competitive sector – its main rivals are BT Cellnet, Orange, and Mercury One-2-One – speed is crucial, and this has greatly inhibited any complacency within the group. 'We make sure we look at all markets all the time,' says Julian Horn-Smith, Managing Director of Vodafone International.

Success began in the UK when the Government awarded to a consortium led by Racal (a firm in the original *The Winning Streak*) the licence to become the UK's second mobile phone network operator, to compete with BT's Cellnet. Vodafone, as part of Racal Telecom, experienced rapid growth as the 1980s saw a huge uptake in mobile phones in the UK. As Vodafone grew, its value exceeded the rest of the Racal group and so Vodafone, after a partial float of 20 per cent in 1988, was demerged in 1991.

In Vodafone's early days, nobody in the fledgling industry had any idea of what mobile telephony would become. No one ever imagined that cellular radio might become the common consumer product that it is today, with penetration of over ten per cent and still rising strongly: 'Back then, we forecast a penetration of something like two per cent after six years, flattening off at 2.5 per cent,' recalls Sir Gerald Whent. Vodafone's head start against BT in those early days comes down to the fact that

Vodafone's vision of the future market was twice that of BT. Both estimates were wildly inaccurate, but BT's was that bit more inaccurate! On the basis of this, Vodafone made a higher initial capital investment in its network, giving it a clear lead against BT's Cellnet as initial demand gave Cellnet major congestion problems. The group does not deal direct with end-users, but with 35 'service providers', and one of the keys to Vodafone gaining market share at the expense of Cellnet in the early years was that its approach was to 'go in as partners with service providers and not master and slave', says Sir Gerald. This brought strong relationships and ensured quality service.

The building of a strong track record in the UK (the largest European market) in terms of technical quality and management expertise gave the group credibility in bidding for licenses overseas. The company now operates in 14 countries and, in terms of levels of penetration, there is huge opportunity for growth.

The group is currently building a digital network to augment its analogue coverage, and this now covers 90 per cent of the UK population. The personality of Sir Gerald Whent has been dominant throughout the firm's success, but his reign has been far from a centralist bureaucracy. His style 'is about keeping people going, and giving them hope and inspiration when things get black, and not letting them get too flamboyant when things are going well.'

NOTES

INTRODUCTION
1 James Aley, 'The Theory That Made Microsoft' in *Fortune*, 26 April 1996.

CHAPTER ONE
1 Herman Simon, *The Hidden Champions* (Harvard Business Press, 1996).
2 E.A. Locke and G.P. Latham, *A Theory of Goal Setting and Task Performance* (Prentice-Hall, Englewood Cliffs NJ, 1990).

CHAPTER TWO
1 Mark Fenton-O'Creery, *Striking off the Shackles* (Institute of Management, Corby, September 1995).
2 Richard Wilsher, 'Loose and Tight' in *The Business Magazine*, March 1996.
3 Hugh Carnegy, 'Struggle to Save the Soul of IKEA' in *Financial Times*, 27 March 1995.
4 'Furnishing the World' in *The Economist*, 19 November 1994.
5 Sandra S. Vance and Roy V. Scott, *Wal-Mart: A History of Sam Walton's Retail Phenomenon* (Twayne, New York, 1994).

CHAPTER THREE
1 Noel M. Tichy and Stratford Sherman, *Control Your Destiny or Someone Else Will* (Currency Doubleday, New York, 1993).
2 A. Davidson, 'The Davidson Interview: Gerry Robinson' in *Management Today*, June 1995.
3 Sandra S. Vance and Roy V. Scott, *Wal-Mart: A History of Sam Walton's Retail Phenomenon* (Twayne, New York, 1994).
4 He is referring here to motivational studies by a number of academics that compare and contrast people with high internal locus of control (belief that they are largely in charge of and responsible for what happens to them) and people with a high external locus of control (who believe they have little opportunity to influence the world about them).
5 Brenton Schlender, 'How Bill Gates Keeps the Magic Going' in *Fortune*, 18 June 1990.
6 'Furnishing the World' in *The Economist*, 19 November 1994.
7 R.C. Christensen *et al*, *Business Policy Texts and Cases*, 7th edn (Irwin, Illinois, 1991).

CHAPTER FOUR

1 Michael Porter, 'What is Strategy' in *Harvard Business Review*, Nov/Dec 1996.

2 R.C. Christensen *et al*, *Business Policy Texts and Cases*, 7th edn (Irwin, Illinois, 1991).

3 James Collins and Jerry Porras, 'Building Your Company's Vision' in *Harvard Business Review*, Sept/Oct 1996.

4 John Mitchell, *JCB: The First Fifty Years* (Special Events Books, Brighton, 1995).

5 Michiyo Nakamoto, 'Sony's Defence of the Living Room' in *Financial Times*, 26 August 1996.

6 Brenton Schlender, 'Brent Schlender, Bill Gates and Paul Allen Talk' in *Fortune*, 2 October 1995.

7 Noel M. Tichy and Stratford Sherman, *Control Your Destiny or Someone Else Will* (Currency Doubleday, New York, 1993).

8 'A Conversation with Roberto Goizueta and Jack Welch' in *Fortune*, 11 December 1995.

9 Donald J. McNerney, 'Creating a Motivated Workforce' in *HR Focus*, August 1996.

10 William G. Lee, 'A Conversation with Herb Kelleher' in *Organizational Dynamics*, Autumn 1996.

11 Ingvar Kamprad, *The Testament of a Furniture Dealer* (IKEA, Almhult, 1976 (revised 1992)).

CHAPTER FIVE

1 Noel M. Tichy and Stratford Sherman, *Control Your Destiny or Someone Else Will* (Currency Doubleday, New York, 1993).

2 Andrew Lorenz, 'Granada Chief Rewrites the Rules' in *The Sunday Times*, 29 September 1996.

3 Ingvar Kamprad, *The Testament of a Furniture Dealer* (IKEA, Almhult, 1976 (revised 1992)).

4 John Mitchell, *JCB: The First Fifty Years* (Special Events Books, Brighton, 1995).

5 Carol Kennedy, 'ABB's Sun Rises in the East' in *Director*, September 1996.

6 Steven E. Prokesch, 'Competing on Customer Service: an Interview with British Airways' Sir Colin Marshall' in *Harvard Business Review*, Nov/Dec 1995.

7 Andrew Lorenz, 'Granada Chief Rewrites the Rules' in *The Sunday Times*, 29 September 1996.

CHAPTER SIX

1 David Clutterbuck and Sue Kernaghan, *The Phoenix Factor* (Weidenfeld & Nicholson, London, 1990).

2 Ingvar Kamprad, *The Testament of a Furniture Dealer* (IKEA, Almhult, 1976 (revised 1992)).

3 John Mitchell, *JCB: The First Fifty Years* (Special Events Books, Brighton, 1995).

4 Betsy Morris, 'The Wealth Builders' in *Fortune*, 11 December 1995.

5 Carol Kennedy, 'The Art of the Profitable' in *Director*, December 1996.

6 Adam M. Brandenburger and Barry J. Nelbuff, 'Inside Intel' in *Harvard Business Review*, Nov/Dec 1996.

7 Hugh Carnegy, 'Struggle to Save the Soul of IKEA' in *Financial Times*, 27 March 1995.

CHAPTER SEVEN

1 Ian Rodger, 'Double Triumph for Young Group' in *Financial Times*, 19 September 1995.

2 Andrew Lorenz, 'Cadbury' in *Management Today*, September 1996.

3 GKN Annual Report and Accounts 1995.

4 Adam M. Brandenburger and Barry J. Nelbuff, 'Inside Intel' in *Harvard Business Review*, Nov/Dec 1996.

5 Noel M. Tichy and Stratford Sherman, *Control Your Destiny or Someone Else Will* (Currency Doubleday, New York, 1993).

CHAPTER EIGHT

1 William G. Lee, 'A Conversation with Herb Kelleher' in *Organizational Dynamics*, Autumn 1994.

2 Alex Taylor III, 'The Man Who Put Honda Back on Track' in *Fortune*, 9 September 1996.

3 James C. Collins and Jerry I. Porras, *Built to Last: Successful Habits of Visionary Companies* (Century Business, London, 1994).

4 Michiyo Nakamoto, 'Sony's Defence of the Living Room' in *Financial Times*, 26 August 1996.

5 Hugh Carnegy, 'Struggle to Save the Soul of IKEA' in *Financial Times*, 27 March 1995.

6 Carol Kennedy, 'The Art of the Profitable' in *Director*, December 1996.

7 James C. Collins and Jerry I. Porras, *Built to Last: Successful Habits of Visionary Companies* (Century Business, London, 1994).

8 S. Marks and I. Seiff, 'Six Basic Principles', c 1930.

9 Noel M. Tichy and Stratford Sherman, *Control Your Destiny or Someone Else Will* (Currency Doubleday, New York, 1993).

CHAPTER NINE

1 David Clutterbuck *et al*, *Inspired Customer Service* (Kogan Page, London, 1993).

2 Steven E. Prokesch, 'Competing on Customer Service: An Interview with British Airways' Sir Colin Marshall' in *Harvard Business Review*, Nov/Dec 1995.

3 Richard Tomkins, 'The Seriously Funny Airline' in *Financial Times*, 11 November 1996.

4 Hugh Carnegy, 'Struggle to Save the Soul of IKEA' in *Financial Times*, 27 March 1995.

5 William G. Lee, 'A Conversation with Herb Kelleher' in *Organizational Dynamics*, Autumn 1994.

6 Patricia Sellers, 'Can Home Depot Fix its Sagging Stock?' in *Fortune*, 4 March 1996.

7 Carol Kennedy, 'The Art of the Profitable' in *Director*, December 1996.

8 David Clutterbuck *et al*, *Inspired Customer Service* (Kogan Page, London, 1993).

CHAPTER TEN

1 William G. Lee, 'A Conversation with Herb Kelleher' in *Organizational Dynamics*, Autumn 1994.

2 Philip Dourado, 'Hi Guys, This is Your President' in *The Daily Telegraph*, 24 January 1997.

3 Richard Tomkins, 'The Seriously Funny Airline' in *Financial Times*, 11 November 1996.

4 Sandra S. Vance and Roy V. Scott, *Wal-Mart: A History of Sam Walton's Retail Phenomenon* (Twayne, New York, 1994).

5 Andrew Lorenz, 'Granada Chief Rewrites the Rules' in *The Sunday Times*, 29 September 1996.

6 Noel M. Tichy and Stratford Sherman, *Control Your Destiny or Someone Else Will* (Currency Doubleday, New York, 1993).

7 William G. Lee, 'A Conversation with Herb Kelleher' in *Organizational Dynamics*, Autumn 1994.

8 Corporate Research Foundation, *Corporate Strategies of the Top 100 UK Companies* (McGraw-Hill, Maidenhead, 1996).

9 Alain Tillier, *The European*, 5–11 October 1995.

10 Sandra S. Vance and Roy V. Scott, *Wal-Mart: A History of Sam Walton's Retail Phenomenon* (Twayne, New York, 1994).

11 Noel M. Tichy and Stratford Sherman, *Control Your Destiny or Someone Else Will* (Currency Doubleday, New York, 1993).

12 William G. Lee, 'A Conversation with Herb Kelleher' in *Organizational Dynamics*, Autumn 1994.

13 R.C. Christensen *et al*, *Business Policy Texts and Cases*, 7th edn (Irwin, Illinois, 1991).

14 *St Petersburg Times*, 24 December 1990.

15 Bill Saporito, 'The Fix is in for Home Depot' in *Fortune*, 29 February 1988.

16 Patricia Sellers, 'Can Home Depot Fix its Sagging Stock?' in *Fortune*, 4 March 1996.

17 Victoria J. Marsick, 'Trends in Managerial Reinvention' in *Management Learning* (Sage, London, 1994).

18 Richard Tomkins, 'The Seriously Funny Airline' in *Financial Times*, 11 November 1996.

CHAPTER ELEVEN

1 Warren Bennis, 'Managing the Dream: Leadership in the Twenty-first Century' in *Issues*, No 9 1989.
2 Noel Tichy and Stratford Sherman, *Control Your Destiny or Someone Else Will* (Doubleday, New York, 1993).
3 Betsy Morris, 'The Wealth Builders' in *Fortune*, 11 December 1995.
4 Corporate Research Foundtion, *Corporate Strategies of the Top 100 UK Companies* (McGraw-Hill, Maidenhead, 1996).
5 John Mitchell, *JCB: The First Fifty Years* (Special Events Books, Brighton, 1995).
6 Matthew Horsman and Paul O'Kane, 'Gerry's Forte' in the *Irish Times*, 1 December 1995.

CHAPTER TWELVE

1 Tim Burt, 'Smiths Industries Set for Overseas Drive' in *Financial Times*, 19 November 1996.

CHAPTER THIRTEEN

1 Julia Thrift, 'A Profile of David Wellings' in *Management Today*, May 1994.
2 William G. Lee, 'A Conversation with Herb Kelleher' in *Organizational Dynamics*, Autumn 1994.
3 John Mitchell, *JCB: The First Fifty Years* (Special Events Books, Brighton, 1995).
4 Ingvar Kamprad, *The Testament of a Furniture Dealer* (IKEA, Almhult, 1976 (revised 1992)).
5 Patricia Sellers, 'Can Home Depot Fix its Sagging Stock?' in *Fortune*, 4 March 1996.

CHAPTER FOURTEEN

1 D. Miller, 'What Happens After Success: the Perils of Excellence' in *Journal of Management Studies* 31:3 (1994), pp 325–58.
2 R. Cowe (ed.), *The Guardian Guide to the UK's Top Companies* (Guardian Books, London, 1993), p 427.
3 R. Cowe (ed.), *The Guardian Guide to the UK's Top Companies* (Guardian Books, London, 1993), p 427.
4 'The Scuttling of Sir Nigel' in *Evening Standard*, 16 December 1993.
5 'Trafalgar braces for bad news' in *Financial Times*, 14 December 1993.
6 R. Cowe (ed.), *The Guardian Guide to the UK's Top Companies* (Guardian Books, London, 1993), p 427.
7 R. Cowe (ed.), *The Guardian Guide to the UK's Top Companies* (Guardian Books, London, 1993), p 387.

8 R. Cowe (ed.), *The Guardian Guide to the UK's Top Companies* (Guardian Books, London, 1993), p 43.

9 A.J. Almaney, 'Wang Laboratories Inc.' in T.L. Wheeler and J.D. Hunger (eds), *Cases in Strategic Management*, 4th edn (Addison-Wesley, Massachusetts, 1993), p 75.

10 A.J. Almaney, 'Wang Laboratories Inc.' in T.L. Wheeler and J.D. Hunger (eds), *Cases in Strategic Management*, 4th edn (Addison-Wesley, Massachusetts, 1993), p 75.

11 A.J. Almaney, 'Wang Laboratories Inc.' in T.L. Wheeler and J.D. Hunger (eds), *Cases in Strategic Management*, 4th edn (Addison-Wesley, Massachusetts, 1993), p 76.

12 Wolfgang Munchau, 'Lingering Death of AEG a Lesson in Mismanagement' in *The Financial Times*, 20 December 1995.

13 Wolfgang Munchau, 'Lingering Death of AEG a Lesson in Mismanagement' in *Financial Times*, 20 December 1995.

14 J.R. Anchor, 'Fisons plc' in C. Clarke-Hill and K. Glaister (eds), *Cases in Strategic Management*, 2nd edn (Pitman, London, 1991), pp 352–67.

15 'Fisons Takes Action After Improper Sales Practices', in *Financial Times*, 23 November 1993.

16 J.R. Anchor, 'Fisons plc' in C. Clarke-Hill and K. Glaister (eds), *Cases in Strategic Management*, 2nd edn (Pitman, London, 1991), p 356.

17 'Turnaround Man Gets a New Fix', in *Financial Times*, 6 January 1995.

CHAPTER FIFTEEN

1 R. Cowe (ed.), *The Guardian Guide to the UK's Top Companies* (Guardian Books, London, 1993).

2 'Sainsbury Fights the Rot as Profits Slide Again' in *The Sunday Times*, 2 February 1997.

3 Corporate Research Foundation, *Corporate Strategies of the Top 100 UK Companies of the Future* (McGraw-Hill, Maidenhead, 1995).

4 'Sainsbury Fights the Rot as Profits Slide Again' in *The Sunday Times*, 2 February 1997.

5 'Sainsbury Fights the Rot as Profits Slide Again' in *The Sunday Times*, 2 February 1997.

6 'Sainsbury's Profit Alert Shocks City', in *The Daily Telegraph*, 25 January 1997.

7 Peggy Hollinger, 'Sainsbury: Supermarkets; Super Margins; Superseded' in *Financial Times*, 30 October 1996.

8 Peggy Hollinger, 'Sainsbury: Supermarkets; Super Margins; Superseded' in *Financial Times*, 30 October 1996.

APPENDIX

1 Corporate Research Foundation, *Corporate Strategies of the Top 100 UK Companies of the Future* (McGraw-Hill, Maidenhead, 1995).

2 Boots Annual Report and Accounts 1996.

3 *Financial Times*, 29 March 1995.

4 N. Brown Annual Report and Accounts 1996.

5 Carrefour Annual Report and Accounts 1994.

6 Carrefour Annual Report and Accounts 1996.

7 Electrocomponents Annual Report and Accounts 1996.

8 Ingvar Kamprad, *The Testament of a Furniture Dealer* (IKEA, Almhult, 1976 (revised 1992)).

9 A. Fisher, 'High Flier Soars Above Placid Pond: SAP's Rise is Unprecedented' in *Financial Times*, 4 August 1995.

10 A. Fisher, 'High Flier Soars Above Placid Pond: SAP's Rise is Unprecedented' in *Financial Times*, 4 August 1995.

11 The Lex Column, *Financial Times*, 19 October 1995.

12 Andrew Lorenz, 'Siebe's Snowball' in *Management Today*, April 1995.

13 'Profits Drop Causes Global Ripple of Fear' in *Financial Times*, 12 December 1994.

14 Southwest Airlines Annual Report 1995.

15 Richard Tomkins, 'The Seriously Funny Airline' in *Financial Times*, 11 November 1996.

16 Elizabeth Sartain, Vice President of People in Southwest Airlines Annual Report 1995.

INDEX